THE GYPSY QUEEN DREAM BOOK AND
FORTUNE TELLER By MADAME JUNO

WHAT THIS BOOK IS ABOUT

" I had a vivid dream last night."

Who has not heard this phrase ? Who has not wondered what the dream foretold ? It must be remembered that people have believed in dreams from time immemorial.

Madame Juno, the Gypsy Queen, gives the true interpretation of every dream you are likely to have. She has striven to avoid that most provoking quality about dream-books, the error of omission. She has aimed at completeness.

In addition to dreams she deals with fortune-telling by cards, dice, dominoes, moles and marks, palmistry, tea-leaves, coffee-grounds, charms and spells.

To *The Gypsy Dream Book* has been added the Oraculum, or Book of Fate, which Napoleon confessed that he was in the habit of consulting.

THE
GYPSY QUEEN
DREAM BOOK

AND

FORTUNE TELLER

BY

MADAME JUNO

THE GYPSY QUEEN

INCLUDING FORTUNE TELLING BY

CARDS	DICE
MOLES	DOMINOES
PALMISTRY	TEA-LEAVES

COFFEE-GROUNDS

WITH CHAPTERS ON

SPELLS	CHARMS
INCANTATIONS	CEREMONIES

TOGETHER WITH

NAPOLEON'S

BOOK OF FATE

HERBERT JENKINS LIMITED
YORK STREET LONDON S.W.1

A
HERBERT
JENKINS'
BOOK

Fifth printing completing 24,506 *copies*

PRINTED IN GREAT BRITAIN BY PURNELL AND SONS
PAULTON (SOMERSET) AND LONDON

CONTENTS

I.—DREAMS AND THEIR INTERPRETATIONS 7

II.—HOW TO TELL FORTUNES BY DOMINOES 193

III.—HOW TO TELL FORTUNES BY DICE .. 194

IV.—HOW TO TELL FORTUNES FROM THE
HAND 195

V.—HOW TO TELL FORTUNES BY MOLES .. 199

VI.—THE MOON—JUDGMENTS DRAWN FROM
THE MOON'S AGE 204

VII.—HOW TO TELL FORTUNES BY CARDS .. 207

VIII.—HOW TO TELL FORTUNES BY TEA-
LEAVES, OR COFFEE-GROUNDS 212

IX.—CHARMS AND CEREMONIES 216

X.—CHARMS, SPELLS AND INCANTATIONS .. 221

XI.—FORTUNE-TELLING GAMES WITH CARDS. 222

XII.—THE ORACULUM, OR BOOK OF FATE CON-
SULTED BY NAPOLEON 224

DREAMS

AND THEIR INTERPRETATIONS

Abase.—To dream that you abase yourself to those with whom you associate, shows that you commit some indiscretion or folly, which you afterwards bitterly regret.

Abbey.—A sign of increasing wealth and comfort ; you will gain much success in your life.

Abdicate.—To dream of the abdication of a king or queen shows astounding news of royalty and unlooked-for events in foreign countries.

Abdomen.—To dream of this being painful, or swollen indicates danger of an internal disorder.

Abhor.—A feeling of abhorrence in a dream means you have good reason for it, and that you had best avoid the person for whom you have the feeling of abhorrence.

Abroad.—To dream of being abroad under pleasant conditions predicts changes and important events, probably leading to your going abroad, where you will find your true happiness in a romantic love affair.

Abscess.—If the dream points to an abscess in the mouth, an urgent warning to pay a visit to the dentist is given ; if in other parts of the body, the warning is for the dreamer to consult a doctor.

Abscond.—To dream of absconding shows that if you follow your present course of action you will have cause to regret it ; you may have need of hiding.

Absent Friends.—Dreaming of those who are absent, means that you will certainly hear news of them immediately ; if a train were seen in the dream, a journey will bring about a meeting with the absent friends.

Absinthe.—To be drinking this in a dream is a clear warning to avoid all drugs.

Abstinence.—For a man to dream of signing the pledge promises good success in a new opening ; for a woman, happiness in some plan dear to her heart.

Abundance.—To feel that you have such abundance of wordly possessions that you need have no fears for the future, warns you not to be reckless, or you may lose all you have through extravagance.

Abuse.—For a woman to dream that she is abused and insulted by one of the opposite sex, shows that her own conduct is at fault, and the dream is a warning that if she desires the respect due to her sex she must behave in a manner to deserve it ; if abused by more than one man it shows that she will have unpleasant business dealings leading to disputes, causing her much vexation ; for a man to dream of abuse and insult from one of the opposite sex shows that he richly deserves it ; if from several women, it is a warning that he may soon be looked upon as a notoriously undesirable character.

Abyss.—To be looking into an abyss points out to you that it is necessary to be very cautious in any new undertaking which you may be contemplating, or you may find yourself in the depths of despair.

Academy.—If you are in an academy of pictures it shows much appreciation of art and a desire to study it; refined tastes, independence, and love of solitude.

Accident.—If you dream of an accident to yourself be sure that it is a warning to guard against its happening by avoiding that which in your dream caused the accident, *e.g.*, water, machinery, fire, or whatever appeared in the dream ; if you see an accident happening to another and recognise that person, if possible, give a warning of the danger in which you saw them.

Accounts.—For a man to dream of accounts shows a tendency to make money the chief object of life, and an inclination to hoard it ; for a woman it shows cares and worries caused by extravagance.

Accuse.—To dream that you are accusing someone of a lie, bad habit, or unkindness, indicates that you had better be on your guard, or you may be hearing the accusation applied to yourself.

Ache.—To dream that you are aching is a warning against chill ; to dream that you have an aching heart foretells distress and misfortune through the affections.

Acorn.—To dream of this shows health and strength, gain through industry, a sowing of which you will see the reaping, increasing knowledge in those matters most interesting to you ; good fortune and ease are predicted by the repetition of the dream.

Acquaintance.—To make a new acquaintance in a dream

is very satisfactory whether it be a man or woman, for they will mean much to you and will become dear to you.

Acquisition.—To dream of acquiring such things as you had thought of as barely possible, is a favourable sign that you may certainly hope for them.

Acquit.—If you dream of being acquitted of a charge made against you, it assures you that the uprightness of your character will be apparent to everyone.

Acrobat.—To be performing as an acrobat shows that you like an audience for everything you do.

Acrostic.—To be dreaming of an acrostic will mean problems and difficulties coming to you, about which you must seek advice.

Acting.—To take part in a play with a number of people around you is a sign that you have a taste for acting and would succeed in that profession ; if a spectator, much pleasure in a place of amusement ; on a stage without taking part in the acting, means that your interests and desires will be centred on someone in the dramatic profession.

Activity.—Dreaming of this means a mind and body so full of energy that even in sleep there must be activity; if you dream of it in connection with a large number of people, or a building your activity leads to a successful career in a public position ; if associated with a small room packed with people and furniture, it shows that you will not have much scope for your energies, and will in consequence weary those with whom you associate by your restlessness.

Actress.—To be married this dream provides a warning against jealousy ; to the lover, a temporary disagreement.

Adder.—This is a bad sign in a dream foreshowing treachery by those you trust, and hidden dangers ; if the snake appeared to be advancing towards you it would be an omen of illness ; if seen coiled, near a form of a man or woman, beware of that man or woman for they are a danger to you.

Adjutant.—To dream of being offered the work of an adjutant, is a sign of a rise in position in whatever capacity you are employed.

Admiration.—To dream of receiving this from one of the opposite sex, means that you will be gratified by much admiration and attention and that your desire for popularity will be realised ; if you are admiring one of your own sex it shows loyalty in friendship, faithfulness in love.

Adoption.—To dream of being adopted assures you of a future well provided for ; to dream of adopting children shows that you behave generously in a case of distress.

Adornment.—To dream of adorning yourself in jewels

is a sign of increasing wealth and position ; if in rich apparel, gratified ambitions ; if in black velvet your prosperity will come late in life.

Adrift.—If in the dream you are floating in water, it is a sign of distress probably caused by the illness of those whom you love ; if you are adrift in a boat without means of steering it, a weak and irresolute character causing trouble and grief to others is indicated.

Advancement.—To dream of this is a hopeful sign of a successful career.

Adversary.—To dream that you have an adversary of the opposite sex foretells to the unmarried, opposition to, and obstacles in the way of marriage.

Adversity.—To dream of adversity is the " coming event casting its shadow before it "—a calamity awaits you.

Advertise.—For a young man to dream of using this method of obtaining a suitable wife, denotes that he will enter into negotiations with a matromnial agency as a joke, and will eventually find himself placed in a compromising situation from which he can only escape by sending his obituary notice to the prospective wife ; for a young woman this dream portends that in her anxiety to marry she has recourse to this method of obtaining a husband.

Advertisement.—To be reading such in your dream is a sign of an unexpected legacy.

Advice.—To be receiving advice in your dream is a sign of reliable friends, whom you may trust in all difficulties.

Affluence.—To dream of a condition of affluence signifies a contented and happy disposition ; it also shows comfort and ease.

Affronted.—To feel affronted in your dream is a sign of being touchy, and too ready to take offence at trifles.

Afraid.—To feel afraid of a man in a dream foreshows that some man, perhaps as yet unknown to you, will be the cause of anxiety in your life, though there may also be some happy associations with this man ; to be afraid of a woman is a sign of difficulty caused through one who may be unknown to you at present, but who will exercise a powerful influence over you in the future.

Africa.—To dream that you are bound for that country signifies that an unexpected opportunity arises which enables You to travel, and it will be through this that you find your future happiness ; to dream of Africa and to see a bird flying, foretells that you will soon receive news from someone in that country.

Agate.—For those born in March to dream of this stone is a lucky sign, for it is one of the birth stones for that month ; for those not born in March it is a sign of sombre tastes and a dislike of bright colours in flowers or dress.

Age.—To dream of age when quite young is a sign of trials and disappointments in youth, and that your happiest time will be late in life ; to dream of youth when it has long since left you, shows health and youthful joy in life and that happiness and contentment will remain with you.

Agony.—To feel this in a dream is a bad sign showing severe attacks of pain and illness.

Agreement.—If in a dream you are signing an agreement against your will, it shows that you are being led into a blunder and that the consequences of your folly will be costly.

Ague.—To dream of ague warns you to beware of alcoholic drinks ; to dream that you are suffering from it cautions you to avoid risk of chills.

Air.—If it is clear and you feel buoyant it is a sign of happiness and good fortune ; if the air is foggy and you feel oppressed it shows calamity and sadness ; if it is filled with sweetness and delicious scents you will find true happiness in love and marriage.

Airship.—To dream of being in one which remains stationary, indicates that you will have but little success in your life unless you endeavour to come out of the rut into which you have fallen ; if the airship moves at great speed it warns you to beware of speculation or you may lose all you possess.

Aisle.—For a young woman to dream that she is escorted down the aisle of a church in company with a young man, portends that she will become unpopular with the male sex and will have to depend upon women for her friends.

Albatross.—To see this bird flying over water would mean distress for those at sea ; it is a bad sign for sailors or those associated with them, meaning sadness and sometimes death.

Alder.—To dream that you are under an alder-tree shows changes and much variety in you life, brought about by unexpected means.

Alderman.—To dream that you are an alderman means that you will be held in high respect by those amongst whom you live and work ; to dine with one, proceed with caution and you will become prosperous.

Alligator.—This is a bad sign of personal danger and distress, possibly caused by those nearest to you ; it also shows much mental disturbance and worry ; if it pursues you a catastrophe is near.

Almanac.—To see an almanac in your dream is a sign of

anxiety as to the date for an expected event, *e.g.*, a party, a wedding, etc. ; if one date on the almanac is clearly seen and the other figures are indistinct, be sure that the one which you distinguish easily is the day for you to choose ; a date seen in a dream is always of importance.

Almonds.—These signify festivities and social enjoyment ; to eat them shows good and generous friends, presents, and prosperity.

Alms.—To dream of almsgiving shows that there is need for you to be more generous in your dealings with others.

Alphabet.—To be saying the alphabet in your dream, is a sign that you have need to be more thorough in all you do, or you will never make much success : attention to detail and method are necessary ; to be reading the alphabet aloud shows a desire to study languages.

Altar.—To dream that you kneel before an altar foreshows sorrow and distress.

Altar Cloth.—To dream that you are present at a wedding ceremony and the altar cloth appears torn, is a sign of coming tribulation in your family ; to dream of making an altar cloth is a sign that in the future you will desire to become a sister or nun.

America.—To dream of America, with water to be seen, shows that you may expect to be travelling to that country ; an event of much importance in your life will probably result from this voyage.

Amethyst.—To see this beautiful stone in a dream is a fortunate sign to those born in December, January, or March, as it is one of the birth stones for those months ; for others it is a sign of sadness, and frustrated hope.

Amputation.—To dream of an amputation is a bad sign of serious damage to a limb through disease or injury.

Ancestor.—To dream of an ancestor is a warning against neglect of those with whom you live ; be more considerate of them and give heed to their warnings.

Anchor.—A very pleasant sign in a dream, meaning good and loyal friends, constancy in love, and the realisation of your wishes ; an emblem of safety to a sailor.

Anchovy.—This dream signifies that you will be liable to have trouble with your teeth, which will become loose ; or you will suffer from inflammation of the roof of your mouth or gumboils, necessitating your living chiefly upon a liquid diet ; to eat anchovy means that you are critical and dainty with regard to your food.

Anemone.—To dream of anemones is a sign of an event in the early autumn : sometimes it indicates a death taking place at that season ; to be picking anemones is a sign of heartache, and a longing for those things which are just out of your reach.

Angel.—To dream of this vision shows radiance, high ideals, happiness and peace.

Anger.—To feel anger in a dream foretells a quarrel with someone near and dear to you.

Angling.—To be doing this without catching a fish means that something which you are planning to do will be a failure, and will give you much disappointment ; if you land a fish success awaits you.

Animals.—A large number of animals shows that your lot will be cast with those who farm ; if the animals appear fat and healthy you will lead a prosperous life ; if they are small and thin your life will be one of toil and care.

Ankle.—To see it slender means that you will become a notably graceful dancer or skater ; to see it swollen foretells an injury ; if it is weak and bending you may expect an attack of illness, leaving you enfeebled and aged in appearance.

Annoy.—To dream that you are annoying someone shows a tendency to petty spite and retaliation.

Anthem.—To be listening to a beautiful anthem shows an exalted idea of life and a high standard of living.

Ants.—These show energy, industry, and power to carry out your plans with success ; dreaming of these insects warns those who annoy you to keep out of your way ; winged ants attacking you is a sign of trials and vexation caused by those around you.

Anvil.—Your strength and energy will bring you success.

Anxiety.—To be in this state in your dream means a warning against allowing yourself to become fussy, fidgetty and worried over trifles.

Ape.—This denotes malicious and dangerous persons whose tongues are to be feared ; it also shows despondency, care, anxiety, and fraud.

Apoplexy.—To dream of apoplexy is a serious warning to take life more quietly, and if you feel any sensation of illness to consult a doctor.

Apparel.—See **Dress.**

Apparition.—This usually means a warning : sometimes bad news.

Apples.—A pleasant sign of happiness, cheerful conditions, and social entertainments ; if seen growing in an orchard they signify a delightful event in the apple season ; to be eating apples shows health, sweet temper, and good fortune.

Apricots.—These near you show pleasures, a smooth

unruffled life, free from worry ; they also foretell good weather ; seen growing in a garden they signify happiness and delight, coming in the apricot season, if in a recognised garden it will be in association with that place ; an apricot stone in your hand means that you have had that which was full of sweetness : memory is all that now remains.

Apron.—If a young woman dreams that she has torn her apron, she may expect to have a serious dispute with a school friend, who through jealousy, has tried to make mischief with her friend's lover and has done her best to bring about a broken engagement ; to mend it, signifies the making up of a quarrel ; to see one starched and folded indicates the arrival of a new maid ; a dirty one, household duties and monotony ; to wear a clean one means that you will take up some new work, possibly nursing.

Arab.—For a young woman to dream of seeing an Arab, means that she will become friendly with a man who will appear to be eminently respectable, but later on she will find out, in a curious manner, that he is anything but desirable as a companion, and the friendship will end abruptly.

Arch.—Things which you desire are developing in the wished-for direction ; the arch is a sign of hope ; your ambition may be gratified in a most unexpected manner ; for a man to dream that he walks under an arch with one of the opposite sex, means that he will have much opposition to encounter in his love affairs ; for a young woman this dream portends, that she will be vexed by the attentions of a man for whom she has a strong distaste.

Archbishop.—To see an archbishop in cope and mitre denotes that some friend or relation will rise to a high position in the church ; if he uplifts his hands a time of peace and quietness is foreshown.

Architect.—If you dream of becoming an architect it foretells success and monetary advancement through house property ; if you are consulting an architect you will leave your present house and buy a new one.

Arm.—To dream of an arm is a sign of love, care and protection, strength and generosity ; if the arm is withered and lean, the loss of a valued friend is predicted ; an arm stretched out towards you shows a new influence that proves to be a life-long source of love and joy ; to dream of your arm being helpless and limp shows a risk of damage to it ; if swollen and red, a warning of a sting or poison is given ; a baby's arm foretells a birth.

Army.—To see an army victorious shows triumphant

public news ; if the army is defeated it will mean bad news from foreign countries causing national consternation.

Arrow.—This shows damaging criticism ; if the arrow points towards you the unpleasant talk is directed against you ; if it points away you are accused of causing mischief and distress by your gossip and unkind words.

Artichoke.—To see these growing means secret trouble ; to eat them, sadness, disappointment, and delay.

Artist.—Dreaming of an artist shows associations with those who study art, also a happy nature finding much beauty and joy in life ; to sit for an artist warns you of being over susceptible to flattery and tells you to beware of those who fill your ears with praise.

Arum Lily.—To see a sheaf of these with the form of one of the opposite sex, shows marriage at the time of year when arums are in flower ; if holding one in your hand, your hope and desires will be fulfilled ; if laid on a bed, it predicts death.

Ascend.—To dream of ascending a steep hill or cliff indicates a need for rest ; it also shows much energy and determination to reach the desired goal, but you must expect to meet with obstacles.

Ashes.—To see a heap of ashes shows grief, loneliness, and disappointment ; to lovers it is an omen of estrangement.

Asphodel.—To see a bunch of asphodels in a dream is a pleasing sign of peace and quietness.

Ass.—See **Donkey.**

Aster.—A settled and placid state of mind and sound judgement are indicated by this dream ; your life will go smoothly though possibly it may be somewhat monotonous ; white asters in a wreath or cross show death for a woman ; purple asters in either of those forms, death of a man.

Asthma.—To dream that you have asthma is a warning to be careful or you may find yourself with a bad attack of this malady.

Asylum.—To dream that you are visiting an asylum is a bad omen : someone near to you is in danger of a mental breakdown ; to dream of being an inmate is a grave warning to the dreamer against excitement or giving way to temper.

Atlas.—To dream that you are studying an atlas means variety, travel, a life full of interest, and love of sightseeing ; for a merchant it signifies new commercial transactions with distant parts of the world ; to a workman, that he will be offered some lucrative situation in a distant part of the country.

Auction.—To be at an auction means a love of buying for its own sake, apart from the use or need of the purchases.

Author.—If you dream that you are an author it means an ambition to become one ; if dreaming of one or more authors it signifies association with writers who become valuable friends to you.

Automaton.—Dreaming of this shows bondage and servitude to a hard taskmaster.

B.

Baby.—Holding a naked baby always shows distress, sometimes great disappointment caused by those you love ; to others a naked baby is a sign of money worries.

Bachelor.—For a married man to dream of being a bachelor denotes that he is losing the affection of his wife through his own fault ; more courtesy and attention should be paid to her ; for a single man to dream of bachelorhood is a sign that ere long he will be prepared to give up that state for married life.

Back.—To dream of your own back as bent and weak shows troubles which weigh you down ; to see it upright and strong means health, power, a successful career, and popularity.

Backbite.—To dream of backbiting is a warning to be more careful and considerate in your talk.

Backdoor.—To dream of trying to get in by the backdoor warns you against deceit, and doing things of which you would feel ashamed were they known by those whose good opinion you care for ; for a maid to dream that she meets her lover outside the backdoor, portends that he is likely to get into some difficulty which will necessitate his changing his present abode, causing her much vexation and disappointment.

Backgammon.—To be playing this shows that you have a rival who may be the cause of your quarrelling with a friend ; to play with a stranger and you win means unexpected developments of plans leading to great success.

Bacon.—If cured and hanging up in a large quantity it means that your provision for the future is wise, for troublous times are coming through bad seasons and lack of money ; to be eating bacon shows luck and profitable business.

Badger.—For a maid or bachelor to dream of a badger means a life of freedom, health and success ; it also signifies a single life ; for the wedded this dream indicates regret that they did not remain unmarried.

Bagpipes.—To hear the music of bagpipes is a prelude to sorrow and woe ; to see them means failure in work or business.

Bailiff.—A bailiff appearing in your dream is an unpleasant sign of urgent need of money ; you will encounter much worry and distress through demands which you are unable to meet.

Bakehouse.—For a young man this dream signifies poverty for his parents in their later years and that if he is unable to support them they must depend upon charity ; for a young married woman it is an unfortunate dream showing that her husband will shortly lose his present employment, and that they will suffer much anxiety from lack of money.

Baker.—To dream of this or of a baker's shop is a good omen of success before making an application for a new post or for a rise in your salary ; to all dreamers it is a sign of gain and luck.

Baking.—For a woman to dream of baking bread shows thrift, a busy life but one of cheerfulness and success ; if the bread becomes burnt, misfortune and trials in the home ; if it will not rise, but appears to become smaller a bad harvest and failure of crops is foretold.

Balcony.—For a girl to dream that she is on a balcony with her lover foretells an interrupted courtship, as sudden illness will attack her lover and keep him an invalid for a long time : but after his recovery the marriage will soon be arranged and she will spend a blissful time in nursing him back to health.

Bald.—To dream of baldness is a warning of illness which will affect your hair : there will be danger of losing it ; if it appears in round patches use precautions when going in a train or tram, etc., or you may find yourself with an attack of ringworm ; for a young woman to dream that her lover is bald is an ominous sign of severe illness from which he may not recover.

Ball.—If at a ball with a feeling of pleasure, you will be a social success and will derive much satisfaction from all your amusements.

Ballet.—To see this shows gaiety, frivolity, passing pleasures.

Balloon.—To see this floating about you in a dream means that you attempt much but achieve little ; to be in one shows that you are easily carried away by a passing enthusiasm for experiments or study, but it has no lasting interest for you and finally vanishes as the balloon in the clouds.

Banana.—To be eating bananas in your dream shows gratification, and the occurence of those things which give you most pleasure ; to see them growing promises much happiness and success in your love affairs.

Bandits.—If you attack them you may rely upon your own judgement and vigour ; if they attack you beware of danger ; if you see them only it warns you against losses through robbery.

Bandy.—To dream of having bandy legs is a warning to be cautious, or you may have such rheumatism as will make it difficult for you to walk.

Banishment.—To dream that you are banished from those whom you love shows misunderstanding and sadness, but it will be of short duration only.

Bank.—For a youth to dream of being in a bank shows that he will become an employé at a bank ; if looking into one in which piles of cheques and notes are to be seen it indicates unexpected good fortune.

Bankrupt.—This is a bad omen of failure and loss ; it warns you to use every effort to recover your position and avert total failure.

Banner.—This is a symbol of a prosperous life for a man, and of a wealthy marriage for a woman.

Banns.—To dream of hearing banns of marriage shows that you will shortly hear of an engagement which will give you much pleasure.

Banquets.—This dream signifies promotion, and of rising to a position of eminence.

Baptism.—To dream that you are present at a baptism, shows to the married the birth of a child who will be delicate as an infant ; to the unmarried, that they will benefit by the death of a godparent.

Bar.—To dream that a bar is placed over you shows a fretting under restrictions which you consider unnecessary ; to leap over a bar, enthusiasm and achievement ; to dream that you are called to practise at the Bar is a good omen of success in your profession.

Barber.—To dream of a visit to the barber shows that there is a new interest coming into your life which will lead you to be most particular as to personal appearance.

Barefoot.—To dream of being barefoot is a sign of ill-health and weariness, also of anxiety about money matters.

Barley Bread.—To eat it signifies good health, comfort, and pleasant plans for the future.

Barley Field.—To walk through it and see the barley wind-swept foreshows distress and trouble : it may be that you have a bad illness or that you will mourn for relations or friends ; if the barley is upright and green you may expect a joyous surprise.

Barmaid.—For a young man this dream denotes that he will soon be obliged to leave his present occupation and possibly emigrate to a foreign country where he will find it uphill work to pay his way, but perseverance will bring him good success ; to dream of marrying a barmaid indicates that he will find an easy billet not requiring much skill nor mental effort.

Barn.—If filled with grain, good fortune, a prosperous marriage, freedom from care, and happiness ; empty, calamity and losses.

Barrels.—If full you will become prosperous ; if empty, monetary loss through carelessness or speculation.

Basin.—If full, you may expect small ailments and minor worries ; empty, domestic annoyance.

Basket.—Domestic duties and family cares ; if full, presents.

Basket of Flowers.—Happiness and contentment, fulfilled desires.

Bassoon.—To hear a bassoon in your dream foreshows a large meeting at which you are called upon to speak ; to be playing on this instrument implies that your energy exceeds your wit.

Baste.—To baste meet in your dream means that you are inclined to seize on the best of everything before offering to share it with others ; to the lover it proclaims comfort and prosperity in marriage.

Bath.—To dream of being in cold water signifies a severe chill ; if the water is very deep and covers you, beware of a skating accident ; if it is so hot that you burn yourself you are warned of coming separation from those whom you love ; to be bathing without being undressed shows domestic difficulties causing you much discomfort ; to see a bath means grief or dismay.

Bats.—A bad sign in a dream, showing sickness and trouble in the home ; also an omen of death.

Battle.—To take part in it shows a hard struggle with misfortune, but, unless you fall, final success.

Battling.—To be battling against an unseen object shows that your fears for the future are unnecessary : much which you dread will never happen ; to be battling against the wind foreshows a hard struggle and uphill work, but by persevering final success.

Bayonet.—This is a sign which you should fear : it shows danger of wounds, operation, and pain.

Bay Tree.—To dream that you are under a bay tree shows a taste for chemistry and knowledge of distilling ; to see it growing predicts that bitterness will mar your pleasures ; to physicians and divines this is a dream of good import.

Bazaar.—To assist at a bazaar with a feeling of pleasure foretells that you will have many admirers, and that when your marriage takes place it will be to a wealthy man ; to make purchases at a bazaar signifies a well disposed nature, with more capacity for talk than for wisdom.

Beam.—An unbroken beam means a successful opening in a new career ; if it falls upon you, disaster and loss of position ; broken, predicts sorrow.

Beans.—To be eating them shows a frugal mind and simple tastes ; to be holding some in each hand, quarrels and disputes with relations.

Bear.—If you are attacked by it, you will be persecuted by enemies ; but if it is running, happiness is in store for you.

Beard.—If it is long and thick it shows health and strength, but an idolent nature, a source of vexation to those around you ; a black beard denotes disgrace ; red, an impetuous somewhat dangerous character ; white, illness of an elderly relative or friend.

Beating.—To dream of beating a person or animal shows a temper which needs controlling, or it may lead you into doing that which you will afterwards bitterly regret ; for the married to dream of being beaten by one of the opposite sex shows disgrace ; to the lover a broken engagement.

Beauty.—To dream of great beauty in persons or scenery shows high ideals and desire for the best in life.

Bed.—To see a bed in an otherwise empty room shows a change of residence ; in a furnished but unfamiliar room, a visit to a strange house ; seen with fruit or flowers, pleasure through the visit, and the time of year at which it takes place is foretold ; a bed seen stripped means a removal from the house ; with bedding disordered and with a human form in it predicts a bad illness with high temperature for that person ; a form seen on a bed with a bandage round the head and jaw means death ; if with a patch of crimson on the chest, from hemorrhage ; flowers in profusion laid on a bed indicate death as would a cross or wreath ; to buy a bed foreshows illness ; to sleep in a strange bed, a journey.

Bed Clothes.—To dream of bed clothes is a sign of sloth and dislike of lending a helping hand to those around you ; to the wealthy this dream forecasts an unfortunate change in circumstances.

Beef.—If you see a piece of beef in a dream be sure that financial worries await you ; to eat it roast, a kind welcome ; boiled, melancholy.

Beehive.—To dream of this shows eloquence, mental capacity, and much energy in forming new schemes and carrying them through.

Beer.—To be drinking beer from a tankard denotes that

you have reason to fear it, or you may become a slave to the habit ; to see it warns you against betting or lotteries.

Bees.—These signify success through your own ability and mental power : you will have many friends and enjoy life to the full ; if you are stung it shows that you have a friend who is not to be trusted ; to see bees flying away from you into their hive, enemies ; for a lover to dream of being stung portends mischief ; to the married, enmity and coldness.

Beeswax.—To see a quantity of this indicates that you may expect to receive a large sum of money or a legacy ; to use it denotes that you are orderly, industrious, and scrupulous in all matters.

Beetles.—To see them running on a floor or up a wall indicates that you will have trouble with these pests ; it also means that domestic trouble is at hand ; if they crawl upon you it foretells that you will be slandered and abused by those whom you thought of as friends ; to kill them implies that you will be able to discover the chief culprits in the mischief and will be able to bring them to book.

Beetroot.—To see it cooked denotes that someone will try to do you a bad turn, but it will fail of its object and will rather benefit you ; to eat it, the existence of a rival who will strive to carry off your lover ; to plant it, vitality, energy and a hopeful disposition.

Beggar.—To dream of being a beggar shows great misfortune in money matters ; to see many beggars, an epidemic of illness among the poor.

Begging.—To dream that you are begging and in want gives a warning against extravagance, or you may find yourself badly in debt.

Bella donna Lily.—This flower is a very pleasing symbol in a dream, meaning hope, love, happiness, and the leading of of an upright and honourable life.

Belle.—To dream that you are the " belle of the ball " implies that you will soon meet with a vain self-opiniated young man who will endeavour to engage your affections by fulsome flattery ; if you are wise you will avoid having anything to do with this fellow ; for a man to dream that he dances with the chief beauty at a ball signifies that he may expect trouble caused by jealousy among his women acquaintances.

Bellows.—To use them insures you against failure from lack of perseverance or energy ; to see them, an endeavour to make the best of a bad business.

Bells.—To hear these ringing in the distance shows desires and longings for a happiness which you feel might well be yours, but something necessary to it is lacking ; if the bells are very near and loud it shows the maturing of events that will bring you great joy and the realisation of your dearest wish ; to ring them means that for a temporary pleasure you bring upon yourself a lasting sorrow.

Bet.—To dream of betting shows that you will suffer from your own imprudence.

Bier.—To see this in your dream foretells a death ; if the bier is seen placed in a house which you recognise the death will be for one of the members of that household ; if the bier is seen placed in a church it will probably indicate that the death is one of which you are told, and will not be a personal sorrow.

Bigamy.—For a woman to dream of committing this crime implies that her bahaviour is open to criticism, and that she is likely to earn a bad reputation for herself unless she amends her ways ; this dream would have much the same meaning for a man.

Bilberry.—Eating bilberries in a dream shows a sharp tongue and harsh nature.

Bill.—To receive a bill which you cannot pay denotes pressing money worries ; if you pay it at once it shows gain through a satisfactory bargain.

Billiards.—To dream that you are playing billiards means popularity and social success ; to see it played, pleasure followed by regret.

Bird of Paradise.—Difficulties and trials are vanishing, and a future of comfort and pleasure will be yours.

Birds.—Flying towards you indicates that news of an important event is near you ; to see them flying round and upon you is not a good sign showing sadness and vanishing hope ; if many are seen circling high in the air happiness will be yours after a time of waiting ; to hear birds singing is a sign of joy coming for you in the spring or early summer.

Bird's Nest.—To find a bird's nest in your dream indicates a very pleasant discovery leading to a fortunate enterprise, brought about to a large extent by your own patience and ability ; it is a good omen of love and realised ambition, new, friends and increased fortune.

Birth.—To dream of this means a piece of news most interesting to you.

Birthday.—To dream of your birthday foreshows a happy event taking place on or near that date ; for a man it signifies a happy life crowned with increasing success and prosperity.

Biscuits.—To dream of biscuits means a loss of appetite ; to eat sweet biscuits, pleasant events.

Bite.—To dream that you are bitten foretells jealousy and spite.

Black.—Is a bad sign, showing grief, death, distance, weariness, and disappointment.

Blackberries.—If picking them with ease and in large clusters it foretells an event of much importance to you occuring in the autumn ; if picking them with difficulty and many scratches it shows delay and disappointments.

Bleat.—To hear the sound of the bleating of sheep is a sign of sadness, loneliness and parting ; the bleating of lambs means cheerfulness and good news.

Blasphemy.—If you dream that you are cursing, it foretells bad fortune ; if you are cursed, misfortune or disgrace.

Blind.—To dream of blindness is a serious warning not to over strain your eyes; to lead the blind indicates that you will become of much use in the world and noted for your acts of charity.

Blinds.—To dream of pulling down the blinds in your home is a sign of sorrow ; to see blinds half down in many houses is a sign of national mourning.

Blood.—To see this is a sign of tragedy ; to lose blood a warning of serious illness.

Bloodstone.—A lucky sign to those born in April or November.

Blows.—To give blows is a sign of a dispute which is likely to end in a law suit ; to receive them, a catastrophe.

Blue.—This is a pleasing colour to see in a dream showing joy, hope, love, and the fulfilment of your desire.

Bluebells.—To see these in the winter foretells a very early spring ; they also signify a somewhat pronounced type of character and appearance, full of charm and optimism : bluebells seen in connection with a recognised figure would probably mean joy in connection with that person : to dream of a large patch of them shows an event bringing you much satisfaction in the spring ; to pick them is a sign that much of the happiness of your life is of your own making.

Bluebottle Fly.—To dream of this insect shows irritation and worries in the home ; if it settles on you, there will be jealousy aroused by your success.

Boar.—To dream of this animal shows much energy and push, though not always in the right direction to gain unqualified success ; it is also a symbol of obstacles.

Boat.—With a smooth blue sea, a pleasant outing and success in a new enterprise ; with a rough sea, turmoil ; on a river with a cloudy appearance, troubles.

Bog.—To dream of a bog is a sign of hindrances in the way of your intended pleasures.

Bolts.—To be unfastening bolts in your dream shows that you will master your enemies and that you will always be welcomed by your friends and will invariably meet with a cordial reception.

Bomb.—To see this in a dream foretells disaster, or news of an explosion and loss of life.

Bones.—To dream of a large number of bones shows that you will study anatomy ; it also displays a taste for learning and investigation ; to hold them means misfortune surmounted with courage.

Bookcase.—To be dreaming of an empty bookcase shows that if the bookcase were full you would not be troubled to read the books ; if it is full you will study many subjects and be eager to learn at all times.

Books.—To be reading a large number of books denotes a desire for knowledge and capability of acquiring the same ; to see a row of books out of your reach, shows a half-formed desire to cultivate a mind allowed to be idle through lack of energy and perseverance ; to be reading a book with a large clear print indicates a very intelligent mind, judgment, and balance ; to see a new book in a bright-coloured binding implies a desire to become an author : if the colour of the binding is a good one, such as blue, your ambition will be gratified.

Bootblack.—To be a bootblack in your dream is a sign of failure in your work ; to be employing a bootblack shows careful attention to detail in all you do and say.

Boots.—If you see many pairs of new boots it shows fortunate business, a good income, and the gratifying of your tastes and pleasures ; old boots, an unfortunate enterprise, ending in failure ; to put on new boots signifies an entanglement in your love affairs.

Borrowing.—To be borrowing in your dream is a sign of carelessness with regard to money and other matters.

Bottles.—A number of empty bottles is a warning against indulgence ; bottles full of wine show an extravagant taste that is likely to bring you to ruin ; broken bottles mean trouble in the home, also cuts and bruises ; several small bottles predict illness.

Bound.—To dream that you are bound is a sign of much disturbance, anxiety of mind and fatigue of body.

Bouquet.—This is a fortunate symbol ; if one of the opposite sex presents you with a large bouquet of choice white flowers it denotes a happy love affair, ending in marriage ; if a woman is given a bouquet by one of her sex it shows that she will become a public benefactor ; to hold a bouquet of white flowers and with the form of a man appearing in the dream, predicts that you will soon be a bride ; to be wearing a bouquet means that you have gathered the best from life and must now be content with its memories ; to destroy one, separation ; to throw it away, vexation.

Bow and Arrow.—To be using a bow and arrow in a dream shows that you will be the means of injuring others by unkind words, spite and gossip ; if the arrow points towards you it denotes unpleasant talk of your personal affairs which may do you harm.

Bower.—To dream that you are in a bower into which the sun is shining, proclaims great happiness in love.

Box.—To see a small locked box in a dream shows that you will find something which you had lost ; an empty open box foretells trouble in a love affair ; full of useful goods, satisfaction and comfort.

Boy.—For the married who have no son this shows that they may hope for one ; for the unmarried woman to dream of many boys shows that she will become the wife of a schoolmaster, or that she will work amongst boys in the cause of charity ; to see a boy who has a haggard careworn face of misery indicates remorse for the past.

Bracelet.—To dream that a gold bracelet is placed upon your wrist means that you will soon receive a good present ; to see several bracelets, that you will buy one as a wedding gift for a friend ; a broken bracelet, loss ; to find one, a discovery made too late ; to break one, the severing of a bond ; to throw it away, life-long regret.

Branch.—To dream of a large branch of a tree is a sign of much independence, and of success in carrying out an enterprise, the larger the branch the greater your success ; to see it severed from the trunk shows separation and partings from those near to you ; to be under a branch which is falling on you means a crushing blow to your desires ; to be sitting on a branch denotes movement and changes which are very pleasant in their results.

Brandy.—To drink it gives warning to abstain from alcohol ; to see it means degrading pleasures.

Bray.—To hear the braying of donkeys shows that you will surprise those around you by your sagacity and the independance of your views.

Bread.—To see a large number of loaves is a warning against waste : a shortage of corn is threatened ; if water is also seen it denotes great scarcity of food abroad, serious disasters causing the lack of it ; if the bread is black it shows famine; spotted bread means danger of plague; if holding a loaf in your hand, there is risk of those things which you regard as necessities becoming luxuries; loaves of bread with crossed swords above them predict mutiny and disaffection among those whom the world trusted.

Break.—To dream of breaking is a sign of misfortune in this direction: you will probably break something which you value; to dream of breaking a tooth warns you to be careful or it will happen; glass, a danger from bad cuts; coal, hardship and trials.

Breakfast.—Eating this meal alone shows discontent with your surroundings; with others, that you will say things for which you will afterwards be sorry.

Breast.—For a mother to dream of this shows that she will sorrow for her children.

Brewing.—To dream of brewing foretells trouble and mischief coming from unsuspected causes.

Briars.—To be entangled in these shows that impatience leads you into committing acts of folly, thus putting yourself into ridiculous positions from which you find it difficult to extricate yourself; to be passing through briars without scratches shows ingenuity in avoidance of disagreeables, and a path smoothed for you by friends.

Bribe.—To be offering a bribe in a dream is a sign of a weak and hesitating character, unable to face any situation needing courage.

Bride.—If you dream that you are a bride, and the form of a man known to you appears, you may feel assured of marriage to this man; to dream of this, and of being dressed in sombre attire, shows a marriage late in life; without the form of a man appearing it predicts an unhappy love affair and broken-hearted disillusionment; to see a bride is a warning of a rival in your affections.

Bridesmaid.—To dream of being a bridesmaid is a sign of much happiness and pleasure; if a man appears to be standing beside you, it predicts the meeting with someone when a bridesmaid, to whom you will become the bride.

Bridge.—Crossing one with deep dark-looking water beneath shows trouble, a sorrowful heart, and tears; picking a white violet as you cross the bridge shows death of a woman, a purple violet, death of a man; to see a wooden bridge foretells honour and achievement; an iron one, obstacles

Bronchitis.—To dream that you have this distressing illness should be taken as a warning against unnecessary risk of chill; to dream of bronchitis, but not for yourself, is a warning of serious illness for a relation or friend.

Brooch.—To see a broken brooch is a sign that you will lose one of much value ; to see one lying in your hand, a good present ; to wear a strange one means that you will make a discovery greatly to your advantage, and will in time turn it to good account in the development of a patent.

Brood.—For parents to dream of a brood of chickens gathered under the wing of a hen predicts that they will have many anxieties with their children.

Brook.—To be crossing a brook in your dream shows that having made up your mind to a course of action you carry it through with ease ; to be sitting beside one denotes doubt and hesitation over some question ; if a man sits with you the doubt is in connection with him and tears and quarrels will follow.

Broom.—To dream that you carry one shows that there is need for you to be careful in the choice of your friends.

Broth.—To be drinking broth in a dream shows to the young a small attack of illness or indisposition ; to the elderly, the return of good fortune.

Brother.—To dream of a brother who is far away is a sign that he is near you in thought and that you will shortly hear news of him ; to dream of a brother when you do not possess one shows that you will make a good and staunch friend.

Brow.—To dream that your brow is puckered is a sign of care and anxiety caused by those around you ; if it is smooth, white, and broad, you will have a life of comfort and will gain those things which you most desire ; for a girl to dream that she is seated with her lover upon the brow of a hill foreshows an unsuitable marriage and a life of friction and dissimilar tastes.

Brown.—To dream of brown indicates an ordinary life without much variation ; an unambitious character which is easily content with the present and without aspirations for the future ; to wear it means misplaced confidence.

Buckle.—If a woman dreams of losing a buckle, she may be sure that an important arrangement which would have been of great assistance to her will fall through in an unforeseen manner and cause her much disappointment and dismay.

Bugle.—To blow a bugle shows a desire to arouse admiration and notice from all whom you meet ; to hear one means that it is time you became more energetic and industrious ; if a man sees a bugle but does not hear it he will become a soldier or sailor, if a woman, she will probably marry a soldier or sailor.

Bugs.—To dream of these is a warning to take precaution or you may see one upon yourself.

Building.—To dream of being in a large building which

appears dark, cold, and vault-like, and you wander up and down stone stairs which have impediments causing you to stumble, tells of crushing trials and difficulties hard to bear ; a large building seen from outside with the sun shining upon it shows lucky news and prosperity in connection with a building.

Bull.—An ill omen of misfortune ; if in company with someone near and dear to you and the bull rushes towards you it shows that you will suffer much heartache and sorrow through this dear one ; if alone, it denotes that the worst troubles of your life must be borne in secret, without the solace of sympathy ; being pursued by a bull predicts attacks of pain or foreshadows an illness.

Bullet.—To dream of a bullet being in you is a warning to be careful with firearms.

Bullock.—To see a drove of bullocks shows you that strength and courage are needed to carry you through the troubles ahead of you.

Bull's Eye.—To be scoring a bull's eye shows you that you will make a reputation by your skill and accuracy.

Bumble Bee.—This shows a cheerful disposition making the best of everything, easily gratified tastes and pleasures, many friends and social success ; to pursue one is a sign of travels.

Buoy.—This is a sign of hope, a very pleasant symbol in a dream ; you have a good friend in all weathers.

Burglars.—To dream that burglars are in the house warns you to be careful and not put so much trust in the honesty of your dependents or you may have an unpleasant discovery ; if you see a burglar entering a house known to you, give a warning to the owner to be cautious against robbery.

Burial.—To be present at a burial is a sign of sadness, heaviness of heart and loss ; if you see the burial taking place at a distance and the sun shines upon you it means that you will benefit through the death of someone.

Buried Alive.—To dream of being buried alive is a sign of your being placed in a position of great danger and fear, after which you will suffer severely from shock ; it also indicates a poor state of health and a need for more leisure.

Bury.—To bury an object in your dream is a sign that you are afraid of being found out in some act of yours which you hope is a secret.

Burning.—To see houses burning in a street shows a disastrous fire in a crowded quarter, causing widespread misery ; to see one house burning near you is a grave warning of danger from fire : this dream warns you of the urgent necessity for taking every precaution against fire ; to see your bed burning is an omen of personal danger from it, much suffering, or loss of life ; a large building or church in flames shows damage to them caused by fire ; to see a large number of letters burning shows that there are things in your life which you desire to conceal ; to be burning newspapers means independence of public opinion, but a possibility that your name will one day appear in the newspapers in connection with an unpleasant case ; to be burning a document implies legal business which will not be to your advantage.

Bush.—To sit beside one, irreparable folly ; to see one, invitations and social enjoyment.

Business.—To dream of transacting some business with a feeling of satisfaction shows that you embark on a new enterprise which proves fortunate ; if with a feeling of doubt, beware of attempting a venture for some time to come for it would lead to failure.

Butcher.—To dream of a butcher shows that you encounter some suffering animal who has been badly treated ; to see an animal being slaughtered, that you hear of a horrible cruelty possibly a murder ; to be shaking hands with a butcher denotes a detestation of his trade, and that you become a vegetarian.

Butter.—To dream of a large amount of butter means good fortune and success through agricultural industries ; a small piece of butter on a large dish foreshows a bad hay harvest, failure of crops and scarcity ; to be eating it, much appreciation of the good things of life and a desire for the best of everything.

Butterfly.—This shows gaiety, social success, lightheartedness, power of attraction and many admirers ; to the lover it speaks of inconstancy.

Buttermilk.—To drink this in a dream shows care and thought for personal appearance and success through your own charm ; to give it to another, a happy plan ; to see it in a pan, good fortune.

Buttonhook.—An exchange between friends, successfully organised plans, and a propitious meeting.

Buttons.—To see many buttons all of one size lying scattered around you signifies much business for you to transact, needing great accuracy and causing a certain amount of worry ; if the buttons vary in size and shape there will be many suggestions as to arrangements and business without anything definite being settled ; for a maid it means that she will marry a man many years her senior ; for a bachelor, that he will not marry until late in life.

Buying.—To be buying food in your dream is a warning

to be careful with your money for you will be in need of more than you possess before long ; buying clothes, furniture, or jewellery is a sign that you will have plenty of money to spend.

C.

Cab.—To dream of driving in a hired cab is a sign of gloom, sadness, and mourning ; to see one at your door is also a bad sign foreshowing difficulties, and departures causing dismay.

Cabbage.—To be cutting cabbages with frost upon them is a sign that in spite of diligence in work and thrift in all ways you will never become very rich ; for the maid it signifies marriage with a man who by profession is a market gardener ; he will not make his fortune in this business and will demand much of his wife's time and attention in helping him in his work although it will be distasteful to her ; to be eating cabbage shows discontent, a poor state of health and finance.

Cabinet.—If you are examining a cabinet in your dream it will mean an unexpected and fortunate discovery giving you much pleasure and satisfaction ; to open a secret drawer means wealth and unthought-of prosperity.

Cabinet Maker.—To dream that you are a cabinet maker shows a power of invention which you may put to good purpose by the use of your hands ; to dream of marrying a cabinet maker denotes that you may look for trouble through the extravagant habits of your husband.

Cackle.—To dream that you hear the cackling of geese, shows that you may expect to hear of the arrival of friends or relatives whom you have not seen for some time and whose presence will prove rather trying to you ; for a married woman to hear the cackle of ducks means a busy life and large family.

Cad.—For a man to dream that he is called a cad shows that he had better mend his manners or he may hear unpleasant truths ; for a woman to dream she is associating with a cad means that there is need for improvement in her own behaviour or she may experience unpleasantness from the opposite sex.

Cage.—To see several birds in a cage indicates that a variety of causes prevents you from obtaining your dearest wish ; should the cage door open and the birds fly out towards you it signifies that all obstacles will shortly be removed and very pleasant news and great happiness will be yours ; an empty cage shows that you will shortly possess a pet bird who will live but a short time.

Cakes.—To dream of making these with currants foretells pleasant society, invitations ; to be making them with many raisins shows an unexpected episode leading to happiness ; with almonds, good fortune ; almonds and icing, a wedding ;

pink and white icing, a christening party ; with lemons, a tea party at which you meet with those who annoy you by their remarks ; carraway seed, pleasure with your dearest friend ; a variety of spices, hospitality to those from abroad from whom you hear many interesting stories ; to see cakes upon a dish denotes the making of new friends and social success.

Calendar.—If you search for a date in an almanac which seems difficult to find it portends that you will soon be fixing the date of your marriage, but if the dream ends before the date is found you may have cause to cancel your engagement.

Calf.—To see one in a dream shows a need for kindness to animals ; a calf with its mother, a need for gentleness with children.

Calm.—To dream of feeling perfectly calm in a trying situation shows that you will find yourself in need of calmness before long.

Calumny.—Dreaming that you are the victim of a calumny denotes that you are too much inclined to be on the look-out for slights and to imagine that you have a grievance.

Camel.—To see these animals crossing the desert means weariness, frustrated plans, endless delay, burdens which must be borne ; to see camels near shows wealth that comes to you after a long time of waiting from an unexpected source abroad ; if a man appeared in the dream it would indicate wealth coming through a marriage late in life ; if riding on a camel it denotes travel in foreign countries ; to be walking on foot behind a camel implies toil, failure, and sadness.

Cameo Brooch.—To dream that a cameo brooch is given to you shows that you will hear of a small legacy from an elderly relation or friend ; to break one, family disputes.

Camp.—To see a large camp in a dream is a sign that you will visit a military station and gain much pleasure and make new friends ; for a girl it foretells marriage with a soldier ; for a youth, military service.

Camphor.—To dream of camphor gives a warning against cold in the head ; to break it denotes good advice given to you which you will despise.

Canal.—To be near a canal in your dream shows dissatisfaction with your life, depression, unavoidable monotony, and a dreary outlook ; to fall into one means that you are, or will be, placed in an environment entirely uncongenial to you.

Canary.—A canary shows a cheerful disposition always making the best of things, many friends, a sociable nature, and love of talking ; if it alights upon you a sudden departure or arrival is notified.

Candle.—To be buying coloured candles shows festivities ; to be buying ordinary candles means household duties which bore you ; to be lighting a candle repeatedly which goes out predicts that for the present you must expect trials and worries ; to be looking at a lighted candle of which the wick bends over till it forms a double flame shows clairvoyance and mediumistic power ; if the whole candle bends and breaks, loss and misfortune ; for a girl to watch a candle being lighted foretells that she will soon receive a proposal of marriage : for a bachelor, that he will inherit a legacy.

Candlestick.—You have need to look at things from a wider point of view ; there is much to be learned ; to make the best of yourself you must cultivate perception.

Candy.—To dream of eating this shows that you have a nature which is easily persuaded by means of a little flattery, for that you will never tire nor question the motives of sincerity of those who thus flatter you ; some day you will experience the falseness of these blandishments, and will realise that it is wiser to show firmness, and not be cajoled by those who find your good nature useful to serve their own ends.

Cane.—To dream of a cane shows that you are disposed to be harsh on those who annoy you and are lacking in kindness to the young.

Canker.—To dream of a canker is unpleasant showing that those things which you fear, such as losing the love of one dear to you or the loss of privileges which you now enjoy, will come upon you.

Cannon.—To see a cannon in the distance shows military or naval display ; with good symbols around it, such as a crown or a star, it denotes honours and promotion for someone dear to you in the Service ; if the cannon is draped with black it predicts the death of an eminent soldier or sailor ; if broken, public disaster ; if near and pointing towards you, personal danger through which you show much bravery ; to hear a cannon foretells war, seen pointing upwards, rebellion.

Cannon Ball.—To see this near is a sign of misfortune and heavy burdens ; if rolling away, it shows that your worst troubles are over and that you may now look forward to better' prospects.

Canoe.—To dream that you are in a canoe with a stranger shows that you will soon make a new friend, with whom you will have much happiness, eventually leading to a joyful love affair.

Canopy.—To dream of being under a canopy means success through the help and interest of those above you.

Canterbury Bells.—To see a large clump of white and

purple Canterbury bells is a sign of your happiness being dependent to a great extent upon others ; if there is more of the purple bell than of the white it is a man on whom it depends : if more of the white bell, it is a woman through whom your happiness comes.

Cap.—To put one on warns you to take precautions in your dealings with those of the opposite sex ; to remove one from your head shows that those things which you desire to hide will become known ; for a maid to receive a cap denotes that she will become a matron.

Captive.—To dream that you are a captive and feeling yourself bound is a sign of sadness ; things for which you are not personally responsible cause you distress and keep you tied to that from which you would fain escape.

Carbuncle.—To dream of this stone shows a severe taste in dress and decorum : a prim unyielding nature, prone to take offence and become sharp tongued ; to dream that you are afflicted with the painful swelling of a carbuncle warns you of a poor state of health, which if not attended to by a doctor will certainly bring an illness upon you.

Cards.—To see a pack in which all the spade cards are showing without red ones is a sign to those who play cards to be cautious, or there will be bad monetary losses ; to those who do not play it would be an omen of sadness, loss, and undoing ; if a pack is seen with all club or red cards it would mean good fortune and success to those who play and to those who do not ; to see the ace of clubs means good news through the post, success and achievement ; the ace of diamonds signifies that you will be gratified by a good present or sum of money ; the ace of hearts, affection and happiness in the home ; the ace of spades, a large town or building ; the nine of hearts is a token of your wish being fulfilled without delay.

Caress.—To dream of caressing someone you love shows that there will be need for your love and care, for illness is likely to attack this dear one, and a time of anxiety awaits you.

Carnation.—To see a bunch of carnations in a dream is a pleasing sign of happiness, love, good friends and health ;' to be given a bunch of carnations shows a faithful lover.

Carpenter.—To be carpentering is a sign of talent in the use of your hands, and of excelling in those things needing accuracy and neatness ; to see a carpenter indicates arrangement of your affairs.

Carpet.—To buy handsome carpets indicates coming good fortune, possibly a new home ; to see your carpets worn and shabby predicts loss of income ; to beat them, innumerable

B

difficulties ; to witness the purchase of a carpet by someone whom you know implies that you will soon hear of a forthcoming wedding in that family ; to see many carpets denotes increased income tax.

Carriage.—To be driving in a comfortable carriage with splendid horses shows that your affairs will prosper, and that you may expect a life of comfort and ease ; if you are in a carriage without horses then your riches will be transitory, leaving you in poverty ; to sit in one which is stationary portends that you will be the victim of scandal.

Carrying.—To dream that you are carrying a heavy weight under which you stagger, is a sign of a burden on your mind, causing you much agitation and distress ; to be carrying a chair means an injured limb ; a child, illness, disappointment, or agitation caused by friends or relatives ; to carry an animal denotes that you will see or hear of a case of cruelty in which you will interfere.

Cart.—To be riding in a cart foretells money losses with much financial worry ahead of you and weariness of mind and body ; to see one coming towards you means that events will be slow in arriving ; things will move in a leisurely manner ; to see one going away shows monotony, boredom, and a tendency always to put off till to-morrow things which could well be done to-day.

Carving—To carve a joint of raw meat is a sign of money worries, the larger the joint the greater the worry ; to carve wood is a sign of development and satisfaction.

Cashier.—To dream that you are a cashier is a sign of a good appointment, involving much responsibility.

Castle.—You may expect good fortune and gratified ambition ; a crumbling castle, disappointment and ill success in love and marriage.

Castor Oil.—To see it growing denotes increasing good looks ; to drink it, unreasonable dislike of someone whom you know by sight only.

Cat.—Dreaming of this animal being near you is an uncomfortable sign of trickery, meanness, quarrels among relations, money matters probably being the disturbing cause ; a cat jumping upon you shows money worries and difficulties ; walking towards you, the arrival of a stranger ; disappearing, that which you feared is passing and will not disturb you.

Cataract.—To dream that you see a cataract of clear bright water foretells peace and comfort in your domestic affairs ; if the water is muddy you must expect misfortune or illness in your family.

Catechism.—To dream of this shows a desire to busy yourself in good works ; a strictly conventional and somewhat dull life is predicted for those who dream of studying the Catechism.

Caterpillar.—You will be criticised unkindly by those who are envious of you, though you have no suspicion that these people are anything but friendly in their feeling towards you ; but there is slyness and deception, and it would be well to be on your guard or you may find unpleasant gossip has been spread about you.

Cathedral.—A very pleasant state of mind ; prosperity, contentment, and happiness with those whom you love are shown by this dream ; to attend a service in a Cathedral implies an exalted position through marriage.

Cat's Eye.—To see this stone in a dream is a lucky sign to those born in July, being one of the birth stones for that month ; for others it shows a treacherous friend.

Cattle.—To see a drove of cattle in a large open space without other signs of life shows changes coming for you, and travel to a new country where you will be very lonely and suffer much from home sickness ; fat cattle denote good fortune ; thin, failure ; to buy them signifies that you must deliberate and consider well before embarking on a new business or project.

Cauliflower.—To dream of cauliflower is a sign of an invitation to dine with a friend ; eating it without sauce denotes dyspepsia ; with sauce, a good appetite ; to see several of them near means infidelity.

Cavalry.—To see a regiment of cavalry in a dream is a sign of gratification and pleasure with those in the army ; to the soldier it is a sign of active service.

Cavern.—To be in a deep cavern which is dark, and in which you cannot stand upright, shows that unless you rouse yourself and use a little more push you will remain in obscurity all your life.

Ceiling.—To dream of the ceiling falling upon you is a sign of overwork and of a tired and worried mind ; it also warns you to be careful not to pass under ladders or scaffolding ; to dream that you can touch the ceiling shows small ambitions easily gratified ; to see it collapse predicts illness or death of a relative or friend.

Celery.—To dream of picking it denotes that hard work will be your lot ; to eat it, a vigorous body and active mind, which will preserve the energies of youth to a ripe old age.

Cellar.—To be in a large empty cellar shows that those whom you accounted friends forsake you when you are most in need of their friendship, for the empty cellar means that a hard fate shuts you out from the sunshine of life ; a cellar full of coal means a well filled purse; full of wine, great prosperity;

if you take a bottle in your hand there is danger of your being tempted to drink immoderately : this dream should be a warning.

Chaffinch.—To dream of this bird predicts spinsterhood.

Chain.—To see a long slight chain around you shows ties that you wish to undo ; a broken chain means adversity ; to discard it, a broken engagement ; to entangle it, a dilemma which will tax your ingenuity to the utmost.

Chair.—To see several empty chairs is a sign of arrivals ; to see chairs piled up one upon the other shows changes in the household.

Chalk.—To dream of this shows that you will go to a place where there is chalk soil which will cause you discomfort ; a piece of chalk in your hand means a taste for drawing caricatures at which you might excel ; to see a large quantity of chalk indicates disappointment ; to a farmer, loss of his cattle.

Chambermaid.—To dream of a chambermaid denotes suspicion and artfulness ; to speak with one, an occasion for fault-finding.

Chameleon.—This shows that you are as changeable as the lizard of which you are dreaming.

Champion.—To dream of being a champion is a sure sign of attaining your desires, though your talent will lie in physical feats rather than in mental achievement.

Chapel.—To dream of being in an empty chapel shows dreariness, dulness, and a monotonous life ; to see it from the outside means that things will turn out better than you had expected them to do.

Chapped Hands.—This is a sign of irritation and constant annoyance in the home, daily vexation and lack of harmony ; it also shows toil and a poor state of health.

Charade.—To dream of acting a charade shows that you often mislead people by your talk ; they misunderstand your motives through your inaccuracy or blundering, and form a wrong opinion of you ; thus you are doing yourself harm.

Charcoal.—To dream of eating charcoal shows an attack of indigestion ; to see it warns you of a threatened chill or indisposition ; to be carrying it means difficulties with your fires or chimneys ; to sit beside a fire of charcoal indicates that you may soon expect to hear good tidings from distant friends or relatives.

Chariot.—To dream that you drive in a chariot surrounded by a crowd shows that you will take part in some public ceremony of importance ; to see a chariot passing by and you are alone, is a sign that your ambitions are many, but are never realised.

Charity.—To dream of charity is a reminder that this virtue is lacking in you ; for a girl to dream that she is charitable foretells that she will bestow her affections upon an unworthy man.

Chart.—To dream of studying a chart means promotion for those concerned with the Navy ; to all seafarers it shows safety and success ; to a woman it signifies perplexity.

Cheated.—To dream that you have been cheated is a warning to be cautious in your business dealings ; to dream that you are cheating is a sign that some day you may find yourself tempted to do so.

Cheeks.—To dream of your cheeks being very red is a sign of a guilty conscience ; of their being swollen, an attack of toothache ; of their being smooth and pink, power of attracting others to you, especially the opposite sex ; it also shows flirtations ; to a business man it is a sign of surmounting obstacles and of rising to a high position.

Cheer.—To dream of cheer and a sensation of joy shows you that such will be yours ; to dream of it with a gathering of people means a visit to a theatre or place of amusement ; to dream of cheer and a disordered table or room is a sign of excess and rowdy pleasures ; to hear the sound of cheering foretells disturbance.

Cheese.—To be eating this shows that you will be entertained by some man who not only provides you with an excellent luncheon, but also much amusement with the good stories which he relates ; a whole cheese denotes a prosperous friend who will bestow good presents upon you ; to grate it means vexation followed by success ; to pare it, incredulity.

Cheesecakes.—To eat them signifies that you are considered good company and you will enjoy the satisfaction of popularity ; to eat them in company with one of the opposite sex means that your love affairs will be numerous and unconventional.

Chemist.—To dream of this predicts illness ; to be serving in a chemist's shop denotes a taste for the profession of dispenser and success in the same ; to steal from it implies a danger of your taking to drugs and the dream should warn you against all opiates ; for a person of bad temper to dream of a chemist's shop speaks of the necessity for controlling it or there may be distressing and serious consequences.

Cheque.—To dream of a cheque sgnifies good money transactions or presents ; to be writing one denotes a legacy ; to tear one up shows loss through carelessness.

Cherries.—To dream of cherries is a sign of a happy event n the cherry season ; to gather white ones means deception by a woman ; red ones, health ; to eat cherries is a good omen for your future and of happiness in love and marriage ; to eat cherry tart, pleasure and enjoyable outings with your friends.

Chess.—To be playing this with a stranger and you win shows a triumph over a difficult matter which has been causing you anxiety ; if you lose the game it foretells failure ; if the figures fall around the board it predicts a quarrel with a friend with whom you are in the habit of playing chess ; to play alone and make rapid and successful moves indicates genius and power to conquer obstacles or enemies.

Chestnuts.—To be eating them raw shows a determination to carry out a scheme which you think will benefit you : if the chestnuts are sound your plan will succeed, if discoloured it will fail ; boiled chestnuts mean that while you hesitate in coming to a decision someone else steps in and snatches a good opportuniy from you.

Chestnut Trees.—To see this tree in blossom indicates an event of much importance and pleasure occuring in the spring : you will probably have some surprises of a delightful nature, and there is little doubt that you will gain your wish ; this tree in leaf without its blossom shows a life of contentment, comfort, and good fellowship with influential friends.

Chicken.—To see many young chickens shows new interests and pleasures ; to see one cooked, hospitality and good friends ; roosting, domestic tribulation ; flying, troublesome matters.

Child.—To see a child asleep in its mother's arms shows severe illness causing much prostration ; a pretty child running means joy ; ugly, a threatened danger ; crying, distress and bad news.

Children.—To dream of many children around you shows troubles : you will find yourself in difficult situations which are impossible to avoid ; if they cling to you the troubles will be greater ; to see many children playing and happy signifies that memories of past happiness are those which must constitute your comfort in the future.

Chimney.—To dream of sitting in a chimney-corner with one of the opposite sex means that you may expect to be married without delay and to have a home of your own ; if the chimney-corner is illuminated by the brightness of the fire your life will be happy and prosperous.

China.—To see a variety of china is a sign of ever-increasing prosperity.

Chinaman.—To dream of a Chinaman shows that you will be brought into contact with someone who appears to be eager to serve you, but in reality is far from being trustworthy.

Chloroform.—To dream of taking this is a bad omen of

coming illness, probably an operation ; to smell it means severe pain ; to see a bottle of it beside you is a danger signal that one day you may be sorely tempted to take poison.

Chocolate.—To be drinking chocolate foretells that you will enjoy health and the comforts of life with but little to trouble you ; to spill it, that you throw away the best chances in life and only awake to this fact when it is too late ; to eat it predicts a present from someone whom you somewhat despise ; to buy it, folly.

Choir.—For a man to dream of singing in a choir shows that in the future he will be in some official capacity in a church ; for a woman to dream of it signifies that she will marry an old love whom she will meet by chance outside a church door.

Choking.—To dream of choking warns you of an attack of quinsy or bad sore throat ; to see another choke means wrath and venom.

Cholera.—To dream of cholera is a sign of an epidemic of severe illness of which you may be one of the victims.

Christening.—For a young man this dream signifies trouble on account of his religious views : he will cause distress to his parents by becoming a member of a new sect which holds strange doctrines.

Christmas.—To dream of Christmas is a sign of some important event taking place at that season ; if pleasant signs are seen in the dream, such as a bunch of carnations or a patch of good colour—blue for instance—you may feel assured of great happiness coming to you about Christmas time ; if when dreaming of this season bad symbols appear, such as black or a cross, it would indicate sadness and misfortune coming at that time of the year.

Christmas Tree.—To see this gaily decorated predicts that the Christmas season will bring about a meeting with some. man to whom you will be introfduced : he will be attracted to you and will become first a devoted friend and in time your lover and husband.

Chrysanthemums.—To see these beautiful flowers of various colours and growing in profusion, shows that a long desired hope in connection with someone dear to you will be realised, probably in the autumn ; white chrysanthemums in a wreath or cross or laid in profusion upon a bed foretell a death occurring in the autumn.

Church.—This is a sign of good friends, courage, honour, and tranquility ; if a cross stands out prominently so that it is the most noticeable feature it foreshadows sorrow ; if you see a cluster of grapes and a sheaf of corn it foretells the death of an old relative or friend in the autumn ; to see a church in a wood denotes a heritage ; to speak aloud in one means disputes.

Churchyard.—To be in one which is unknown to you and without bad signs shows that you will visit some place in the country and will be interested in the churchyard ; if it is familiar and you see an open grave by which you stand, it means the death of a near relation ; if you see this in the distance and the sun is shining brightly you will benefit through a death ; for the married to dream of wandering in a churchyard alone at night foreshows the loss of husband or wife ; to the unmarried, that they will mourn the loss of a dear friend or lover.

Churning.—To dream of churning promises good and successful results in all you undertake ; you will be fortunate and will always take a turn in the right direction for your own happiness.

Cider.—To dream of cider means happy days spent in the country with your friends ; to drink it predicts a distant heritage.

Cigar.—If you smell this it shows successful ambitions, friendship and love ; if you see a man smoking one you will have a wealthy lover ; who will absorb all your thougnts ; to break one in half means a disagreeable incident or a quarrel ; to be buying boxes of cigars implies that you will need a good income to gratify your tastes.

Cinders.—If sitting beside a heap of cinders it shows forlornness, a dreary existence, and poverty ; to gather them up denotes household drudgery, distasteful duties ; to be eating them indicates remorse ; to sift them foretells friction with your relations.

Circus.—To dream of this denotes a nature so absorbed in seeking pleasure that all other interests or duties of life are set aside and a completely selfish existence is the result ; to dream that you are a spectator at a circus implies that you will shortly be enjoying such in company with your friends.

City.—To dream of a large city full of movement shows prosperity ; deserted, a public calamity ; burning, a terrible fire in some large town is foreshown.

Clapper.—To dream that you are using this to scare the birds means that you are offended at small faults or failings in others and are always ready to bring them into notice, but are blind to your own more obvious deficiencies.

'Claret.—To dream of claret is a sign of deriving much pleasure and benefit from good and generous friends ; to drink it means that you may hope for much prosperity if you can restrain the extravagant tastes of those around you.

Clarionet.—To be playing on this instrument in your

dream is a sign of a pleasure which is gratified in an unexpected manner.

Clergyman.—To see him in his robes with a pen in his hand indicates that you will soon be making arrangements about your banns of marriage ; if he advances towards you with outstretched hand, reconciliation and the healing of an old sore are foreshown ; for a young unmarried woman to dream of a clergyman means that she may expect a disappointment in a love affair.

Climbing.—If you climb a tall tree with ease it means long life, health, and success in all you undertake ; if the tree is short you will not attain to more than an average success in life ; if it bends under you but does not break you will have difficulty in mastering the obstacles which you encounter, but your perseverance will be rewarded and you will achieve great things ; to climb a dead tree shows a wasted opportunity.

Clock.—To dream that you hear a clock ticking indicates the probability of over-sleeping yourself, causing you much inconvenience ; to hear a clock striking shows that an event of some importance is developing : possibly the number of strokes which you hear may show the days, weeks, or months, that will elapse before the event takes place ; to wind one is a sign of forethought and carefulness ; to hold one in your hand implies a desire to hurry over the present and arrive at a time to which you are looking forward.

Clothing.—To be clothed in garments of curious shape in which you feel grotesque indicates that you will probably become eccentric as you grow older and will be laughed at by your friends ; to be walking out of doors in night attire shows a worried state of mind, turmoil, and anxiety ; to be clothed in rags, misery and privation ; to buy rich clothes, beauty and pleasure.

Clouds.—These show disappointment and failure of plans ; clouds appearing low down over a house mean misfortune and distress to the inhabitants of it ; black and angry-looking clouds, approaching disaster, probably breaking up that home ; dark clouds over a large building with many people seen moving around it indicates a public calamity ; if a tongue of flame shoots from the loud, a disastrous fire ; vivid copper-coloured or red clouds foretell an earthquake and violent storms ; two clouds some distance apart, disunion ; light fleecy clouds, serenity and pleasant conditions.

Clove.—To dream of cloves shows a desire for appreciation and a wish to appear at your best on all occasions ; also a pronounced taste in colours and in dress.

Clover.—This is a fortunate sign of coming happiness ;

to walk in a field of clover promises the attainment of your heart's desire.

Coach.—If drawn by chestnut or white horses you may look forward to a time of ease and luxury ; by black horses the wealth you will enjoy is of a temporary nature only, and you will mourn the loss of it ; to alight from a coach warns you against an act of folly or a harmful indiscretion.

Coal Mine.—For the unmarried to dream of looking down into a coal mine is a sign of misfortune in love and marriage ; to t e married it foreshadows doubt and transitory happiness.

Coals.—If burning brightly you may expect comfort and good fellowship ; if put out by water, damage and loss through a fire.

Coal Scuttle.—To be carrying one full of coal shows that you will adapt yourself to unaccustomed circumstances requiring much energy ; an empty coal-box signifies domestic difficulties and vexation causing discomfort and annoyance.

Coat.—To dream that you are helping someone into a coat shows sadness caused through a parting ; hurriedly putting on a coat, an unexpected urgent message necessitating your presence elsewhere ; to tear it distressing news ; to tear the sleeve, failure in a new enterprise ; a new dress coat denotes the pleasures of life.

Cobbler.—To dream that you are a cobbler shows a life of ardous and ill-paid work, poor health, and a struggle to make both ends meet.

Cock.—To hear one crow is a sign of forthcoming good news and of conquest and triumph ; to see one in the house shows prosperity and the carrying out of successful plans.

Cockatoo.—Dreaming of this bird indicates a troubled state of mind, disturbances in the home and some vexation with friends.

Cockchafer.—If one flies upon you expect sudden news of a somewhat disagreeable nature ; to see many cockchafers flying denotes a bad harvest season.

Cocoa.—To dream of drinking cocoa predicts a tendency to dyspepsia and a nervous condition, also much need of warmth and comforts ; to be buying it shows care for others, good nature and kindness ; to see many packets of it means that you will live in contentment and that cares of the past will no longer trouble you.

Cocoanut.—To dream of a number of cocoanuts shows a visit to a fair ; to see them growing, travel and interesting discoveries ; to eat them, a dissatisfied mind ; to crack one means a love of birds and power of taming them.

Coffee.—To be drinking it alone shows indisposition ; in company with others, congeniality and social pleasures with the opposite sex ; to be making it, dependence on creature comforts ; black coffee, dissipation.

Coffee House.—To dream of eating in a coffee house is a sign that your pleasures are marred and hindered through lack of money.

Coffin.—If a coffin is seen very near it predicts death of a relative or great friend ; if in a house known to you it shows death or grave danger to a person in that house ; a coffin seen with purple upon it signifies the death of a man, with white the death of a woman, with snowdrops the death of a child or infant, with a sword the death of a soldier, with a flag a sailor; to dream that you are in a coffin is a very bad sign, showing danger of trance or a cataleptic condition.

Coke.—To see a fire of coke is a prediction of coming difficulties through lack of work and consequent money worries ; to buy it, vexation and discontent.

Cold.—To dream of intense cold denotes a disagreeable change in the weather ; to dream of feeling chilly means that you will meet with a cold reception from someone with whom you particularly wish to be friendly.

Collar.—To be wearing one which feels tight and stiff shows a swollen throat, possibly mumps ; a black collar, legal business through a death ; a gold collar, riches and honour ; for a girl to dream that she puts on a stiff white collar before the glass, denotes that she has a timid admirer who hesitates to approach her but will eventually do so in an awkward and hesitating manner.

Collar Bone.—If you dream that your collar-bone is protruding and painful it is a warning to avoid anything which might be likely to damage it ; to dream of it as normal shows a present of a necklace or neck ornament.

College.—For a boy or girl to dream of this shows that the desire for college life will be gratified ; for the mature to dream of it shows success and attainment through study and perseverance.

Colliery.—For a young woman to dream that she is in a colliery signifies that the chief ambitions and desires of her life will not be realised and she will be compelled to be satisfied with more moderate wishes ; for a young man this dream foretells achievement and wealth after a time of toil and anxiety.

Colonel.—For those connected with the Army to dream of the colonel shows to those in subordinate positions a need for more attention to discipline : to officers a hope of promotion ; for a colonel to dream of one predicts changes in his position ;

to a girl this dream foreshows that she will have an elderly lover.

Colour.—To dream of a mixture of many colours is a sign of a temperament depending largely on existing environment; becoming cheerful and gay in a congenial atmosphere and amidst beautiful surroundings, but mournful and out of heart in a gloomy house or on a dark day; it also implies change and movement, variety in life, many friends, and social pleasures.

Combing.—To be combing your hair shows that things are going smoothly for you; if knotted and the comb breaks it predicts trouble, failure, and disappointment; to comb the hair of a friend denotes a misplaced confidence.

Comedian.—For a youth or a girl to dream of being a comdeian shows a desire to become an actor or an actress; to dream that you are a comedian and receive applause promises you good success in the profession.

Comet.—To dream of a comet shows favourable weather, unusual and interesting events, successful enterprises; to the lover it is an unfavourable dream forecasting blighted love and separation.

Companion.—For those who are alone in the world to dream of having companionship shows a new interest coming into their life which will prove to be of much value and comfort.

Campanulas.—To dream of blue campanulas denotes that hope is centred on one desire: this flower assures you of the certainty of obtaining your wish; white campanulas mean contentment, peace, and happiness in your life.

Compasses.—This dream would show that you may expect to travel to far distant countries and to spend your life in most interesting activity.

Competitor.—To dream of competing in races, jumping, or swimming, with a sense of failure and exertion gives warning that if such competition is attempted it will lead to unpleasant results in the way of an accident or a bad strain.

Compliment.—If you receive a compliment in your dream you will shortly meet with someone who will pay you much attention; to a lover it is significant of foolish jealousy.

Concert—Dreaming of a concert of beautiful music foretells much enjoyment with a great friend; for those who are ill to dream of being at a concert proclaims their recovery.

Concertina.—To see this being played in a dream is a sign of contact with those who jar upon and irritate you and shows lack of harmony in your surroundings; to play it, dilatory habits and feeble wit.

Confectionery.—To dream of varieties of sweets and confectionery is a sign of a profitable undertaking bringing the gratification of small desires, much gain and prosperity ; to be eating them shows the pleasures of children ; to buy them, hospitality.

Confront.—To dream that you are suddenly confronted by one who has acted deceitfully towards you shows that your lack of moral courage allows you to keep silence and pass over the deception when a good opportunity of speaking is given you.

Congregation.—To dream of attending a service and being the sole congregation would show that your chief interest in life will be associated with a church and with those who officiate in its services ; to see a large congregation dressed in black indicates a funeral of some important personage.

Conjurer.—For a man to dream of conjuring shows a talent for sleight-of-hand which he would do well to take up as a profession ; for a woman it denotes cunning and deception.

Consumption.—To dream that you have consumption is a bad sign and should lead to care and precautions against this disease ; to see a patch of bright red on the chest is a sign of danger from hemorrhage.

Conundrum.—To dream of a conundrum will usually mean that you have composed or solved one ; if someone is asking you to solve conundrums, be sure that you are going to meet with a bore.

Convolvuli.—To dream of white convolvuli shows feelings of sadness : love and hope which have lasted but a short time now leave memory only to which you cling.

Cooking.—To dream that you are cooking points out that it would be well for you to learn to be useful for one day you will probably be in need of such practical knowledge.

Corks.—Dreaming of corks shows the power of adapting yourself to your company and of proving yourself useful in awkward situations.

Corkscrew.—To dream of this signifies that curious and unusual turns of fate in the past have caused some of the present difficulties in your life ; to use a corkscrew indicates inquisitive people who trouble you with question .

Cormorant.—To dream of this bird shows agility, swift decisions, and the achievement of your end through the power of rapid thought and work.

Corn.—To see corn blooming with the sun shining upon it foretells that events are maturing which will bring to you your heart's desire ; it is also a sign of wealth and successful undertaking.

Corncrake.—To hear this bird in a dream foretells radiant happiness, even if it be but transitory : the events that bring this about will occur in the early summer ; to see a corncrake running towards you shows important news from the country, possibly necessitating changes and journeys.

Cornelian.—To dream of a red or white cornelian would be a lucky token to those born in June as it is one of the birth stones for that month ; for those not born at that time it means that small events will be their lot in life.

Corner.—To dream that you are in a corner from which you seem unab e to move shows that you unintentionally offend a great friend ; to a lover it predicts delay in marriage.

Cornet.—To be playing a cornet means that you must be content with a small measure of success in all you undertake ; to hear it portends family strife in which you will be involved.

Cornfield.—To be standing in a cornfield of unreaped corn is a sign of full and lasting happiness coming to you in the summer ; if the corn is reaped and in sheaves it shows illness and sadness, possibly death for an old person ; to be reaping the corn predicts that you bring sadness and ill-health on yourself by your own folly.

Corns.—To dream that you have corns proclaims the unpleasant fact that your friends speak unkindly of you behind your back.

Corpse.—To see a corpse near you foreshows the death of a relation or dear friend ; to see one near water or floating in it predicts death by drowning ; with a pistol by it, a tragic death ; with a bottle, death from poison.

Cottage.—To dream of a cottage in which you appear to be living with a feeling of pleasure foretells happiness and contentment in a marriage on a small income ; for those who live in luxury to dream of a cottage with a feeling of sadness shows severe monetary losses.

Cotton.—Dreaming of cotton spinning shows that you will acquire an interest in cotton manufactories, proving a piece of good luck for you ; if you see an abundance of cotton it will mean a fortunate monetary investment.

Cough.—To dream that you are troubled by a bad cough implies that you will certa n'y have one, possibly an attack of whooping cough.

Counterpane.—To see it torn predicts illness and mental derangement of someone near to you ; too small shows everyday difficulties ; too large that you will hit upon a good plan ; for the housewife to dream of a counterpane foreshows an emergency in which she will need to have all her wits about her.

Country.—To dream of this is a pleasant sign of forth-coming pleasure and the maturing of a happy plan ; for those who live in the country this dream would hint that they must make the most of the present for it is likely to be the best and happiest time of their lives.

Courtship.—For the unmarried to dream of a happy court-ship is a sign that such will be theirs ; for the married to dream of this shows a somewhat restless and unsettled state, result-ing from a lack of harmony and understanding between husband and wife.

Cousin.—To dream of your cousin shows that an event of importance will shortly happen to the one of whom you are dreaming : the probability of the event turning out to be a pleasant or a sad one must be judged by other indications in the dream.

Cow.—To dream of cows shows a calm and contented state of mind, peaceful and prosperous days.

Cowslips.—To dream of picking cowslips implies that your life will be as sweet as the fragrance of the cowslip ; to see them growing, joy ; to the married it foretells a birth.

Crabs.—To see several of these predicts strife, disputes, and family disagreements possibly leading to legal interven-tion ; to be eating them shows an undiscovered taste which now affords you much pleasure ; to be catching them denotes a successful life full of good opportunities.

Cradle.—This foreshows a birth ; a broken cradle sorrow and anxiety about a child ; a black cradle, a bad illness and your hope shattered.

Crape.—To dream of crape is a sign of sorrow, bereave-ment and grief.

Crazy.—To dream of being crazy is a warning that you must strive to be calm on occasions that prove trying to your self-control ; to dream of it in connection with those around you shows a severe mental shock and strain.

Crew.—To see the crew of a vessel lying or sitting about the deck shows mutiny ; if they are rushing hither and thither it denotes a great storm ; to see them with bare arms Indicates the outbreak of an epidemic for which there is vaccina-tion ; with bare heads foreshows a funeral at sea.

Cricket.—To hear this insect indicates the arrival of an unexpected visitor who has an unceasing flow of conversation ; if it jumps towards you it shows that a surprising piece of news awaits you.

Cricket.—To dream that you are playing cricket shows a

love of outdoor life, a good and honourable friend or lover, social pleasures and popularity.

Cricket Bat.—To dream that you are holding a cricket bat means to a man or woman a desire for fair play in all matters.

Cries.—To dream that you hear cries of distress shows that someone dear to you is in urgent need of your presence ; the cry of an infant brings sad news.

Criminal.—To dream that you are a criminal means disgrace and ruin.

Crimson.—To see a patch of crimson shows a daring and passionate nature ready to take any risks in a venture of love ; reason is sometimes outbalanced by excitement which leads later on to occasional fits of despair ; crimson and gold predict honour, a rise in position and wealth.

Crinoline.—To dream that you are wearing a crinoline is a sign that fashion is a most important consideration with you and which you follow to excess ; to buy one means that unless you retrench in your expenditure you will have but a pittance to spend upon your dress.

Crochet Work.—To dream that you are doing crochet work shows a mind rivetted on personal affairs and trivial events.

Crocuses.—To dream of crocuses shows a state of delight and happiness which will be yours in the early spring ; crocuses are an emblem of joy ; to be picking them promises radiant happiness in love.

Cross.—To see one shows that you meet with many obstacles and hindrances in the way of your desires ; to see a black one predicts sorrow through the death of someone far away ; a red one, murder ; a gold one, episcopal honour ; to be wearing a silver cross means that you will become a member of a Community.

Crown.—A golden crown placed upon your head foreshows advancement and honours ; a position of power and wealth will be conferred upon you ; a crown of silver assures you of good health and a long life ; if crowned with green leaves it means that friends and fortunes forsake you ; with brass or iron indicates illness or sorrow.

Crows.—To see several crows in your dream is a sign of death ; if they are resting on a house the death will be for one of the inmates of it ; to see them circling round a tree in leaf foreshows an event causing you grief which will occur in the early spring ; if the tree is bare it will happen in the winter ; if one alights upon or near you it signifies the refusal of an offer of marriage.

Crumpets.—To be eating them indicates an afternoon's

pleasure spent in the company of congenial friends ; to see a dish of them, an invitation to a tea party.

Crust.—To dream of many pieces of crust shows you that waste is going on in your household ; if you are eating the crusts it implies a tendency to meanness, and a disregard of those who are less fortunate than yourself and who badly need assistance.

Crutches.—To dream of using crutches is a sign of an accident or an illness which causes lameness for the time being ; to buy them shows that a friend or relation will meet with an accident which will necessitate the use of crutches ; if you break or burn them it means a joyful recovery from illness.

Crysolite.—To dream of this is a lucky sign to those born in July or September, as it is one of the birth stones for those months ; this stone is a symbol of a simple childlike nature, innocence, and high ideals.

Crystal.—If looking into a crystal it shows a great desire to see into the future, the power for which you probably possess ; if the crystal appears dark it will indicate that the future which you desire to anticipate is best unseen ; if it is clear and sparkling it shows that your desires and hopes will be realised.

Cuckoo.—To hear a cuckoo in your dream is a sign of a happy meeting with someone dear to you in the springtime ; if you see a cuckoo on a bare tree it foreshows a hope destroyed.

Cucumber.—To be eating this in company with strangers shows an unexpected invitation giving you much enjoyment ; to see several of them growing denotes a new plan successfully carried out ; to pick them, prosperity and social success.

Cup.—An empty cup proclaims a time of anxiety ; a full one tells of splendid opportunities coming your way which will ensure your future success.

Cupboard.—To dream that you are shut up in a cupboard shows a trying condition of life from which you cannot at present escape ; to be opening a cupboard in which food is stored predicts a necessity for shopping ; to open it and find it empty means that you will have a disappointment in your money affairs ; to find it full proclaims abundance ; if the doors open of themselves it betokens illness for the bread-winner of your family.

Curate.—For a boy to dream of becoming a curate is a prediction of his choosing the clerical profession ; for a girl to dream of a curate shows that she will fall in love with one ; for a woman, that her interest is bound up in a curate and in parochial matters and that she is apt to bore others by her persistent talk on these topics.

Ourlew.—To hear this bird signifies a desire for those things which are beyond the possibility of your obtaining, a restless nature fretting against constriction and limitation ; to be searching for a curlew's nest shows a striving for a tainment against tremendous odds ; if you find it success is yours ; if your search is vain you must expect failure.

Ourrant Cake.—To dream that you are eating currant cake shows an invitation to a tea party where you will make a new friend in whom you will find much satisfaction.

Ourrants.—To be picking currants shows a very satisfactory ending to a matter about which you had some doubt : the happy solution of it probably occurs in the summer ; to be eating large clusters of white currants in company with one of the opposite sex to whom you give a bunch predicts that you will shortly fall in love and that your feeling will be entirely reciprocated ; to be eating red currants indicates affection, friendship, happiness in love and marriage ; black currants, tranquility and good fortune, the comforts of life and marriage with someone of mature age ; to be eating currant tart denotes satisfaction and unexpected pleasures ; to see a tart uncut foreshows an invitation which will bring you much enjoyment.

Ourtain.—To dream that you are hanging several curtains is a sign of a new home ; to be hiding behind a curtain means a desire to know everyone's business and to pry into secrets,to see a curtain pulled across a window indicates that someone is hiding a matter from you which would be to your advantage to learn ; if you touch the curtain the information will be revealed to you shortly.

Oushion.—To dream of arranging cushions shows pleasure through new possessions ; if you arrange them for a man or woman it foretells an illness for a relation or friend that will cause you anxiety ; a cushion in rags foreshows a bad attack of sciatica or lumbago.

Oustard.—To be eating custard in your dream is a sign of illness possibly measles or chicken-pox ; if you are making it the illness is for someone near you ; to drink it indicates future trouble with your teeth and much expense with dentistry

Cypress.—To be under a cypress tree shows despair and the death of a cherished hope ; to be climbing one which bends under you means that you make your troubles harder to bear by your own attitude towards them and by anticipating them ; to be cutting a cypress foretells that you bravely face a great difficulty and overcome it by your own endeavours.

D.

Daffodils.—To see large clusters of these flowers indicates that a long-desired hope is about to come to pass ; to be picking them with a feeling of light-heartedness predicts that a great joy in connection with someone dear to you will occur in the spring ; to see them in the form of a cross or wreath foretells a death which will probably take place in the spring-time.

Dagger.—If the dagger is near and pointing towards you it would be a bad sign of danger from wounds or an operation ; if it is at some distance and pointing away it shows a much less personal danger ; to have one in your hand predicts that you will one day need to defend yourself against personal violence.

Dahlia.—To see a large cluster of dahlias of all colours is a sign of events and changes of importance occurring in the early autumn ; white dahlias in a circle or cross foreshow a death, possibly of an old person ; to pick them is a sign of thrift and the rapid increase of your income.

Dairy.—To dream of being in a dairy where you are surrounded by pans of milk and rolls of butter shows a new agricultural enterprise which will bring you great success ; if you are in a dairy which has nothing but empty pans and no butter, be sure that your venture will be a failure ; if you skim the milk and taste the cream you may expect riches from an unexpected quarter.

Dairymaid.—To dream that you are milking cows or making butter shows that you will take up land work which will prove to be both successful and profitable ; to a young man this dream signifies that he will meet with a charming girl who will become his wife and that they will live in the country and prosper in the management of a dairy farm.

Daisies.—To dream of daisies shows that you have an attractive child-like nature, finding happiness in simple pleasures ; to dream of making a daisy chain means that you attract someone to you of the same nature as yourself who will become all the world to you ; to make one and tear it to pieces proclaims that you will forfeit your happiness through your own mistake.

Damsons.—To dream of eating damsons shows family friction and disputes ; to pick them, complication of your affairs.

Dance.—To be dancing is a pleasant omen of coming joy and gratification, good news and happiness in love and friendship ; to be a spectator at a dance foretells a great disappointment and a failure.

Dancing Figures.—To dream that you see figures dancing

in happy abandonment shows that your hopes and desires will be fulfilled and that many changes will occur, all tending to your success ; this dream also denotes social pleasures, gaiety and lightheartedness.

Dandelion.—To dream of eating dandelion leaves is a sign that you had better be careful or you may find yourself with an attack of liver disorder ; to dream that you are picking the flower foreshows solitude and poverty ; to dig them up, unexpected news of the marriage of an old friend.

Danger.—To dream of being in danger shows that you will one day be in need of great courage and coolness in an emergency : " forewarned is forearmed " and you will escape from it unhurt ; to see someone in great danger and be unable to save them means that you will witness a fatal accident.

Darkness.—To dream of being plunged into black darkness shows sadness, heartache, and that you must tread a path of great difficulty and disappointment ; to walk in it, that you will be summoned by an urgent message to go to the assistance of someone in trouble.

Dates.—To be eating dates denotes a pleasure which does not come up to your expectations ; to be cooking them, discretion ; to be counting date stones means that your past mars your future ; to be picking them foreshows travel in foreign lands under happy circumstances.

Daughter.—For the married who have no daughter to dream of one shows that they may hope for the fulfilment of this desire ; for those who have a daughter it predicts that she will cause them some anxiety.

Day.—To dream of a special day of the week usually means that an event of some importance will take place upon it ; if good signs appear in the dream you may anticipate a pleasure if gloomy signs you must prepare for misfortune ; if you dream of a beautiful clear day it is an omen of delight.

Dead.—To dream that you are dead is a sign that you are out of health, and that you need rest and change or you may have a bad illness ; to see someone known to you lying dead is a warning to prepare for severe illness to attack that person ; if pleasant signs appear in the dream, such as the sun shining, it will be an assurance of ultimate recovery from it.

Dead March.—To hear the Dead March in your dream shows the death of someone of importance for whom you will hear the Dead March played in reality.

Death Tick.—To hear this in a dream is a warning of illness and trouble for you or yours ; if it is persistent and loud, death for a near relative is predicted.

Debt.—To dream that you are in debt warns you to guard

against extravagance and gambling, or you may find yourself in financial distress ; if a debtor is paying you be on your guard against lending money.

Decorate.—To dream that you are decorating a public room shows that new opportunities of pleasure or advancement in life will open out for you ; if decorating a church it means fresh interests and the making of new friends ; the time of year at which this will occur is indicated by the flowers that you are handling, *e.g.*, daffodils the Spring, chrysanthemums the Autumn, and so on.

Deeds.—To be examining deeds shows inheritance of property ; to be signing them, the disposal of a property or business ; to be destroying a deed denotes a transaction of which you are ashamed.

Deer.—To see a herd of deer running away from you shows that your ventures in new directions of work or business end in failure ; if you kill one it means that you will hear of scandal in your neighbourhood ; if you chase one, a fruitless effort to undo your mistakes ; to see one dead, that you will be the innocent cause of distress to a dear friend.

Delicate.—To dream that you are delicate warns you not to think too much about your health or you may become fanciful and a chronic invalid.

Delight.—To hear the word delight in a dream is a hopeful sign that you will shortly feel in this pleasant state.

Delphiniums.—To see a group of blue and white delphiniums is a pleasant sign of true happiness and fulfilled desires ; if these flowers are bent to the ground and broken it means frustration and sadness ; to be holding large sprays of them signifies that you find your happiness in marriage.

Dentist.—To dream of the dentist shows that you have need to consult him at once.

Desert.—To dream that you see the desert warns you of the fact that those things which you most desire in life can never be yours ; to wander in the desert implies that you will cling persistently to your hope all through life although you may know it to be a fruitless one ; the figure of a man or woman appearing on the desert shows that there is someone at a great distance, and possibly unknown to you at present, who will be of much importance in your future life.

Desk.—To dream of opening a locked desk which does not belong to you and of finding in it something that gives you a feeling of pleasure, shows that you make an important and beneficial discovery, opening up a way for personal advancement ; if you are sitting at the desk you will receive a letter which will bring both pleasant and upsetting news ; to shut it indicates that you will lose a friend with whom you have corresponded for years ; to see a stranger at the desk means consultation with a lawyer.

Despair.—To dream of being in a state of despair indicates vexations and trials over which you will lose your temper.

Dessert.—To see an array of various kinds of dessert is a pleasing sign of coming happiness, the things which you desire will be obtained ; it also shows festivities and enjoyment, hospitality and good friends.

Destroy.—To dream of destroying a letter unopened means that you will be vexed by an anonymous correspondent ; if you destroy a cheque, or other form of paper money, that you will have to spend money on replacing something which you have lost or broken ; to destroy a ring, a broken engagement or unhappy marriage ; to destroy a book shows a feeling of disgust and contempt with yourself.

Detective.—If you dream of being followed by a detective be sure that you will put yourself into a damaging position unless you pay heed to your conscience and cease your present actions ; to dream that you are interviewing a detective means that you will have some unpleasant episode in your life.

Detesting.—To dream of detesting someone is a sign of a jealous and spiteful character which makes life unpleasant for those around you.

Devil.—Dreaming that the devil is near you gives warning that a reformation is much needed or you may find yourself so tightly in the grip of bad influence that it will be almost impossible to extricate yourself ; to see the devil fleeing from you shows a victory and escape from a subtle danger.

Devotion.—To feel intense devotion to a person in your dream is a sign that an absorbing affection is coming into your life.

Dew.—To dream of this denotes a trouble or disappointment that will disappear as rapidly as the dew in the sunshine ; to walk in the dew predicts happiness to lovers and success to the business man.

Diadem.—To be wearing this ensign of Royalty shows that your ambition is realised beyond your expectation : wonderful good fortune and influential friends assure you of an unusually successful career.

Diamonds.—To dream of these precious stones is a specially lucky sign for those who are born in September, as they are one of the birth stones for that month ; diamonds are good symbols for all dreamers showing wealth, rich friends, and happiness in marriage.

Dice.—To be playing with dice is a sign that you will be enticed into a hazardous amusement or undertaking which may bring upon you severe losses.

Difficulty.—To dream of being in a difficulty in a thoroughfare or on a journey warns you that you will probably find yourself placed in an awkward situation : it would be well to be cautious in a crowd or when travelling, thus mitigating, or possibly avoiding, a troublesome incident ; if the difficulty lies with those around you it means that you will be drawn into unpleasant discussion.

Digging.—To be digging a piece of ground that is clean is a sign of thrift and industry which will be well rewarded by good luck and gain ; if it is heavy and full of weeds it shows that troubles are in store for you ; to dig a well is a sign of a valuable discovery ; to dig a ditch or trench, illness ; to dig a large bare piece of ground indicates a doubtful undertaking in a new country ; to be digging for gold and finding none means that you stake your all on a chance and lose it, if you find a lump of gold great good fortune and success will be yours ; if you lose or break your tools it implies an outburst of temper ending in a quarrel.

Dinner.—To be dining alone at a table laid for several persons and with a scanty supply of food on it shows that you must be content with your lot in life for the present, but that in the future you will have cause for rejoicing ; to be a guest at a dinner party with a feeling of satisfaction implies that hospitality gives you enjoyment : if with a feeling of weariness it means that you will be a social failure.

Diploma.—To dream of gaining a diploma shows that you will attain to much success and proficiency in your work.

Dirt.—To see a heap of dirt or rubbish near which you endeavour to avoid but cannot, denotes that gossip and slander will be spoken of you : in spite of doing your best to disprove it there will be serious obstacles in the way of establishing your innocence ; to clear away a heap of dirt shows that you are the means of preventing the spread of an unpleasant story or piece of mischief ; to be building up a heap of dirt or rubbish means that you are a danger to society through your tongue and bad influence ; to fall on to a mud heap, poverty and despair.

Discussion.—To be taking part in a heated discussion shows to the married a state of turmoil in the home, family disputes and disagreeableness ; to the unmarried, friction with friends or lover.

Disease.—To dream that you have a contagious or horrible disease is a bad omen of that which may overtake you : if a good sign appeared in the dream it would foreshow your recovery.

Disgrace.—To dream of public disgrace is an unpleasant sign of that which may come upon you, possibly through no fault of your own ; to dream of being in dire disgrace warns you to give up your present amusements and companions or you will find yourself shunned by relatives and friends.

Disguise.—If you dream of being disguised it shows that you will one day have need of this in order to avoid the consequences of what you have done.

Dish.—To dream that an empty dish is in your hand is a sign of greed ; to break one is a foretaste of a greater loss ; to be carrying one, anxiety in household matters.

Dispute.—To dispute with one of the opposite sex shows petty jealousy leading to a disagreement ; to dispute a question with one of your own sex after which you turn away in anger predicts a severed friendship.

Distance.—Dreaming of great distance is a prediction that your truest happiness is yet to come.

Distress.—To feel this in a dream means a condition of trials and anxieties ; if you see someone in great distress and you appear to be looking on with indifference, it indicates that you are the cause of much distress.

Ditches.—To fall into a ditch full of muddy water shows that you will narrowly escape a more serious accident ; if you cross a ditch there are troubles in your path caused by those around you ; if the ditch is dry it is your own blundering which causes the difficulties ; to see a ditch without crossing it means that you usually find a way out of awkward situations.

Diving.—To dream of diving with a feeling of horror warns you against attempting it ; if with a feeling of pleasure, a great and unexpected piece of news which will lead to a fortunate discovery awaits you ; to the lover it reveals deception.

Diving Bell.—To dream of a diving bell forecasts that you may one day find yourself in danger on the sea or river.

Divorce.—For the married to dream of this is a sign that there is need for amendment or there may be dishonour and shame ; for the unmarried it gives warning that their conduct is far from pleasant and that there is just cause of complaint from those in authority.

Docks.—To dream of being in a whipping dock with a feeling of forlornness shows a voyage to a distant country, probably to make a new home there ; if with a feeling of happiness and excitement, it means a voyage ending in great success and joy, probably through marriage.

Doctor.—For a youth or girl to dream of being a doctor

shows a taste for that profession, and that it would be well to follow it ; for the mature to dream of a doctor proclaims that there is need to seek medical advice.

Dog.—If a strange dog jumps upon you in a savage manner it is a bad omen of misfortune and of a life of anxiety, bitter disappointment, and unhappy love affairs ; if it bites you will be wise to avoid making friendly advances to strange dogs : this dream also means family misfortune and money troubles ; if the dog runs toward you but passes by, you will avoid a calamity ; if you chase one you will be called upon to face a difficulty or danger needing much courage ; if one follows you at some little distance, barking and snarling, it shows adverse conditions and the thwarting of life's chances ; if a dog comes up to you in a docile manner and licks your hand, those things which have been the cause of much trouble in your life hitherto will soon have passed and you will be free to enjoy a time of happiness and comfort ; to see dogs fighting means turmoil and dispute ; fighting with a cat, bickering and irritability ; to play with a dog means that you will suffer for past folly ; to hunt with one, a hopeful outlook ; to lose one, dismay or lack of success ; to hear one howling predicts danger ; barking, sudden alarms and quarrels.

Donkey.—To see a donkey running away from you shows that there is danger of your becoming such a bore that your friends will avoid you ; running towards you means the arrival of an event or piece of news which has long been waited for, and your patience is at last rewarded ; to hear one braying is a sign of defiance, and indicates that you follow your own ideas whatever the result may be to others ; to see its ears, scandal ; to see one heavily laden, gain and profitable business.

Dolphin.—This dream shows a cheerful and optimistic character ; it also means gaiety and pleasure on the sea or river.

Doves.—If a dove is near it means a personal message of happiness and an assurance of faithfulness in love ; to see several of these birds shows calm peaceful circumstances, high ideals, beauty of mind, great affection, and progress ; if they are feeding from your hand it indicates that your desire is now about to be fulfilled ; for the business man to dream of doves is a fortunate omen of success ; to those who are ill or anxious this dream would bring comfort and hope.

Dowry.—For a man to dream that he has received a dowry with his wife indicates that it would be unwise to allow him to have the management of her money affairs for he would certainly sqaunder her fortune.

Dragon Fly.—If it is flying towards you it foreshows

tidings of unexpected occurrences, changes, and unlooked-for events ; if one alights upon you it predicts varied interests, new friends, and advantageous opportunities.

Draughts.—To dream of playing draughts shows that you have a rival who is not easy to dispose of ; to play with one of the opposite sex, disappointment in love.

Drawer.—To dream of an empty chest of drawers shows that you will go on a visit ; to be searching vainly in a drawer for something you cannot find means the loss of a valuable which causes you much vexation ; to find your drawer open denotes insecurity of your property or money.

Dreams.—A dream within a dream indicates that there is a special message of warning to be given or a piece of useful information of importance to you ; to dream of the dead usually means that you will receive news of some bad illness or trouble for their surviving relations.

Dress.—To dream of new clothes is a sign that you will shortly be wearing them ; for a youth to dream that he is in white denotes that he will follow a profession that necessitates a white garment, such as a clergyman, surgeon, etc., ; for a girl to dream of being in bridal attire when she is not engaged to be married, is a sign of a troubled love affair possibly never ending in marriage ; if this eventually takes place it will be after many years of waiting when youth is past ; if a matron dreams that she is in a wedding dress it reminds her of a past happiness and love, which now are waning ; for a man or woman to dream of being dressed in black foretells mourning ; in gorgeous apparel, an increased income and association with the rich ; for the prosperous to dream of threadbare, shabby clothes tells them to beware of speculation or extravagance, or such clothing may be their lot ; a dirty dress signifies approaching dismay.

Drinking.—To be drinking water from a large glass means vigour, honesty, truth, and interest in mechanism and electricity ; if you are given water to drink, an illness causing fever and a parched mouth is foretold ; if you are giving water to another the illness will be for that person ; to be drinking milk from a large glass shows that you may expect comfort, tranquility, and happiness in love ; to be given milk from a jug predicts danger of illness, possibly typhoid or weak lungs ; for a girl to receive a drink of water from a man assures her of a speedy marriage.

Driving.—To dream of driving with a stranger shows an unpleasant episode or danger coming from an unsuspected source ; with someone known to you and with a feeling of sadness predicts estrangement and parting ; with a feeling of pleasure, new and happy plans ; to be driving a horse which you cannot control means that against your will and better judgment you will be drawn into a friendship, and possibly an engagement, which will lead you into difficulties.

Dropsy.—If you dream of having this disease it would certainly be a warning to consult a doctor should your health appear to be unsatisfactory in any way.

Drought.—For a farmer this dream portends misfortune to his crops, or an accident to himself ; to others it is an omen of failure and the thwarting of plans.

Drowning.—To dream that you are drowning is, in the first place, a warning that unless you are cautious you may one day find yourself in great danger through water ; it is also an indication of worry, agitation, and of inevitable troubles which seem overpowering ; to be struggling is a sign of a desperate effort to escape a fate which you have brought upon yourself.

Drummer.—For a man to dream that he is a drummer foreshows popularity and a successful public career ; to a woman this dream brings social success, a large following of friends and admirers, and power of gaining her own ends.

Drums.—The hearing of drums signifies triumph, success, hilarity, and fame ; muffled drums, death of a famous soldier.

Drunkenness.—To dream of being drunk is a sign of a weak will and debased nature ; to dream that a drunken man is near shows that you may lead others into bad habits by your own follies.

Ducks.—Dreaming of ducks promises success in work, a busy life, good sense, and profit ; if you catch one, you are warned of a snare which will be laid for you.

Duel.—To be present at a duel indicates that you are the cause of a very serious quarrel which leads to strife and unpleasantness in a love affair ; to fight one signifies an antagonism which may lead into an outburst of violence ; to dream that you are killed in a duel brings dishonour and disgrace.

Duet.—If you are singing a duet with one of the opposite sex it means that you will shortly neet with someone of musical tastes to whom you will become a dear friend and you will have many pleasant meetings and happy hours together ; to be singing or playing a duet with one of your own sex shows a subtle and unsuspected rival ; to hear a duet beautifully sung or played foreshows a musical treat in store for you ; if it is badly played or sung perplexity and annoyance in business matters are predicted.

Dumb.—For the elderly this dream should be one of

warning against overwork and strain ; for the young it means fear or a bad shock.

Dungeon.—To dream of being shut up in a dungeon from which there seems no escape, shows that there will be events in your life, the consequences of which you will often struggle to evade, but will find it impossible ; to shut the door of a dungeon on a man or woman foretells that you will allow someone to suffer for your misdeeds whilst you go free ; to see a dungeon signifies perplexity and doubt in a love affair ; to the married, domestic tribulation.

Dusk.—To dream of the dusk shows that there are things in your life which are best kept out of sight.

Dust.—To dream of a thick dust being over you shows that you would be better appreciated by your friends if you paid more attention to your personal appearance ; for a girl to dream of dusting a room tells her of a short engagement owing to the fact that her lover will receive the offer of a new appointment necessitating his removal to a distance, and the wedding will in consequence take place without delay.

Dwarf.—For those who are big and strong to dream of being dwarfed is a sign of a coming humiliation which will make them appear small and foolish in their own eyes and in the sight of their friends ; to dream that you are married to a dwarf is a sign of marriage to someone who is deficient in size or in wit ; to talk with one portends calamity and possibly disgrace for someone dear to you.

Dye.—To dream of using a dye for yourself shows that you adopt an entirely new and somewhat startling style of dress and possibly change the colour of your hair also ; to see another using a dye means that you are jealous of the good looks of another and are constantly wondering by what methods you can improve your own appearance.

E.

Eagle.—To see an eagle flying above you is a sign of changes through distant causes, increasing power and knowledge, and wealth from an unexpected source ; if it is flying from you and you see a patch of bright colour or the sun shining, it shows wealth and honour after a change of residence ; an eagle with disordered feathers and drooping wings denotes the downfall of a monarch ; if a vulture is seen also it predicts the death of those in powerful positions ; if you see a flying eagle with outstretched wings swoop down and settle on a large tree or wide space of ground conquest and acquisition of territory are predicted ; two eagles fighting foreshows war ;

a dead eagle, public loss and mourning ; to see one in a cage signifies an unusual episode in public affairs.

Eagle's Nest.—To dream of finding an eagle's nest is a sign that you will attain to a position of power and wealth through your own ability and determination to overcome obstacles ; to seek for one but without success shows that your ambitions will not be gratified ; to see one on which an eagle *is* sitting predicts association with those in places of authority and honour : it also denotes a life of ease and wealth.

Ear.—Dreaming of an ear that is large and ugly shows that you will hear of scandal and abuse ; to see a normal ear means that you will receive some interesting and pleasant piece of news or valuable information ; to dream that your ears are cut off is a sign that you are indiscreet in your talk and will offend some of your relatives or friends by disclosing their confidences ; singing in the ears denotes false rumours.

Ear-ache.—To dream of ear-ache warns you of an attack of this painful malady.

Ear-rings.—If ear-rings are given to you by a man it shows ardent love ; if by a woman, admiration and generous affection ; for a lover to dream of buying ear-rings predicts the displeasure of his sweetheart ; for a girl to buy them means the humiliation of unrequitted affection.

Earthquake.—To feel this in a dream invariably shows that such will take place ; to see one foretells the news of a serious earthquake causing havoc and loss of life ; to dream of being in the midst of an earthquake but remaining unharmed foretells sorrow, loss, and misery followed by a time of peace.

Earwig.—Dreaming of earwigs is a sign of uncomfortable discoveries in the home, trouble with domestics, deceit and prying.

Easel.—To dream that you are sitting opposite an empty easel shows that you will one day sit for your portrait to be painted ; if you are working at an easel on which a large piece of canvas is stretched it means a talent for painting that might well be turned to account ; to purchase an easel is a sign of marriage to widows and maids ; to the married, increase of worldly goods.

Easter.—To dream of Easter with a feeling of joy shows that some new happiness will come into your life about that time ; if with a feeling of sadness, or symbols of sadness, it means that sorrow or some trouble will come upon you at Easter-time.

Eating.—To dream of this shows a somewhat grasping nature, eager to seize on the best, and leaving the less desirable things for others ; to be eating from a large pudding means greed ; to eat a loaf of bread hunger and a scanty larder ; to eat boiled fish indicates delicacy and probably an illness in which fish will form a part of your diet ; to eat fried fish which is crisp denotes satisfaction and good opportunities, but if it is badly cooked and greasy, domestic troubles are foreshown.

Eating House.—For the business man this dream predicts the offer of an appointment which will involve much travelling ; to a woman, dissatisfaction with her surroundings.

Eavesdropping.—To dream that you are eavesdropping denotes that you practise it or will do so at some future time ; this dream also shows a carping nature always on the lookout for the means of creating gossip and making mischief ; to see someone listening at a door warns you of the fact that such is the habit of a person who may do you much harm by trickery and deceit.

Echo.—Dreaming of an echo shows that there is a lack of reality in your character and that you are constantly adopting some new pose in imitation of those who are, for the time being, your companions ; for a lover this dream foretells the ending of bliss and a broken engagement.

Eclipse.—This is a bad sign of public and private calamities and a stormy atmosphere ; to see the sun eclipsed indicates the ruin or death of a man : the moon eclipsed denotes equal danger to a woman.

Eel.—To be catching eels foreshows labour and a strenuous life ; to be eating them means malicious tongues and treacherous friends ; to be selling them denotes poverty ; a dead eel shows misfortune.

Eggs.—Finding a nest of hen's eggs shows success in a new undertaking and profitable business ; if the nest is empty be cautious and do not enter rashly into a suggested plan ; to find a nest of ducks' eggs means achievement through industry and your own ability ; to be carrying eggs in your hand warns you to be wary in all matters of business ; to eat them is a sign of escape from a threatened disaster.

Elbow.—To dream of it as bent or painful warns you of an injury to your arm ; if you see it round, smooth, and white it signifies admiration and affection from one of the opposite sex ; if rough and red you may expect to encounter opposition and trials that will tax your strength and patience to the utmost.

Elderberry.—Dreaming of this tree signifies to the youthful pleasant prospects in the future, health, vigour and ardent affection ; to the middle aged it promises peace, health, energy and success.

Elephant.—To dream of this splendid animal is a sign of power ; if it is seen with a sheet of water or with natives, it probably denotes travel in hot climates ; if with the form of a man known to the dreamer it shows promotion for that man ; if you mount an elephant it means that a rise in position and good fortune will be yours ; to see an elephant approaching you means happiness and stability in love and friendship ; to see a herd of them signifies amazing news of a discovery in a distant land which will probably lead to a profitable investment on a large scale.

Elm.—To dream of a large elm tree in full leaf is a sign of prosperity, and coming happiness ; if the elm is bare it means that there will be a long waiting for your pleasures and that life will be advanced before your best days come to you.

Elopement.—To dream of eloping shows that your lover is likely to prove of so unreliable a character that if you marry him you will probably have reason to regret it ; for the married to dream of it is a sign of unhappiness and disloyalty.

Embrace.—To dream of embracing your relatives shows departures and arrivals ; if you embrace a stranger it means that you will travel and come into contact with many persons, one of whom will become dear to you ; to dream of the embrace of a lover predicts constancy and a love which is wholly yours ; the embrace of children denotes great affection for them and happiness in their company.

Embroidery.—To dream that you are at work on an important piece of embroidery which is developing exactly as you intended it to do, shows an ambition to master a subject or piece of work that appears very difficult to you : if the silks do not break and you work easily your ambition will be satisfactorily carried out, if they break or become entangled and the work seems to be at a standstill failure and disappointment are before you.

Emerald.—To dream of this stone is a lucky sign for those born in March, May, and September, as it is the birth stone for these months ; it is a pleasant symbol at all times meaning promotion and success to a man, hope and security to a woman; an emerald is a token of wealth and foreshows this to those who dream of it ; sometimes it means a good present of jewellery.

Employment.—To dream of seeking employment shows that a new plan will not succeed.

Enemy.—To dream that you have an enemy is a sign that you have made one although you are quite unaware of the fact.

Engagement.—To dream that you are engaged, without seeing bad signs in the dream, shows to a bachelor or maid that they may hope for this happiness ere long ; for the widow or widower this dream foreshows a second marriage ; for a parent it means a coming wedding in the family ; to dream of an engagement and see a frog or toad is an indication of scandal in connection with it.

Engine.—To dream of an engine running alone and slipping off the lines denotes trouble on the railway, strikes, and discontent ; if coaches are attached to it an accident is foreshown.

Engrave.—To dream of engraving your name on stone shows that you will be instrumental in bringing into prominence someone who will prove to be of great use in the world and of value to many : your intervention on behalf of this individual will thus be of wide-spread importance ; if you are engraving your name on metal it denotes a profitable offer that you would do well to accept.

Enjoyment.—To feel enjoyment in a dream is a sign that such will be yours ; to the lover it foreshows a courtship unmarred by jealousy or strife.

Enlist.—For a youth to dream of this is a sure sign that he will one day join the colours ; for a man or woman to dream of it indicates a new venture requiring a complete change of life.

Enterprise.—To dream that you are engaged in a great enterprise which leads to fame is a sign of an ambitious nature, full of energy in carrying out projects ; if good symbols appear in the dream such as a star, or crown, then you may feel assured of the success of your enterprise ; if gloomy or bad symbols are seen it would be wise not to embark on this venture.

Entertainment.—To dream of performing at an entertainment at which there is no audience shows that you will not be a brilliant success from a social point of view ; for a maid to dream that she enjoys herself at some place of entertainment portends that at a concert or theatre she will meet with a man who will eventually become her husband ; to the married this dream signifies improvement in affairs and contentment.

Envelopes.—To dream of piles of envelopes around you denotes a correspondence which causes you annoyance ; if the envelopes are red great anger will be aroused by their contents and there will be a risk of libel ; if an envelope with a black edge is seen you will hear news of a death ; a white envelope with gilt upon it denotes an invitation to a wedding ; an envelope without a stamp, a begging letter ; an envelope with a crown or lion upon it signifies a letter of congratulation on some achievement or an offer of a good promotion.

Envy.—To feel this in a dream indicates that there is an unreasonable jealousy in your mind of which you would do well to get rid.

Epaulets.—For a soldier or sailor to dream of these is a sign of promotion ; for a civilian to dream of them denotes an unexpected turn of fortune ; to a maid it suggests that her affections will be given to a soldier or sailor who will rise to high rank through his proficiency.

Epicure.—To dream of being an epicure and seeing luxurious food and drink around you shows that as a result of greed, costly living, and indulgence, you will come to the plainest of fare, though meanwhile you recklessly enjoy the dainties for which you crave.

Ermine.—To dream that you are dressed in ermine shows association with those in high and powerful positions who bring success and honour to you through their influence ; this dream also gives a general indication of comforts, riches and power.

Errand.—To dream that you are sent on an errand against your will and with feelings of annoyance shows that an unpleasant task lies before you and that you will come in contact with disagreeable people ; a difficult errand which you carry out satisfactorily promises you a good reward and a present of money.

Eruptions.—To dream of an unsightly eruption or blotches shows that you will be likely to suffer from an ailment producing skin trouble and a rash ; it warns you against chill and indiscretion in diet.

Escape.—To dream of escaping from a man or woman shows that there is a menace to your peace of mind through some person ; to escape from a window foretells a danger of fire.

Eucalyptus.—To dream of standing under a large eucalyptus tree shows a desire to evade such things as demand energy and to spend your days taking merely a languid interest in your surroundings and occupations ; to be picking it signifies that you endeavour to conceal your real feelings under cover of assumed hilarity ; to be drinking oil of eucalyptus denotes a dread of infection ; to dream of its scent implies a desire to forget the past and enjoy the future in spite of the drawbacks around you.

Evening.—To dream of this with a feeling of pleasure or with good symbols appearing indicates some specially happy incident of an evening in the company of someone you love ; if with a feeling of sadness or signs of gloom appearing it is on omen of misfortune and sorrow, probably in connection with those nearest to you.

c

Evergreens.—To dream of picking evergreens shows regret for the past and little hope for the future.

Everlastings.—To dream of these flowers is a sign of patient hope whilst there is but little to hope for ; if they are seen in a wreath or cross it would indicate a death.

Examination.—To dream of an examination when nothing of the sort awaits you means that you will be put in a position of responsibility needing judgment and knowledge.

Examine.—For a youth or girl to dream of passing through the ordeal of being examined without being able to find answers to fit the questions, shows that rest is needed or when the time of examination comes there will certainly be a failure ; if you dream of passing through it with ease and without faltering it predicts a most successful test from which you emerge with flying colours.

Exchange.—To dream that you exchange a photograph with one of the opposite sex is a sign of a friendship that will ripen into love ; to exchange an animal signifies that you will speculate with a farmer and lose ; to exchange a child shows that you will lose one.

Exciseman.—To dream that an exciseman is in your house shows an unexpected demand for money which appears to you unreasonable and which you find very inconvenient to meet ; if you dream of an exciseman in connection with some-one known to you it signifies the offer of a good post for that individual.

Excuse.—To appear to be making excuses in your dream indicates a somewhat shifty nature with but little regard for truth when it is found to lead to personal inconvenience.

Execution.—To dream of an execution shows that you will be told some dreadful piece of news which will cause you great distress.

Executor.—To dream of an executor means that you will benefit by a legacy.

Exercise.—To dream of taking violent exercise shows a desire to achieve success in the face of many obstacles and difficulties ; if the exercise is half-hearted and appears to be aimless it implies that a lack of concentration will mar your efforts.

Exhausted.—To dream that you are exhausted when you have no reason for being so shows that you sometimes cause a feeling of exhaustion in others by your restless and fussy habits.

Exile.—To dream of being an exile is a sign that you will go through much tribulation for one whom you love.

Expedition.—To dream that you are about to set out on

an expedition accompanied by many people foreshows an event of much importance that will lead to a new career.

Eyebrows.—To dream of eyebrows shows that you will meet with someone who has very much marked and thick eyebrows : this characteristic will attract your attention at once, and the casual meeting with this individual will bring a powerful influence into your life.

Eyeglasses.—To dream of eyeglasses shows that you are slow to see faults in yourself but very quick to perceive them in others.

Eyelid.—To dream of swollen eyelids foretells that you may suffer from them ; to see smooth white eyelids shows that you will fall in love at first sight with someone who has noticeably good eyelids.

Eyes.—To dream of beautiful eyes gazing into your own shows fidelity, depth of character and love : it is also a sign of penetration and the solving of difficulties ; if you see eyes glaring at you it means that you will meet with someone whose eyes are noticeably unpleasant and who will prove to be venomous towards you ; to see squinting eyes is an unfortunate omen that someone near and dear to you is developing defective eyesight ; to dream of your own eyes being very sore and painful denotes illness affecting your eyes ; to dream that you have lost them is an urgent warning to consult an oculist.

F.

Face.—To see many familiar faces around you shows that you will receive an invitation to a party or wedding; to see many strange faces foreshows journeys ; to see the face of someone known to you appearing harrassed or white means news of trouble or of illness for this friend or relation ; to see a face distorted and swollen predicts severe illness affecting the face ; swathed in bandages shows an accident ; to see a beautiful face which seems close to you indicates that you will meet someone of whom this dream face is a representation and with whom you fall in love at first sight ; to see your own face in a mirror signifies an illusion rapidly dispelled.

Factory.—To dream of being in a factory where all the machinery is at work but no workers are to be seen, shows a coming strike of great national importance causing inconvenience and threatening disaster.

Failure.—To dream of failure in connection with a thought-out plan warns you not to attempt it ; to dream that you are a failure in every way shows that there is need of more self-reliance and energy or you will certainly not meet with any measure of success.

Fainting.—To dream of fainting in the street or in a crowded thoroughfare is an omen of a sudden indisposition which will attack you, probably when out on business or pleasure ; to dream of fainting in your home shows a slight ailment from which you will soon recover ; to dream of tending someone who has fainted means that you will be called upon to give assistance to a person whom you find in a prostrate condition.

Fair.—To dream of being at a fair foreshows an outing in company with those who are somewhat boisterous and rowdy.

Fairy.—To dream of meeting a fairy who promises you all you can desire, warns you that you should be cautious in listening to the persuasions of those who endeavour to drag you into doing things which you feel are unsuitable or undesirable ; to meet a bad fairy who predicts all manner of evil for you warns you of an enemy who will do you some harm at the first opportunity.

Faithless.—To dream of being faithless to someone who is dear to you shows a rival who is likely to overthrow your happiness.

Falcon.—Dreaming of this bird warns you to be on your guard, for you have an enemy.

Falling.—To dream of falling an immense depth and then finding yourself enclosed by steep cliffs without any apparent outlet, indicates trials that seem overwhelming and will wellnigh drive you to despair ; if you seem to emerge from the depth into which you fell, then you may hope to find a way out of your troubles and to experience a more peaceful condition of life ; to dream of falling a short distance and being able to ascend easily shows a temporary discomfort through which you come triumphantly ; to dream of falling downstairs or falling in a street, warns you that you should be careful to try to avoid the occurrence of these accidents.

False.—To dream of someone in whom you trust being false is a hint to you not to be so entirely trusting in the future or you may have a sad awakening.

Fame.—To dream that you have attained to fame shows that your ambitions for the future will be realised through your indomitable energy and determination.

Famine.—To dream of experiencing a famine is a sign of coming distress and shortage of food.

Fan.—This shows a love of admiration, frivolity, pleasure with the opposite sex, flirtations.

Farewell.—To say farewell or to hear another say it, is an omen of sadness, an aching heart, and painful news.

Farm.—To dream of a farm where herds of cattle are to be seen is a sign that an unexpected turn of events takes you to farm life, bringing you success and prosperity.

Farmer.—For a youth to dream of being a farmer shows that he will in the future become one ; for a girl to dream of farming shows that she will probably emigrate and become a farmer's wife.

Farthing.—Dreaming of a farthing shows a miserly mind ; to hold a farthing in your hand means a sad state of poverty and a sore need of friends.

Fast.—To dream you are considered fast shows that there is good ground for that opinion.

Fat.—If you dream of being fat when you are not so, you may be sure that you will become very stout unless you take precautions against it ; to be eating fat shows that you will overcome obstacles and let nothing stand in the way of attaining your desire ; to cut off fat and put it aside shows that you are often your own enemy and frustrate the good things that might come to you by your blundering and lack of foresight

Fates.—To dream of fate being against you warns you not to undertake a new enterprise or business without first carefully investigating its merits ; this dream should also warn you against trying to make elaborate plans for carrying our a scheme of personal interest to you, for it would almost certainly be a failure ; to dream that fate is working in your favour is a hopeful indication of success and happiness for you.

Father.—To dream of your father shows that you should look to him for counsel and advice ; to dream of him with a feeling of remorse indicates that he needs your care and affection.

Fatigue.—To dream of being over-tired when you have done nothing to cause it means that after a time of agitation and exertion you will be well rewarded and will the more enjoy the time of ease which follows.

Fault.—To dream of committing a fault warns you to be careful or you may be led into some folly that will afterwards give you cause for much regret ; to accuse someone dear to you of a fault shows that you will one day feel remorse for your habit of criticism.

Faun.—To dream of a faun shows that those dependent on you may suffer through your adventures, which are doomed to failure.

Favour.—To dream that you ask a great favour of a stranger denotes a loss of your time in seeking what you cannot obtain ; to ask a favour of one of the opposite sex denotes failure in obtaining your desires.

Fear.—To dream of fear shows that you will be placed in a position needing courage and that you will face it with coolness and bravery ; to dream of frightening others shows cowardice and a weak irresolute character.

Feasting.—To dream of feasting signifies the gratification of small pleasures and tastes.

Feathers.—To dream of large and handsome feathers shows a good present, sometimes of money ; to dream of small white feathers denotes something which you fear but will meet with courage ; to see waving white plumes shows promotion and honour.

Feeble.—To dream of being very feeble and unable to help yourself foreshows a coming illness which will leave you in a weak condition.

Feet.—To dream that your feet are sore foretells delay and frustrated plans ; if they are cut off, pain and injury ; if you dream of many feet it means that one of yours is in danger to burn your foot shows a danger of scalding ; to dream that they are dirty or misshapen, predicts illness and misfortune ; if your feet appear to be light and you seem to be dancing you will have much pleasure and good friends ; to see feet or a foot at some distance from you denotes a journey : this dream also signifies understanding.

Fence.—This shows that there is but a step between you and success.

Ferns.—To dream of ferns shows dignity and peace, a steadfast and reliable nature ; dreamed of in connection with a man or woman they would indicate someone in whom you may place implicit trust and through whom much happiness will come to you.

Ferret.—This dream denotes mischief sown by gossip ; it also shows a love of prying into other persons' affairs and thrusting a finger into each pie.

Ferry Boat.—Dreaming of crossing a wide river in a ferry boat shows that your difficulties will be smoothed away by the aid of good and useful friends.

Festival—To dream of a festival with a feeling of pleasure shows that there will be a special happiness in your future to which you may look forward and which will come in connection with a festival.

Fetters.—To dream of fetters shows that you have bound yourself to someone who will prove to be nothing but a clog upon your life.

Fever.—Dreaming of fever shows that there is danger of an attack of it ; if strawberries or strawberry leaves are seen on the chest it denotes scarlet fever ; if pans of milk are seen in the dream it probably means an attack of typhoid fever.

Fiddle.—To dream that you hear beautiful music from this instrument denotes happiness and peace in your surroundings ; if you hear discordant sounds it indicates a lack of harmony with your domestic life ; to be playing the violin shows that you will take up some new enterprise in which you will score a brilliant success.

Fiddler.—To dream that you hear a fiddler playing shows a desire for amusements, probably dancing ; if your wish is not gratified you will become restless and dissatisfied with your surroundings and may take up with undesirable friends ; for the elderly to dream of a fiddler reminds them of past happiness and the necessity of doing their best to give pleasure to their children.

Field.—To be in a large field from which you seem unable to emerge shows that, by the interference of those around you you are driven into a position that you greatly dislike ; to be in a field that is full of flowers is a sign of joy ; to be in a ploughed field means a sorrowful heart ; to see several large fields of grass shows pleasure and prosperity ; if a notice board is seen warning trespassers off the fields it denotes that you will probably inherit some land ; to see a small field that has many paths and patches of bare ground shows a loss of income through agricultural investments ; seeing apple orchards with the trees in blossom denotes a visit to the country in the spring ; fields of mowing grass show a visit to the country in the summer fields of scarlet poppies mean that you will have much enjoyment in the summer-time with those most congenial to you ; fields of hops show trials, vexation, and sleeplessness.

Fife.—To hear music from the fife indicates that you will probably take a long journey to say farewell to a soldier who is about to rejoin his regiment for foreign service ; to be playing on the fife shows that you will take up some work or interest from which you will derive much satisfaction.

Fight.—To see men fighting signifies serious quarrels among those with whom you live ; to see men fighting in a street shows that you are likely to come in contact with an unpleasant episode ; to see women fighting shows jealousy and an ungoverned nature.

Figs.—To eat good sound figs signifies joy , happiness, and an abundance of the good things of this world ; to dream that a fig is given you by one of the opposite sex denotes a friendship which will ripen into love and probably end in a happy marriage : should the wedding take place soon after this dream the lovers will be likely to experience some fortunate surprise at their wedding ; for those in business to dream of figs is an omen of success and prosperity ; to be eating mouldy or defective figs shows that your pleasures will be marred by some disagreeable incident.

Figures.—To dream of any number above one and below seventy-eight is said to portend good fortune to the dreamer, but forty-nine is considered a specially lucky number ; numbers above seventy-eight are uncertain except three hundred and forty-three which is always a lucky number ; to some people the number thirteen is invariably one of misfortune, must be judged with regard to the dream as a whole in order to arrive at the correct meaning ; the figures sometimes indicate special events which will happen on the particular date shown in the dream or they may specify a sum of money coming to you : the latter is often the meaning of numbers in a dream ; figures seen by a cross or wreath of flowers foreshow a death which will probably occur on the date indicated by the figures.

File.—To dream that you are using a file shows that circumstances are arising which will need adjusting with skill and tact in order to preserve harmony and good-will.

Find.—To dream that you find a lost possession is a sure sign of your doing so.

Fine.—To dream that you pay a fine shows an error of judgement from which you suffer some inconvenience.

Finger.—To dream that your fingers are painful and swollen shows that you will suffer in some way with them, it may be from gout, chilblains, or some other ailment affecting the fingers ; if you burn your fingers it warns you to be careful to try to avoid this ; to cut your finger slightly without its bleeding shows that you had better interfere less with other people's affairs or you may be led into a quarrel bringing serious consequences upon yourself ; to cut your finger deeply signifies injuries and small accidents ; to see more than five fingers denotes new relations.

Fire.—To be looking on at a fire means a grave warning of danger from it ; this is one of the most ominous signs and should be regarded as an urgent need for caution against fire ; for a householder it indicates the wisdom of insurance or, if already insured, of increasing its value ; if you set fire to a house or building in your dream it shows that you gain your own ends by dishonest means.

Firearms.—To dream of firearms near you is a sign of tragedy and sorrow ; to be using them indicates a quarrel of a longstanding nature which may one day lead you into committing an act of violence ; to see another using them mean that you may be called upon to bear witness in a case of murder.

Fire Engine.—To see a fire engine advancing towards you denotes a risk of fire and personal loss of property ; if the engine is going away from you it shows that the fire is one of which you will either hear or see.

Fire Escape.—If the fire escape is near you it would show a grave warning of danger from fire or explosion ; if at a distance the danger is less personal.

Fireside.—To dream of sitting at the fireside alone and by an empty grate or a lifeless fire foreshows a sorrow which you must bear alone ; to be by the fireside with a cheerful glow and people around you shows that your happiness and pleasure are bound up in those near to you.

Fireworks.—To dream of fireworks indicates that there is a risk that you will be easily deceived by outward appearances and will waste your substance continually in buying cheap imitations of genuine articles ; to be letting off fireworks shows a desire to associate with those who now ignore you ; if a firework explodes it means that you will commit some folly which will bring upon you a severe censure.

Firmament.—To dream of this as blue and cloudless predicts tranquility, a cherished hope about to be realised, and fair weather ; to see it looking murky and grey shows depression, disappointment, trials, and general gloom ; if it is looking black and angry it means turmoil, unrest, and confusion ; to see it orange-coloured indicates wrath and snowstorms ; a pink rosy glow shows love, trust, happiness, and good weather ; a mackerel sky, fickleness, deception and windy weather ; white only to be seen indicates obscurity, mystery, and foggy weather.

Fish.—Fish seen in the sea denotes a cruise or news from abroad ; a starfish by itself means a piece of good luck for you. To dream of fish lying in heaps on the shore shows great storms ; fish seen in quantities far inland indicates a flood.

Fishing.—See '' Angling.''

Fits.—To dream of fits is a bad sign and means that there is a danger of such attacking you or someone closely connected with you.

Flag.—To see a flag waving foretells disturbances, rebellion, war ; if you carry one it portends glory and honour ; a flag at half-mast on a church shows the death of someone of importance associated with the church ; a flag half-mast on a large public building, the death of a well-known and important person ; to be standing by a flag with a small gathering of people around you signifies that you become and

C*

enthusiast on certain subjects and attract a small following of those who share your views ; unless you endeavour to modify your enthusiasm it may lead you into disagreeable disputes with those who have no sympathy with you.

Flagon.—To dream of drinking from a flagon means that you never feel quite satisfied with persons or things as they are.   ●

Flames.—To dream of being enveloped in flames is a warning of a fire from which you escape in peril of your life ; to see them bursting from a tree signifies a violent thunderstorm in which trees and buildings are struck by lightening ; to see flames bursting from the ground denotes an earthquake ; to see an empty house in flames foreshows total loss, destroyed hope, and despair.

Flattery.—Dreaming of someone who offers you much flattery warns you to be on your guard or you may find yourself drawn into a snare.

Fleas.—To dream of these pests is an unpleasant signal that one is near you.

Fleet.—Dreaming of the Fleet if you are not already associated with someone in the Navy, means that something of much interest and importance to you is likely to occur in connection with the Naval profession ; for those who have relations or friends in the Navy it predicts good promotion for them ; to dream of a fleet of fishing boats in full sail is a sign of advancement and increase of wealth, new plans and ideas which put into practise will bring you much success.

Flesh.—For those who are poor and whose food is scanty to dream of becoming fleshy signifies improved conditions : fortune will smile upon them and the comforts of life will be theirs ; for those who have abundance to dream of wasting shows a danger of serious illness ; to see the flesh yellow predicts an attack of jaundice ; if it is covered with large spots or scabs chicken-pox is predicted ; to see it looking sunburnt shows health, vigour, and enjoyment.

Flies.—To dream of a swarm of flies shows disorder and lack of cleanliness ; to dream of flies settling on you denotes anxieties and worry which are accentuated by your being possessed of a fidgetty and exacting nature ; to kill them is significant of coming illness.

Flirting.—To dream of flirting shows that you derive much pleasure and satisfaction from it and have little regard for the harm that may come upon others through this habit.

Floating.—To dream that you are floating in water with a feeling of sadness shows that there is a vast space between you and your desires : it also denotes illness for someone you love ;

to be floating with a feeling of well-being shows a calm uneventful existence which is nevertheless a happy life.

Flood.—To see a flood in a dream indicates the coming of heavy rain and bad floods ; it is also a forecast of sadness and trouble.

Floor.—To dream of a floor from which planks are missing shows the loss of a relative through death ; to be lying on a floor means danger of a fall and a broken limb ; to scrub a floor indicates minor worries and petty vexations.

Flour.—To see flour in large quantities is a bad omen indicating the illness or death of a great friend ; to be buying flour by the sack shows illness and sorrow in the home ; to be idly sifting flour through your fingers indicates trifling with serious questions thus endangering your future happiness ; to be weighing a meagre supply of flour means adversity and money worries ; to see flour with black spots in it predicts a bad harvest season and a serious shortage of flour.

Flowers.—To see them growing in profusion shows much happiness in your life ; to see a variety of bright-coloured flowers means that unexpected events lead to a joyful meeting with someone you love ; to be gathering sweet scented flowers denotes a love that is fully reciprocated.

Flute.—To dream that you hear this in the distance foretells news of a birth ; to be playing on it shows that you take the ups and downs of life as they come, meeting difficulties with a smiling face ; it also shows a clinging to past memories that are dear to you.

Flying.—To dream of flying means that there is much that you wish to leave, and to have that you cannot obtain ; things desired are far distant causing a restless condition.

Flying Angel.—To see this vision in a dream is a token of peace, love, and joy that is swiftly approaching you.

Fog.—To dream that you are in a dense fog means that you will certainly experience this discomfort ; it also shows that it would be wise to wait for a while before embarking on a new venture.

Folly.—To dream that you commit some folly which is likely to bring about unpleasant results, warns you to give more consideration to matters which you already have in hand.

Font.—See '' Baptism.''

Food.—To see food in the larder or spread out on a table shows financial difficulties : the more the food the greater the difficulty.

Fool.—To dream that you are considered a fool by those whose good opinion you value shows that your tendency to self-consciousness leads you into doing and saying somewhat awkward things, thereby rendering yourself liable to be deemed a fool.

Football.—For a man to dream of a football shows that he will one day excel in this game ; for a woman to dream of a football shows a love for sport and for doing everything in common with the opposite sex.

Footmen.—To see several footmen in attendance on you predicts that you will become very prosperous ; if the footmen are standing at an open door beyond which you see scarlet or crimson cloth it shows that you will be present at a state function or court ceremony.

Fop.—To dream of a fop means that you will come into contact with such a one whom you will find agreeable even whilst you despise his foppery ; for a man to dream that he is a fop shows a vacuous mind and idle habits.

Forehead.—To dream of your forehead as remarkably handsome suggests that you possess great spirit ; if it is very much rounded it signifies good fortune and ability ; if large and full it shows eloquence, courage and power ; if it is small and much wrinkled it implies an harassed state of mind, difficulties, and obstacles ; to dream you have a forehead of steel or iron shows that you bear a feeling of extreme hatred towards someone who you consider has done you an injury.

Forest.—To dream that you are in a wood or forest with birds and flowers about you has many pleasant meanings : happy meetings with those most dear to you, love and fulfilment, desires coming to pass, satisfaction ; if the wood is dark and dreary, without flowers or birds, it is a bad omen, showing loneliness, an aching heart and disappointments ; if rain falls upon you illness is foreshown.

Forge.—To dream of being in a forge shows a need for refinement and for reconstructing your ideas on many subjects.

Forgery.—To dream of committing forgery is a sign that someday you will be sorely tempted by stress of circumstances to do so.

Forget-me-Not.—To be picking a bunch of forget-me-nots reveals the attainment of a cherished hope ; to be given this flower by one of the opposite sex denotes that you will find your truest happiness in love and marriage ; to see masses of this flower growing shows hope, love and joy, pleasure in nature, and a time of special happiness which will probably occur in the late spring.

Fork.—To see this warns you of those who constantly flatter you : it would be well for you to be on your guard or you may one day awake to the fact that all this flattery was used as a tool to harm you.

Forsythia.—To be picking large sprays of this flowering shrub denotes that you may reasonably expect to obtain those things that you most desire : a time of sunshine and happiness is before you and the events that lead to this will probably occur in the spring.

Fortune.—Dreaming of a fortune is a hopeful sign that you will inherit one.

Fortune-Telling.—To dream of consulting a fortune-teller shows that before long you will do so ; if you have a feeling of pleasure in the dream you will hear what you desire, if with a feeling of gloom the " fortune " will be disappointing.

Fountain.—To dream you are beside a fountain of clear water is a most favourable omen indicating happiness and success in love and marriage, prosperity in business and good fortune in all you undertake ; if the waters are muddy or discoloured it foretells your good luck will be mixed with vexations and troubles ; to be drinking from a fountain shows a craving for knowledge and for penetrating into mysteries ; to be drinking from a fountain of dark-looking water denotes strange matters coming to light which lead you to suspect and distrust those with whom you are closely associated.

Fox.—Dreaming of a fox shows that you have an unsuspected enemy, possibly disloyal dependents ; sometimes it means theft and trickery ; seeing a fox pursued by hounds would mean that danger is rapidly approaching you or yours.

Foxgloves.—These flowers denote ambition ; if they are bending and breaking it shows defeat ; if they are upright in large clusters, attainment ; a large patch of white foxgloves means calm, a serene state of mind, pleasant events and happiness in love.

Fraud.—To dream of being defrauded by those around you or with whom you may work shows that it would be well for you to use some precaution in your dealings with them.

Freemason.—For a Freemason to dream of being expelled from the Order shows that there is some doubt as to the wisdom or fitness of the course which he has taken in some matter ; for one who is not a Freemason to dream of becoming one denotes the making of many new friends who will prove loyal and faithful ; if dreamed of with an expanse of water or a ship to be seen it foretells a visit to the East

Freesia.—Dreaming of these sweet-scented flowers in masses shows beauty of mind, high ideals, and a cherished hope likely to be realised in the springtime.

Friend.—To dream of a great friend is a sign that the friendship is deep and will be life-long.

Friends.—To dream of those friends whom you constantly see usually denotes something of importance happening in connection with them, or that an unexpected piece of news is told you by one of them ; to be amongst many friends shows popularity, social pleasures and the assurance of loyalty and affection from your friends

Frightened.—To dream you are frightened without apparent cause shows that you will escape from a danger with nothing worse than a bad shock ; if you are frightened by a man, avoid lonely places ; if by an animal, be careful not to meddle with one.

Fritillary.—To see a profusion of these beautiful flowers is a sign that you will probably pay a visit to Oxford in the early summer, where they may be seen growing wild ; to be picking them shows a happy memory and associations with someone in the past.

Frog.—If several frogs are seen in the garden or field it denotes wet weather ; if they are in a room or near you it signifies unpleasant sights and stories ; to see several frogs near you foreshows sickness and grief, and with other gloomy signs such as clouds it would show a danger of melancolia.

Frost.—To dream of frost in the summer indicates a spell of abnormally cold weather ; to dream of it in the winter shows that you will probably wake to find the window covered with frost ; sometimes to dream of frost predicts an event to be expected in the winter, the nature of which event must be judged by other signs in the dream.

Frown.—To dream of frowning shows that you have a bad habit of doing this which annoys your friends.

Fruit.—Dreaming of various fruits seen in clusters is very pleasant and means that things are developing which will tend to your success and happiness ; it is a sign of comforts, pleasures, increased income, and general advancement.

Frying Pan.—To dream of frying pans is a sign of household cares, drudgery, and uncongenial work.

Fuchsias.—To see masses of fuchsia blossom denotes pleasant meetings and reunion after separation from relatives or friends.

Fun.—Dreaming of what you may consider " fun " is a sign of pleasure in practical jokes and noisy enjoyment.

Funeral.—To dream of attending a funeral, dressed in black predicts bereavement ; if you seem to be alone it is the funeral of someone specially dear to you, husband or lover ; if you are looking at a funeral from a distance, without other signs of grief, it shows the death of someone whom you know but slightly, and if a patch of bright colour or other good symbol appear, it means that there is some benefit to you through the death ; a funeral seen passing along a road in which flowers or buds of trees are to be seen, would mean a death taking place at the time of year indicated by the flowers or the buds of the trees, as for instance the buds of a chestnut showing the spring ; to see a funeral by a station or with a train shows that a journey will be taken for it.

Fur.—To dream of being dressed in costly furs shows riches and much comfort in life ; to see a piece of sable on a coat or dress means mourning.

Furniture.—To be buying new furniture shows a removal to a new home ; if the furniture is poor and shabby, it shows thst you will experience much difficulty in your home life, and that poverty will be your lot.

G.

Gag.—To dream of a gag being in your mouth is an unpleasant omen as it probably predicts a visit to the dentist and a gag being used ; to be inserting a gag for yourself shows that there is need for you to be more reticent in your talk.

Gaiety.—To dream of gaiety with a feeling of pleasure denotes that a time of social enjoyment is before you ; if with a feeling of distaste, it means that you will have the gaiety, but it will bring you nothing but disappointment, for you will be conscious of being a failure.

Gain.—If you acquire this by fair means you may hope for wealth ; if by injustice you will lose all you possess.

Gaiters.—For a clergyman to dream of gaiters shows that he will have promotion and will rise to a position of honour ; for a woman to dream of wearing gaiters shows that she will take up some new work which necessitates the wearing of a uniform.

Gallantry.—For a man to dream that he is charming those around him by his gallantry signifies that in reality he bores them by his conceit.

Gallop.—To be galloping on a bay horse denotes impetuosity and a habit of rapid decision which sometimes leads you into small errors of judgement : on the whole you meet with more fortune than of failure ; to gallop on a black horse foreshows a temporary trouble that comes upon you so rapidly that you are quite unprepared to meet it, but it will pass as swiftly as it appeared ; to gallop on a white horse signifies pleasures, good friends, and a love affair which will end in a happy marriage.

Gallows.—To see a gallows near you is a sad omen of great distress and coming tragedy ; if seen at a distance it indicates a tragic event of a less personal nature.

Gambling.—To be gambling with strangers denotes that you would be wise to leave if alone : it may also show that you suffer financially from the speculation of others ; to be gambling with those who are known to you and you are the winner shows a successful investment : if you lose, a serious loss.

Game.—To dream of playing games with a feeling of weariness or boredom shows that you will be called upon to exert yourself in a good cause although the task is most irksome to you.

Gaol.—To dream of being in gaol is an omen of much ill-fortune ; you may find yourself in danger of being there through a blunder , or you may have to go to gaol to see someone near and dear to you who is imprisoned there ; this dream shows that you need much courage and determination to go through the trials ahead of you.

Garden.—Wandering in a large strange garden that appears to be without flowers shows loneliness and separation from those you love most ; if the garden if full of beautiful flowers it denotes joy and the fulfilment of your heart's desire ; if the garden is steep and you walk up and down paths which seem to lead nowhere it means that your happiness will come to you after much waiting and through an unexpected source.

Garland.—To dream that you are wearing a garland of flowers is a sign of happiness, love, honour, and marriage.

Garlic.—To dream of eating garlic shows that you will find it possible to put up with the vexations and vicissitudes of life in an astonishingly cheerful manner ; to be picking it means that you desire to come to the root of some matter of which at present you have only an inkling : if the garlic comes up by the root as you pick it, you will discover the secret : if it breaks off in your hand, it will remain a mystery.

Garnets.—To dream of these stones is a fortunate sign to those born in March, October, November, being one of the birthstones for those months ; for those who are not born in these months this stone signifies delay and obstacles in obtaining their desires although they may hope to have them eventually.

Garotter.—To dream of being garotted is a sign of probable danger to your throat, it may be from accident or from illness.

Garter.—To dream of garters shows a contempt for feminine weakness.

Gas.—Dreaming of seeing gas shows you that someone has

carelessly left gas burning all night ; to smell it is an indication of a serious waste of it.

Gate.—To dream of climbing high gates shows that with perseverance and energy you will surmount all your difficulties, but if the gates break as you climb them it means that an unforeseen incident brings about disappointment and failure ; if the gates appear to open as you approach them, you may feel assured that good fortune and unlooked for success await you ; small gates show daily worries and small obstacles ; swing gates denote pleasure with friends ; massive iron gates indicate misery, disgrace, and imprisonment ; to be struggling to open a gate in desperate haste which sticks fast means that you will be placed in a most awkward position from which you will only extricate yourself by subterfuge and untruth ; to see several white gates shows ease and enjoyment while black gates denote depression and loss.

Gather.—To dream that you are gathering armfuls of flowers shows that you are attracting someone to you who will fulfil your ideals : it is an assurance of happiness, love, and perfection.

Gauze.—To dream of covering your face with gauze indicates an affected modesty which is merely superficial.

Gems.—To see many gems of value means riches ; if they are in the form of a chain it shows that the money will come from a near relation ; scattered gems would indicate money at various times from different sources ; if the dreamer is possessed of gems of value and bad signs appear in the dream, it would be well to guard them carefully or they may be gems of memory only.

Geraniums.—These flowers show a strong will and determined character, very pleasant surroundings, contentment, happiness ; they also denote two natures with a great bond of affection between them.

Ghost.—To dream that you see a ghost is a sign that you are, or will be, in the close presence of a spirit, even though its form may be invisible to you.

Giant.—To dream that you are a giant shows a danger ahead of you to meet which you will need all your strength ; to encounter one and overthrow him denotes a prosperous ending to a risky venture.

Giddy.—To dream that you are giddy warns you of a danger of falling if you attempt to climb inaccessible places.

Gift.—To dream of receiving gifts foretells good luck, pleasures, and success.

Gilt.—Garments covered with gold lace signify honour and association with those in a position of power.

Gimlet.—To dream of a gimlet near to you shows a new enterprise or undertaking.

Gipsy.—To dream of gipsies shows a desire to wander and be free of restraints ; if a caravan appear in the dream it shows that you will have your desire and enjoy a life of freedom.

Giraffe.—This indicates surprising and unlooked-for developments ; if the giraffe is near or coming towards you, you will profit by unexpected means ; if it is going away from you or in the distance it means that you will lose that which you had counted on gaining.

Girdle.—To wear a girdle shows a life of solitude, frugality, and rigid discipline ; to break a girdle indicates that you tire of the restrictions which you have made for yourself, break away from them, and lead a life of pleasure.

Gladioli.—To see these growing in profusion indicates courage in the face of difficulty, love, hope, and tenderness ; to be picking them shows a longing about to be realised ; to be holding a large bunch of them means a satisfied desire and an assurance of true love.

Glass.—To dream of many empty glasses means that you will entertain your friends and delight in hospitality, but that you will meet with difficulties in your arrangements ; to dream of a large pane of glass shows that you are inclined to be too communicative about your private affairs and that some day you will probably find out your indiscretion in an unpleasant manner ; to dream of broken glass denotes a sudden end to an accustomed habit.

Gleaner.—To dream that you are gleaning in a harvest-field shows that you make the best of the circumsatnces in which you find yourself, but you will seldom possess the most desirable things in life : you will gather much that others would discard.

Globe.—To see a globe means that you will have relatives and friends in various foreign countries with whom you will have much correspondence.

Gloom.—To dream of gloom is a sign of a morbid self-absorbed mind, needing a new focus.

Gloves.—To dream of new gloves shows that you may expect a present of some ; to be wearing long white gloves means social pleasures ; black gloves denote sorrow ; cotton gloves, dismay ; to be buying several pairs of gloves shows success and good friends ; to be wearing gloves that have holes in them indicates many disappointments.

Gnats.—Seeing many of these insects denotes worry over an array of small things.

Goat.—A white goat signifies a new enterprise which has

an element of risk about it ; a black goat shows worry in the home and failure of plans ; several goats mean an unfortunate symbol for a sailor.

Gold.—To dream of this is a sign of ambition and a great desire to accumulate wealth ; if you see much gold you will probably become very prosperous ; to be wandering in a gold mine shows that the source of your wealth will be abroad.

Golf.—To dream of playing golf shows absorption in this game and a desire to become a famous player ; to be playing and unable to hit your ball shows that you make no success against a powerful opponent ; to be carrying golf clubs but not using them denotes a life so filled with work that there is no leisure for recreation.

Gondola.—To dream that you are in a gondola with a feeling of delight shows that you will one day be in Italy under the most happy and perfect conditions ; it also predicts contentment and a life of ease and comfort.

Goose.—This dream denotes a venture needing much discussion and arrangement, plans made only to be upset again, a fussy state of mind ; to see geese coming towards you shows the arrival of unexpected and troublesome visitors ; geese seen in the distance indicate an event of interest to you occurring in the autumn ; to be eating goose predicts pleasures and a gratified wish.

Gooseberries.—To dream of gooseberry trees covered with fruit shows a pleasant occurrence in the gooseberry season ; to be picking them when green and being scratched in the process, means that you try to seize a pleasure which does not lawfully belong to you and from which you derive more pain than joy ; seeing a dish of ripe gooseberries near you denotes hospitality and social enjoyments.

Gorse.—To see quantities of gorse in blossom predicts a mild winter and beautiful spring ; to be picking it shows a brave endeavour to make the best of things as they are, although there may be many things which you would desire to be different in your life.

Grain.—To see large fields of grain indicates success in work or business, prosperity, and the maturing of pleasant plans ; to be carrying grain shows that you waste your opportunities by snatching at things too hastily.

Gramophone.—To dream of this shows that you will probably be vexed by being drawn into a somewhat disorderly and noisy pleasure.

Grandchild.—For the married to dream of a grandchild means that they will become grandparents and will find much happiness in their grandchildren.

Grapes.—These denote pleasure and a life of freedom from care ; to be picking grapes shows abundance and fulfilment ; to be eating white grapes means a powerful influence in your life ; black grapes show the capacity for grasping difficult subjects and the amassing of wealth ; a bunch of black grapes close beside you predicts coming illness.

Grass.—To see tufts of bright green grass near to you is a sign of development, pleasant events, and successful plans ; 'if the grass appears withered it means that you struggle to avert a calamity and will meet with disappointment and failure ; to be picking fresh green grass shows a simple unaffected nature finding pleasure in the small events of life ; if the grass is withered it foreshows destroyed hope, affliction and death ; to be eating it denotes poverty and illness.

Grasshoppers.—To see many of them portends a poor harvest ; if several jump upon you it shows a danger from chill ; if you see many of them jumping together it probably foreshows the death of an old person.

Grater.—To dream of using a grater means that you have some bad tricks that set other persons' teeth on edge.

Grave.—To see an open grave into which you look foreshows a great sorrow ; to see a grave with a flower or some kind of fruit upon it would signify that a death takes place at the time of year when that flower or fruit would be in season.

Gravel Walk.—Dreaming of walking on a gravel-walk shows that your path in life is strewn with small obstacles, vexation, and discomfort.

Gravestone.—Seeing this with good symbols indicates that you will gain through a death ; with bad symbols it predicts mourning.

Green.—To see this colour in a mass shows the gift of leading and power to attain to greatness ; it also denotes promotion and a variety of pleasant events.

Greenhouse.—Dreaming of this shows secrecy and things which you desire to conceal ; birds on your hand in a greenhouse mean sadness ; a black-and-white bird, mourning.

Grey.—To see masses of pale shimmering grey denotes that mists and shadows obscure your truest happiness ; it is also a sign of resignation and calm, and of a desire to see beyond the ordinary happenings of the world, to unfold mysteries and hear new things ; dark grey shows commonsense, dignity, and order.

Grey Hairs.—To see yourself prematurely grey-haired is a sign of coming illness or shock which may bring about such a condition.

Greyhound.—This is a symbol of great energy and untiring activity which will bring you much success and good fortune ; if the greyhound is running towards you it denotes favourable tidings of the result of some new enterprise.

Grinding.—To dream of grinding corn shows abundance, the comforts of life, cheerfulness, and gratified ambition ; to grind pepper means vexation and affliction ; to grind coffee shows sleeples ness and a slight indisposition, while nuts denote the aftermath of an indiscretion.

Grind Stone.—To be turning a grind stone shows monotony and vexatious duties ; if the grindstone appears to be turning itself it means that your toil is over and that pleasure and change await you.

Guests.—To receive guests in a dream signifies to those who are not in a position to receive them, that in the future they will be in good circumstances and find pleasure in giving hospitality to a large circle of friends.

Guitar.—To be playing upon this instrument shows a power of attraction for the opposite sex and also pleasant adventures ending in a happy love affair.

Gun.—This is an unpleasant symbol ; if near and pointing towards you it denotes grave danger of a sudden calamity ; with other bad signs a violent death ; if the gun is at a distance it means strife and serious quarrels ; to hear the report of a gun signifies a catastrophe and bad news ; to be handling a gun is an indication that you commit some serious blunder which you never cease to regret.

Gunpowder.—To see a quantity of gunpowder in a dream shows danger of an accident caused by explosion.

Gymnastics.—To be studying gymnastics shows that you will probably take up the profession of a teacher on that subject.

H.

Haddock.—To dream of a dried haddock shows that unless you take reasonable care with your personal appearance you will have the mortification of hearing yourself described as looking somewhat like a dried haddock ; to be eating it means satisfactory arrangements.

Hall.—To dream of hail falling is unpleasant, foreshowing bad weather, personal discomforts, things all awry, and arguments and disagreements over trifling matters ; hail talling upon you shows losses, disappointments, and a troubled life ; hail in your hand means that you are badly in need of a protector, for much which befalls you is caused by lack of consideration on the part of others ; to see the ground covered with hail in the summer denotes anxiety about someone you love.

Hair.—To dream of your hair glossy and beautiful is a sign of new friends and of an admiration which you will find very pleasant ; to see it looking short and scanty shows a grievous disappointment ; if it is matted it means that you will have misfortune and possibly an illness ; black hair cut short signifies despondency, a cranky nature, and a tendency to melancholia ; snow-white hair denotes a severe shock ; red hair shows a passionate ambitious nature, vivacity, and much power of attraction.

Hair-Dressing.—To be dressing the hair of a woman shows a confidence betrayed ; to be dressing your own hair, a desire to propitiate someone whom you have offended ; to have your hair dressed by a woman shows that you have a friend who is desirous for your welfare.

Ham.—To see a ham garnished with a frill and ready for table shows a pleasant invitation, and pleasure with your friends ; an uncooked ham in the larder indicates a need to save for the future or you may be in difficulties ; to eat it denotes that you will become discontented as you advance in years although you have much which should give you pleasure.

Hammer.—This shows breakages and troublesome little duties.

Hammock.—To dream that you are in a hammock with a sensation of pleasure denotes a happy experience occurring in the summer ; to be in a hammock swung under a bare tree shows a mournful ending of that to which you had been looking forward with delight ; to see someone in a hammock under a bare tree indicates the parting of friends or a lovers' quarrel ; to be sleeping in a hammock means that you are apt to give trouble to others by your hobbies.

Hand.—A beckoning hand predicts an important change coming for you, unforeseen occurrences bringing this to pass ; a hand lying close to you denotes oneness of mind with some-one dear to you, care, and protection ; dreaming of beautiful white hands augurs happiness, successful undertakings, and a calm unruffled life ; to dream of ugly red hands shows a nature likely to be soured by bitter disappointments, misfortune, and aversion to present conditions ; a hairy hand denotes subtilty, quick temper, and a rough manner ; a skeleton hand shows the desire to unravel a mystery ; a small fat hand implies greed and gossiping tongue ; to dream of your hand becoming smaller shows a danger or a grief brought upon you by a relative ; to work with the right hand indicates good fortune ; to work with the left hand, ingenuity and capability in seeing both sides of every question ; to take up fire in the hand without being burned means that you execute all your plans without hindrance or obstacle ; to be shaking hands with an array of people shows a gathering at which you will be the centre of attraction ; to see many hands indicates good luck and a powerful position, industry, and gratified ambition.

Handcuffs.—To dream that you have these on your wrist is a very bad omen of misfortune, signifying that in the future you may be bound to someone who will bring disgrace upon you.

Handwriting.—To see handwriting on a wall is a signal of danger to yourself : the words may be legible but if this is not the case other symbols may show you from what danger the dream is warning you ; large writing on a big sheet of paper shows legal documents and that you will have much business to deal with ; to be reading a letter which has a black edge predicts mourning for a relation ; to be writing means the arrival of important news requiring much attention and correspondence.

Hanged.—To dream of being hanged is ominous of a tragic death ; to see a person being hanged is a bad omen of shocking news and a sudden death.

Happiness.—Dreaming of feeling intense happiness is a sign that you may hope for an event which will give you great joy before many months have passed.

Hare.—A hare running towards you shows the return of an absent friend ; to see one going away denotes fear and a troubled mind ; several hares show a profitable enterprise ; dead hares indicate money which had been acquired through industry and is rapidly spent ; a hare close to you shows a journey or a long expedition with a friend.

Harebell.—To see a large patch of white harebells is a sign of a peaceful and placid existence ; a bunch in the hand foretells news of a birth ; a large patch of blue harebells denotes happiness, fulfilled hope, and a faithful lover.

Harelip.—To dream that you have a harelip is an unpleasant omen that you may meet with an accident causing some damage to your lip ; to see this affliction on another shows that you are much disturbed by some unpleasant sight.

‹ **Harlequin.**—To dream of being a harlequin denotes that you weary those around you by your follies.

Harmony.—To dream of hearing beautiful harmonies means peace and bliss in love, good friends, happiness, and contentment.

Harp.—To be playing on the harp denotes a jealousy which leads to a severed friendship ; to hear the harp shows melancholy and predicts the possibility of a nervous breakdown.

Harrissi Lily.—To see these beautiful flowers growing predicts peace, joy, and love ; to be holding them means a wedding ; to see them on or near a bed foreshows serious illness or a death.

Harrow.—To see a harrow at work shows that much of your time will be given to endeavouring to make the lives of those around you smooth and happy whilst you cheerfully spend your days in a somewhat monotonous manner ; to be using a harrow shows irksome duties, loneliness, and a comfortless existence.

Harvest.—To be in a field of corn already reaped is a somewhat sad emblem for the dreamer, showing that you have sown that of which the reaping will be tears : with an aching heart and with obstacles in your path, you must endeavour to make the best of what remains for you ; to see someone who is not working, in a cornfield which has been reaped indicates an approaching bad illness or shock for that person ; to see a reaped cornfield in the distance denotes that you will miss much of the joy which might have been yours through your own folly.

Hat.—To dream of buying several new hats shows prosperity, good luck, presents ; if they are black hats it means sorrow and mourning ; to see shabby hats indicates that you must depend upon the kindness of friends to provide you with pleasure and comforts ; to see many clerical hats denotes an unexpected interest in connection with the clerical profession and the loyal friendship of one who is a clergyman ; to see silk hats shows a funeral ; a Field Marshal's hat denotes triumph, promotion, and prosperity ; a shapeless or torn hat shows a street brawl or accident.

Hate.—To feel hatred towards someone in a dream indicates a danger of allowing yourself to become soured and harsh, thereby possibly bringing hatred upon yourself ; to dream of being hated shows an uneasy mind and a fear of consequences.

Hawk.—This is a bad symbol as it indicates circumstances in which people and things seem to be working against you and placing you in trying predicaments.

Hawthorn Blossom.—To see this growing in profusion shows a great happiness and possibly a complete change in your life which will occur in the early spring ; to be picking it denotes the fulfilment of a desire.

Hay.—To dream of making hay denotes a likelihood of fame, wealth, and influential friends ; to be seated on a haycart means a risky undertaking which may bring about a disaster ; to be raking hay shows a capacity for putting your knowledge to practical use ; to be standing on a haycock means that you like to be considered witty ; to be on a hay rick implies a desire for mastery and preeminence ; to be sitting under a hay rick shows a lack of friends, and pecuniary difficulties ; to be loading hay signifies that there is a doubt in your mind as to how to proceed, but you find the right way and come to a wise conclusion ; to smell newly cut hay gives an assurance of happiness to lovers.

Head.—To dream of having hurt your head gives warning of family troubles ; if you see it bandaged if foreshows an accident ; to be bandaging your head denotes an injury or illness affecting the head of a relative or friend ; to dream of your head as very large denotes a serious illness ; to dream of it as very small means that you will probably lose your memory; to dream of headache shows that self-indulgent habits are likely to ruin your health.

Heart.—To dream of this without bad symbols appearing is a sign of coming happiness through the affections, bringing joy into your life ; sometimes it is an indication of satisfaction through money ; to dream of your heart as being very large or very small is a prediction of serious illness.

Heat.—To dream of extreme heat which distresses you shows that something about to happen is likely to cause you discomfort and to place you in an awkward position ; if the heat passes off and you become pleasantly cool, you will soon be out of difficulty and will even gain by having been through it ; to dream of being in a feverish condition shows an attack of illness or an injury.

Heathen.—To dream of association with the heathen shows that you unexpectedly develop a great interest in missionary work and will probably, if circumstances permit, go abroad and take an active part in this work ; to dream of becoming a heathen denotes that you are likely to bore people by your narrow-minded prejudices.

Heather.—To see purple heather in large quantities means a delightful visit to the country where you will find the heather in bloom ; to be picking white heather promises you much that you desire, good fortune, and a happy love affair.

Heaven.—To dream of a condition of heavenly bliss predicts a joyous event such as the fulfilment of a long cherished hope, good fortune to those who are poor, distinction and honour to the ambitious ; for lovers this dream denotes a happy marriage under the most auspicious circumstances with numbers of congratulating friends and an array of costly presents ; to dream that you are resting in Heaven shows a mind attuned to spiritual contemplation and the power to lead a life of calm resignation in the face of trials and anxieties.

Hedge.—To be scrambling over a hedge with much difficulty reveals that you make great efforts and spare yourself no trouble to attain your ambitions and carry out your plans ; to dream of cutting a hedge shows tasks that you greatly dislike but which nevertheless you must do ; to be jumping a hedge shows good luck : you will surmount obstacles and carry all before you.

Hedge Hog.—To dream of this creature being near you shows that you will be immensely surprised by hearing that someone whom you regarded as a confirmed bachelor is about to be married ; to see the hedge hog in the distance denotes that you must wait for some time for the news which you expect.

Heliotrope.—To dream of this fragrant flower predicts happiness in love, peace and comforts in the home, loyal friends ; to be picking it shows that a right decision brings you a great joy ; if it dies in your hand it means that you will lose your love through long waiting.

Hell.—To dream that you are in Hell or that you see it indicates that your life is a bad one and intimates a serious need of reformation ; to dream of the word " Hell " is a warning to you not to continue in your present habits for they are a danger to yourself and to others.

Hens.—To dream of the cackling of hens denotes that a secret which you have told to a friend has been disclosed to others ; to see a hen near you shows bickering, agitation, and domestic annoyance ; to see a number of hens that appear content is a good omen of thrift, domestic peace and comfort : it also shows a visit to the country ; to see a hen with young chickens round her is a sign of happiness in the home, family affection, and good luck.

Herbs.—To dream of these shows a taste for buying patent medicines and for experimenting with self-prescribed drugs.

Hermit.—Dreaming of a hermit who is at present a stranger to you shows that you will make the acquaintance of someone who lives a hermit life but who will eventually cease to do so through your influence.

Hide or Hidden.—To dream of trying to conceal anything by putting it in some out-of-the-way place is a sign that a secret of yours will be disclosed by a person whom you believed to be reliable and honourable ; to dream of trying to hide an object for which you are unable to find a hiding place shows that you wear your heart on your sleeve and that your endeavours to conceal your feelings or plans are useless for they are apparent to everyone ; to dream of finding an hidden object and of exposing it to view indicates that you will be astonished at some piece of scandal or other information which will be told to you in confidence ; for lovers to dream of hiding things is an omen of unpleasant gossip started by ignorant mischief-makers ; to dream of hiding your face shows a guilty conscience and a desire to obliterate the past ; to hide your hands shows a danger of theft ; to hide your feet denotes sloth and a weak character, with a tendency to keep undesirable company.

Highlander.—To dream of being a Highlander in Scotch costume foretells sound business capability and a plodding contriver in transactions ; to dream of shaking hands with one shows that someone of whom you are fond joins a Highland regiment.

Hills.—To dream that you are climbing steep hills of which you do not seem able to reach the top indicates a condition of worry and difficulty with which you must cope ; if you reach the top it means that you will in time overcome the obstacles in your path and will experience a time of peace and quiet ; to lovers this dream denotes serious hindrances in the way of marriage which will eventually be surmounted ; to be walking down a hill shows a doubt in your mind as to the course of action which you had better follow, but that you finally decide to choose that of the least resistance ; to be running down hill means that you evade a difficult situation by turning your back and leaving others to grapple with its solution.

Hips.—To dream of strong hips shows health, a love of out-door exercise, strength, and vigour ; to dream of your hip being painful or swollen predicts an injury.

Hoe.—To dream of hoeing means that you have more to do than you can well accomplish and that each day things occur which need your attention and increase your work ; it is also a sign of perseverance, good spirits, and health.

Holly.—To dream of seeing a holly tree covered with berries in the summer or spring indicates something of importance which will happen in the winter : unless gloomy signs appear in the dream it may be assumed that the event will be a happy one ; to be picking it denotes an irritable state of mind arising from circumstances of your life which are at present impossible to avoid ; to see a holly tree covered with berries in the early autumn predicts a hard winter.

Hollyhock.—To see a quantity of these flowers growing in a garden which is known to you predicts a visit of pleasure to the country in the summer ; to see them broken and on the ground means a severed friendship or a lovers' quarrel ; to be picking them shows a most satisfactory conclusion to a troublesome matter.

Home.—Dreaming of home when away from it shows that one of the members of your home is needing you ; if you dream of it with feelings of distress it predicts illness or trouble for one of your family ; if you see it with the blinds pulled down it shows death ; to dream of home whilst you are living there shows that you may one day hope to have a home of your own.

Homesick.—To dream of being homesick shows that you will have to bear this discomfort, but not for long, for you will become so wrapped up in those who are around you that the home-sickness will vanish and you will enjoy each day of your life.

Honey.—To be eating honey shows pleasures, a happy life, prosperous undertakings, honour, and renown ; to see much honey in the comb shows good success in a new enterprise and also social enjoyments.

Honeysuckle.—To be picking honeysuckle shows that you may hope to obtain your desire in the summer ; to be given a bunch of this flower by one of the opposite sex denotes ardent love and a union of bliss ; to see masses of it growing beyond your reach shows that you will miss your chance of true happiness through no fault of your own.

Honour.—To dream of disputing as to your honour is a sign of its being questioned by someone whose good opinion you desire to obtain : you lose the chance of keeping this good opinion by your folly.

Hoop.—To dream of bowling a hoop is a sign of light-heartedness and freedom from care ; to be bowling it in company with one of the opposite sex shows that your happiness is dependent on that person.

Hornets.—Dreaming of these around you shows danger disguised by a covering of smooth speeches and flattering remarks : the sting is concealed but the mischief-making and slanders have nevertheless the power to damage you.

Horns.—To see horns on the head of another denotes a powerful enemy or at least one who has feelings of animosity towards you which may prove to be unpleasant in their result ; to dream of horns on your own head signifies wealth and importance.

Horses.—To see horses looking sleek and well groomed denotes pleasures, comforts, and loyal friends ; if you are dealing in horses it shows that good luck awaits you in a business transaction ; to see horses galloping in disorder means that events are hurrying towards you over which you have no

control and which will bring about many changes ; to be
driving a horse does not promise anything very good : it often
indicates disagreements and disagreeable incidents ; if the
horse becomes restive and out of control it predicts danger of
a riding or driving accident ; to mount a big handsome horse
denotes a position of honour and power ; if the horse is lean
and ill-groomed it shows that you will not have sufficient
means to carry out your scheme ; to chase a horse predicts
that your best chances will come through leading an outdoor
life in which your boundless energy but somewhat erratic
habits would mingle ; to kick or injure a horse shows a
coward and a bully ; to see a dead one is an ominous sign of
grave danger to you or yours.

Horseshoe.—To see a horseshoe near you promises a most
unexpected piece of good fortune, the achievement of your
wish, and luck in all you undertake ; if the horseshoe is reversed
it means an upset of plans causing much disappointment and
vexation ; a broken horseshoe denotes a dilemma and an
overthrowing of your projects.

Hospital.—To dream of being in a hospital foretells illness
for yourself or for those dear to you ; if you are in a ward for
male patients illness for one of their sex is predicted ; if in a
ward for women it shows illness for a woman ; if you see conspicuous wounds and you help to dress them it shows a danger
of wounds for yourself : if looking on at the dressing of them is
means that you will see someone belonging to you with wound
or injuries ; if you are busily engaged in working in a ward in
which you see a steaming kettle it foretells great anxiety on
behalf of someone dear to you who will have a bad illness
affecting the chest : if in this dream you were to see piles of
cotton wool and bandages it would predict rheumatic fever,
if an oxygen pump it would show heart or lung trouble ; to be
lying in a long ward bare of furniture, of which you are the
sole occupant, denotes an attack of infectious fever for which
you are removed to a fever hospital.

Hotel.—To dream of being in a large comfortable hotel
denotes a visit to one through which great happiness comes to
you ; to be wandering in a mean comfortless hotel shows a
visit which is completely spoiled by uncongenial surroundings ;
to dream of several hotels means travels and enjoyments ;
to dream that you are the proprietor of an hotel signifies wealth
and prosperous transactions.

Hothouse.—See " Greenhouse."

Hounds.—Dreaming of a pack of hounds means to those
who ride or desire to ride that they will realise their wish and
follow hounds ; to those who do not ride or go in for this sport

it predicts a danger of rapidly approaching mental derangement.

Hour Glass.—To see this near you is a warning of personal danger and of sudden severe illness ; to see one at a distance shows that the peril is for others ; if it is seen in connection with a house known to you it denotes a calamity for the inmates of that house.

House.—To see a house without clouds around it is a good sign of successful plans and business; to see a house at a distance from the outside shows a visit of pleasure ; if trees in full leaf or flowers are to be seen the visit would probably take place in the summer, bare trees or trees with snow upon them would show that the visit would be in the winter ; a red house shows congeniality and comforts, a white house shows peace, hospitality, wealth ; a grey house denotes gloom ; a black and white house signifies dignity, beauty, peace, and comfort ; to be wandering in a strange house full of people who are all unknown to you is a bad sign of a harassed state of mind, worries, turmoils, and a poor state of health ; to see a house in which no windows are to be seen denotes death.

Humming Birds.—Dreaming of these shows a love of birds and much knowledge of them ; if they fly round you it foreshows exciting news from a distance ; if they are in a cage it means a present of some pet birds.

Hungry.—To be very hungry in your dream denotes that you will become rich and honoured through your genius and industry ; to eat and be satisfied shows a gratified ambition, and for the lover a speedy marriage.

Hunting.—To be stag hunting shows a fruitless effort to undo the results of past mistakes ; to be fox hunting shows pleasant meetings, sociability, and popularity ; to be hunting on foot shows that your motives are likely to be misunderstood and that you will be unjustly accused of meanness and deceit ; to return from the chase on a lively horse denotes good fortune.

Hurricane.—Dreaming of a hurricane foreshows a gale of great force causing damage around you ; if a boat or ship is seen it predicts shipwreck.

Hurt.—To dream of being hurt in your feelings shows an over sensitive nature which is too much on the look-out for supposed slights ; to dream that you are hurt by a cut or a fall warns you to be on your guard against such accidents occurring.

Husband.—For the unmarried woman this dream shows that she will shortly meet with a man who will probably become her husband ; if good signs appear, such as the sun or crescent moon, the marriage will be happy one : if bad signs appear, such as a cross or lynx, the marriage will be most unhappy and will possibly end in separation.

Husbandry.—To see the implements of husbandry in your dream indicates that the source of your income will depend largely on the produce of the soil and on your own efforts in making the results of the labour satisfactory ; if you see the tools broken and in pieces it signifies failure.

Hussar.—To dream of a man in a hussar uniform shows to the maiden who dreams it that her affections will be given to someone in that regiment ; for a youth to dream of being in this uniform means that he will join the hussars.

Hyacinth.—To dream of the scent of these flowers foreshows a blissfully happy love affair ; to see them growing shows fulfilled desires and gratified ambition ; to pick them indicates a joy which will come to you in the spring.

Hydrangea.—To see these flowers growing in a pot indicates amiability and a desire to make the most of yourself : it also shows appreciation of small pleasures and a cheerful acceptance of things as they are ; to see them growing out-of-doors in masses denotes the fulfilment of a pleasant plan and also social pleasures ; to pick them shows independence, decision, and success in a new enterprise.

Hymns.—To dream of singing or saying hymns signifies that your love and interest are absorbed in one who is a clergyman or some other official of the church ; to be reading an hymn aloud shows an act of kindness to an elderly person ; to be sharing a hymn book with another shows an intimacy which you may have cause to regret in the future ; to be composing an hymn indicates a desire to follow in the footsteps of those whom you admire.

I.

Ice.—To be eating ice shows a danger of illness from a severe chill ; to be skating or walking on ice which has a cracked or thin appearance denotes that you are doing things which have hidden dangers and that some day you will awake to this fact and have cause to regret your present course of action ; if the ice gives way it is a sign that you break a promise recently given to a friend ; if the ice is thick and you skate upon it in company with others it indicates a desire to travel, which plan you may hope to carry out ; if the ice bends under you but does not break it means that you will have many adventures through which you come siuccessfully ; to be breaking ice shows that you will engage on some unprofitable enterprise which ends in failure.

Icebergs.—To see these in large numbers denotes an ambition to become an explorer ; to see several small ones indicates an array of obstacles which spoil your best chances in life ; to see one iceberg signifies an enemy who will take advantage of a superior position to do you an injury.

Iceland Poppy.—To dream of seeing these lovely flowers in masses is a pleasing indication of your happiness ; to be picking them shows love, hope, and peace of mind ; if they die in your hand it predicts that a short-lived joy will be yours.

Icicles.—To see icicles near you is a warning of illness caused by chill ; seen at a distance they show a spell of abnormally cold weather causing damage to crops ; to be holding icicles denotes a frigid and contemptuous attitude towards those whom you consider inferior.

Idiot.—To dream of an idiot is a sad omen that you will come into contact with one who is mentally deficient ; if you are touching the idiot it shows relationship and also indicates the horror which you endeavour not to feel, of one thus afflicted.

Idle.—To dream of being idle shows that you need a well-earned rest.

Ill.—To dream of being ill shows that you have a little illness to go through ; if a bad sign, such as a kettle, accompany the dream the illness will be serious ; if trees or flowers are seen it indicates the probable time of the year in which the illness will take place, for instance, a bare tree would show the winter, snowdrops the spring.

Illumination.—To dream of this augurs success in life and much happiness, but if the lights begin to disappear it means that sorrow, disappointment, and tears will be your portion.

Image.—To see an image near you denotes a tendency to conceit and self-importance and also to harshness of judgement and criticism ; if the image is broken it means that your pride will have a severe fall ; if you break an image if shows that you attempt a short cut to fame but do not meet with much success.

Imprisonment.—To dream of imprisonment is an omen of coming disgrace and dire misfortune.

Imps.—To dream of imps shows that you will be worried and dismayed by perpetual annoyances, some of them trifling but nevertheless very trying ; it also denotes losses and much waste of time in searching for things which you particularly need but cannot find.

Indian Chief.—To see this in your dream indicates speedy news from India ; if the figure has an out-stretched hand it denotes the return of friends or relations from India.

Infancy.—Dreaming of this shows regret for the past as having been the happiest time of your life, and a longing to recall it.

Infirmary.—See " Hospital."

Ink.—To dream of gazing into ink is a sign of clairvoyant power : perseverance would develop it and pictures would gradually unfold themselves before you in the ink ; a pot of ink and a piece of paper near you should encourage you to attempt literary work for these symbols show capacity for such work ; to see an pen in an ink-pot and a blank sheet of paper beside it denotes a troublesome correspondence.

Inn.—To dream of being at an inn is an unfavourable omen as it denotes unsuccessful business and poverty ; to the lover it means the unfaithfulness of his sweetheart ; to the tradesman a loss of business, and dishonest agents.

Inquest.—To dream that you are present at an inquest is a bad omen of a discovery that will give you a severe shock.

Insanity.—To dream of insanity as attacking you or yours is an ominous warning to avoid all such things as might be likely to produce it.

Insects.—To dream of insects crawling on you signifies a nervous condition which is trying to yourself and to those around you ; to see them swarming near you shows agitation and daily worries ; to see them disappearing predicts a time of freedom from care.

Insult.—If you receive an insult in your dream it warns you to be guarded in your words and conduct so that you avoid all occasion for insult.

Intemperance.—Dreaming of intemperance shows that there is need for you or yours to guard against a tendency to this weakness.

Inundation.—To dream of this indicates misfortunes and misery ; to dream of being inundated by letters of appeal on behalf of charity foreshows an inheritance from an unexpected source ; to dream of being inundated by letters of abuse shows poverty and inability to meet your claims.

Invalid.—Dreaming that you see an invalid who is a stranger to you means that you will become a good friend to an invalid who will greatly value your affection ; to dream of someone you know as an invalid foreshows bad news of a brother or sister.

Invitation.—To dream of receiving an invitation written on black-edged paper denotes the postponement of a party on account of mourning ; one written on gilt-edged paper shows an invitation to a wedding ; written on black paper, to a séance ; on pale blue or pink paper, to a dance ; on brown

D

paper, to a lecture ; on green paper, to a political gathering ; on mauve paper, to a dinner-party ; if the invitation appears creased or torn it means that you will not enjoy that to which you are bidden ; if the writing appears upside-down it shows that you will decline the invitation.

Iris.—To see these flowers growing is a sign of much pleasure and happiness occurring in the early summer ; to pick them shows a longing for what has hiterhto been out of your reach but which is now about to be yours.

Iron.—To dream of iron in quantities shows a sound investment which will bring you prosperity ; to see pieces of broken, rusty iron denotes a dismal failure and poverty ; to see pieces of red iron signifies the shedding of blood and is a very unfavourable sign in a dream.

Iron Mould.—To dream of this shows that you will be much annoyed by damage done to some new articles of apparel ; it also indicates disturbance and unrest in the home.

Irritation.—To dream of feeling irritable means that a condition of unrest and vexation awaits you ; to dream of your skin being irritable shows that you will have some troublesome ailment which will cause this discomfort ; to dream of the palms of your hands being irritable denotes unaccustomed work or a new enterprise.

Isinglass.—To be eating this shows a desire to mould yourself in the likeness of someone whom you look upon as ideal ; to be breaking isinglass denotes an entirely new outlook on life and the changing of your former ideas ; to be buying it shows a bad memory for di agreeable duties.

Island.—To be on an island without clouds and without the sea surging up round you shows pleasures and a visit to a place of happy memories ; to be on an island with clouds and with a rough sea dashing up to you indicates mental disturbance, anxieties, and a threatening of illness.

Itch.—To dream of this horrible disease foreshows contact with the squalid side of life.

Ivory.—To dream of having ivory in your hand shows an increase of wealth and the possession of much that is valuable ; to the lover it denotes that his love is set on a beautiful girl ; to buy ivory indicates prosperity and a well-merited reward for past industry.

Ivy. To hold this in your hand is a sign of patience, understanding, and steadfastness ; to be given ivy by one of the opposite sex denotes faithfulness in love ; to be picking it means that you will live in security and peace sheltered by the loving care of those around you, and that you will posses many loyal friends ; to see it growing thickly on a house signifies family affection and happiness in the home ; to see it growing up fruit trees foreshows failure of crops.

J.

Jacinth.—To see this stone near you is a pleasant omen of an unexpected piece of good fortune ; to hold it in your hand shows that you will possess things of much value ; to drop it denotes that through your own foolishness you will lose that which would have been for your happiness.

Jackdaw.—To see one in a cage signifies solitude and monotony ; if one is near you in your dream it shows depe idable friends, sagacity, and knowledge acquired by perservering study ; if one alights upon you it means that you will become famous through a new discovery or the invention of a patent.

Jade.—For all persons this is a lucky stone of which to dream, but especially for those born in June or July as it is one of the birth stones for these months ; to dream of a jade necklace shows delight in a present of jade from lover or husband.

Jam.—Pots of jam show a need for caution against extravagance ; also a probable shortage of all fruits.

Jar.—To dream of many empty jars is a warning that unless you exercise tact and patience there will be unpleasant occurrences in the home with friction and disputes ; to see empty jars around you is a sign of waste and a need for household economy.

Jaundice.—To dream of this malady warns you to take precautions and care, or an attack of it may be your fate.

Jay.—To see this bird of bright plumage near you signifies the cheerful news of the unexpected arrival of someone whom you much desire to see ; if the bird is seen at a distance it means that the news will be delayed ; if you see more than one jay it shows that a much talked-of plan will be successfully carried out.

Jealousy.—To dream that you are causing jealousy between friends or relations warns you to be careful in avoiding the risk of such unpleasantness.

Jelly.—To see various coloured jellies is a sign of festivity and social enjoyment ; to be eating them denotes a time of pleasure and of pain ; to be eating lemon jelly foretells the approach of an illness ; coffee jelly, an attack of insomnia ; calves' foot jelly, great weakness ; pineapple jelly, wealth and success ; to dream that pots of jelly are given to you indicates good fortune, loyal friends, and gratified wishes.

Jemmy.—To dream of this shows a bad attack of tooth-ache.

Jessamine.—This dream brings assurance of great happiness through the loving care of husband or lover ; a large bouquet of it denotes a wedding.

Jew.—To see a Jew near you indicates that through some trickery you will lose a large sum of money ; to be dealing with a Jew signifies a successful transaction of business ; to quarrel with one shows that money matters will be a source of dissention between you and your relations ; to shake hands with a Jew means that you endanger your reputation for honesty by some questionable transaction of business.

Jewels.—To see precious stones near you signifies wealth ; if the jewels are in the form of a ring it means that your riches will come through marriage ; in the form of a cross, through a death ; in the form of a coronet, you will inherit a fortune ; in the form of a bracelet, through good friends and your own endeavours.

Jig.—To dream of dancing a jig with one of the opposite sex denotes a mutual love and admiration ; to be dancing a jig by yourself shows that your heart is bestowed on someone who is at present unaware of your love, but who will fully reciprocate your feeling when you disclose your affection.

Jilted.—To the unmarried this is an unfortunate sign that this fate may be theirs ; to the married it shows jealousy and distrust which are probably not without good reason.

Jockey.—This dream means successful dealing and good money enterprise, luck in races and in speculation ; if you see the jockey fall refrain from betting for you would probably lose heavily ; for a girl to dream that she is in love with a jockey denotes that if she married him she will lead a gay and merry life for a time, but will afterwards endure much worry on account of pecuniary difficulties, brought about through extravagance and reckless living.

Journey.—Dreaming of a journey with someone dear to you shows that such will take place ; if you are on a journey alone and with discomfort and difficulties surrounding you, it means that there will be trouble of some kind necessitating a journey, it may be on account of illness or death.

Joy.—To dream of feeling joyous is an indication that you will hear a joyful piece of news but that you will at the same time meet with petty annoyances which will somewhat mar your delight in the good news ; to see the word " joy " written near you denotes much happiness and the fulfilment of a great desire.

Judge.—To see a judge in a large building means that

you will one day be called upon to appear as witness in a court of law ; if he is seen in a carriage it shows a function attended by a Judge at which you are present ; to see one near you indicates that there is need for alteration in your behaviour and that, if you pay no heed to this warning in your dream, you may one day find yourself having to answer for your conduct in the law courts.

Jug.—This shows domestic trials and difficulties needing much patience ; to see one broken denotes a disagreeable surprise.

Jumping.—To jump high and alight on your feet shows a rise in position ; if you fall it means that you will not reach the goal for which you are aiming ; to jump and fall into mud shows that you will lose your position and bring disgrace upon yourself ; to dream of jumping over obstacles signifies that you will attain to a position of honour through your diligence and ability ; to jump over a high gate denotes proficiency, and over a low gate a lack of enterprise.

Jungle.—If you dream of being lost in a jungle it denotes that you will be placed in a perplexing situation by the curious behaviour of a friend or relation : if you finally emerge from the jungle it means that you will find a successful way out of your difficulty ; to meet with a stranger in a jungle shows that you unexpectedly meet a friend whom you supposed to be far away.

Jury.—To dream that you are a juryman indicates that you will be called upon to serve as such ; dreaming of the jury denotes a case in which you feel much personal anxiety and interest : whether the verdict will be favourable or the reverse must be judged by other signs in the dream.

K.

Keepsake.—This shows that such will be given to you by someone from whom you will be separated by great distance but whose thoughts will always be with you.

Keg.—To see this denotes that you are too fond of your food and drink.

Kernel.—To eat the kernal of a fruit-stone shows a desire to taste all the pleasures which life offers, even if in doing so bitterness is mingled with the joy.

Kettle.—To see a kettle steaming is a sign of illness and unless a human form is seen also the illness is probably for yourself ; it is an ominous sign of trouble ; to see a brass or copper kettle has a different meaning, for these indicate comforts, domestic peace, and social pleasures.

Key.—To dream of holding a large key shows that you will attain to a position of power and honour ; to see a key near you denotes that things will become easier and that your path will be made smooth ; a key seen at a distance means that you will need the assistance of good friends to help you through difficulties ; to lose a key signifies dismay ; to find one denotes that an experiment about which you were doubtful turns out to be a most fortunate venture ; to hide a key indicates dishonesty and treachery.

Keyhole.—To dream that you are peeping through a keyhole shows a prying suspicious character, and the dream warns you of the fact that you will one day be caught at this unpleasant habit ; to dream of another looking through a keyhole at you is a warning that someone near you is untrustworthy.

Khaki.—For a youth to dream that he is in a new suit of khaki or to be buying this material denotes that he will become a soldier ; for a girl to be dressed in khaki or to be buying it, shows that she will seek employment for which she is well suited, under government ; to see a suit of tattered khaki shows disturbances and a danger of riots.

Kill.—To dream that you are killing an animal is a sign that you will get into a violent rage without just reason, and will vent your wrath upon an innocent person ; it warns you to control your temper or you may one day have cause to rue it bitterly.

King.—To dream of speaking with a king denotes riches and honour ; to be following one means that you gain a high position through influential friends ; to see a king on his throne indicates security and peace ; to see him on foot signifies rebellion, anarchy and shameful disloyalty.

Kingfisher.—To see this beautiful bird near you shows the return of someone for whom you have been longing ; to see it flying means surprising news of a happy nature ; if it alights upon you it denotes an unexpected achievement in a difficult matter.

Kiss.—To be kissed indicates disagreeable visitors ; to kiss the hands of a woman shows pleasant prospects and good fortune ; to kiss her face denotes faithfulness in love, courage and devotion ; to kiss the earth shows sorrow and care ; to kiss an infant means a birth ; to kiss a stone shows death.

Kitchen.—To dream of a kitchen shows the arrival of friends ; to be in one means domestic disturbance ; to be in a kitchen which is disordered and dirty shows that a time of worry and turmoil is before you.

Kite.—To see a kite flying shows that pleasures upon which you had counted are vanishing.

Kitten.—To hold a kitten shows a present of a pet ; if it struggles it means thas you will lose it ; to feed one shows the development of a plan which will prove to be satisfactory ; to meet one means the unexpected arrival of a friend ; to chase one denotes a disquieting occurrence which you would fain avoid ; if a kitten runs towards you it signifies that a trifling event may bring about a calamity.

Knave.—To dream that you see the Knave of Hearts card shows an ardent lover ; to dream of a knave with whom you come in contact is a warning against someone who is at present a stranger to you.

Knee.—To dream of your knees being painful or swollen denotes injury or sickness ; to feel them sore or fatigued shows trouble, grief, and delay ; bent knees predict ill-health ; to kneel down indicates devotion, humility, or embarrassment ; to dream of walking on your knees shows much distress for yourself through a dear friend ; to dream that your knees are withered, so that you cannot use them in walking signifies poverty in later years ; to fall on the knees means misfortune in business.

Knicknacks.—For a woman to dream of arranging these in a room is a sign of disturbance and domestic worry ; to a man this dream indicates bickerings and strife over petty matters.

Knife.—This is not a good sign meaning quarrels, bad temper and broken friendship ; a knife in the hand means danger from wounds and attacks of pain ; two knives crossed show an enemy to be feared : a figure by the knife would reveal if the ememy is a man or a woman ; to cut yourself predicts illness ; to sharpen a knife shows that you take in hand an unpleasant task and bring it to a successful conclusion.

Knight.—To see a Knight in armour foretells good fortune, success in love, and the loyalty of your friends ; if you dream of putting on his armour it warns you to be prudent for you may be in danger ; if you remove the armour it means that the danger will pass away without harming you.

L.

Laburnum.—To see this tree in full blossom signifies radiant happiness for which you may hope in the late spring ; to be picking it shows joy, love, and a fulfilled desire.

Lace.—To dream of beautiful lace shows a desire for costly possessions and things which are at present quite out of your reach ; it also means refined and artistic taste ; if you are wearing the lace it signifies that you will become the possessor of some such treasure.

Lackey.—To dream of a lackey indicates that one of your domestics is acting dishonestly and that much of your substance is disposed of to undesirable persons in the neighbourhood ; to dream of the lackey bowing to you denotes that you will be annoyed by the attitude of those around you towards your servants.

Ladder.—To dream of climbing to the top of a ladder signifies advancement, mental and bodily activity which lead you to success, and the attainment of good fortune ; to come down a ladder denotes humiliations and poverty.

Ladies.—To see a lady whom you recognise shows devotion and loyalty ; to see one who is a stranger means a new friend who will be of much influence and interst in you life ; to see many strange women denotes gossip and slander ; to hear one speak without seeing her foretells a departure.

Lake.—To dream of being in a boat on a lake alone proclaims that loneliness will be your lot in life ; if in company with others, but without oars or sail, it shows danger of a boating accident ; to be gazing into a lake from its banks shows a desire to be loved and admired by someone who at present pays you no attention ; to be on a lake with the sun shining and with one of the opposite sex means great happiness through marriage and the spending of your honeymoon in the lake country.

Lambs.—To see them in a field indicates tranquility, and the probable occurrence of a happy event at the season when lambs are seen ; to carry a lamb shows care and consideration for the young and tenderness towards the aged ; to kill one means secret grief ; to find one means a surprising gain in a doubtful undertaking ; to buy one shows amazement ; to eat lamb denotes sorrow ; to dream of keeping a pet lamb signifies that you will lavish your love on someone who is unworthy of it.

Lament.—To dream of lamenting without good cause shows that you are too much absorbed in yourself and that if you gave more heed to the needs of others you would become of more use in the world.

Lamp.—To light one signifies dreariness, dismay and sorrow ; to extinguish one shows a doubtful matter ending in calamity.

Land.—To dream of owing land in foreign countries indicates that you will make up your mind to go abroad and will by hard work achieve a successful career as a farmer ; to dream of owing much land shows that you inherit a small property which you will increase by purchasing land adjoining it ; to see a large tract of bare land predicts travel in far distant countries.

Lane.—If you are wandering in a lane which is dark and narrow and which has high banks it means uncertainty and doubt as to some plan for the future ; if the lane is full of light and has low banks it means that your way will be clear and the future full of promise.

Lapis Lazuli.—A lucky stone of which to dream for those born in April or May ; it also signifies a good present from an unexpected source, pleasant events, and rich friends.

Lark.—To hear the lark singing and see it flying towards you signifies that those things for which you have waited so long are about to be realised ; to see a lark flying high up in the air shows a speedy increase of fortune ; if it flies away from you it denotes the sending of important news to someone dear to you ; to eat these birds means accidents in the house.

Laughter.—To dream of laughter predicts that you begin the day in joy but end it in sadness.

Laurel.—A large laurel tree signifies a successful undertaking, and to the married healthy children ; to be picking laurel leaves means bitterness and the denial of a cherished hope ; a small laurel denotes that you do not avail yourself of good opportunities and therefore lose your chance of success.

Lavender.—Dreaming of lavender means that those things for which you have longed will come at the time of year when lavender is in flower ; if you are picking it, that you will visit a friend in the country and spend a time of peaceful happiness ; to dream of its scent means satisfaction.

Law.—To dream of instituting legal proceedings against anyone shows that there is danger of your losing money by speculation or trade, or that some enemy will injure you bringing upon you trials and vexation ; to dream of being sued or prosecuted foretells a need for care and wariness in your dealings or you may find yourself in an unpleasant position ; for a youth to dream of the Law indicates that he would do well in that profession ; for the mature to dream of it predicts a probability that they may find themselves being called to order through the law.

Lawn.—To dream that you see a bright green lawn is a pleasant omen of success and the attainment of your desires ; to walk on one shows that you find your truest happiness in study and in the development of your talents ; to sit on one means pleasure in the company of your friends ; to see a lawn thick with rank grass signifies that you mar your prospects by inattention to detail.

Lawyer.—To dream of interviewing a lawyer denotes some new and interesting arrangements necessitating legal advice; to meet with a lawyer who holds a document shows an inheritance; to write to a lawyer signifies a doubtful negotiation.

Lazy.—To dream that you see lazy people around you and that you are vexed with them, is a sign of misfortune to some of your relatives who will depend upon you to assist them; if in your dream you imagine yourself to be lazy and sleepy over your work it foretells illness; to dream that you hear yourself described as lazy, denotes that through your hesitation in coming to a decision you will lose the chance of an excellent offer which would have been greatly to your advantage to accept.

Lead.—To dream of a large lump of lead indicates news of a severe illness affecting the brain; to lift it shows heaviness of heart and sorrow; to a girl engaged to be married it foretells deceit and broken promises; to a business man it is an omen of misfortune.

Lean.—To dream of lean and bony cattle is a bad omen as it foretells poor crops to farmers and dull business in other callings; to dream that you see many lean people around you is a sign of distress and poverty and if they appear emaciated it denotes a probable famine; to dream that you yourself have become lean and cadaverous shadows forth a time of anxiety and suspense; a girl who dreams that her lover has grown thin may be sure that their course of true love will not run smoothly.

Learning.—To dream of learning with ease subjects which are most difficult to you when awake assures you that if you persevere you will master them.

Lease.—If you are signing a lease it signifies a change of residence; to be drawing up a lease shows that you will acquire property which you will let; if you are disputing a lease it means that you may look for trouble with your landlord.

Leather.—Dreaming of a quantity of leather, or articles made of leather, denotes that you will meet with insult and unpleasantness without being able to avenge them or justify yourself; to smell it shows a taste for good possessions and beautifully bound books.

Leaves.—To dream that the ground is covered with green leaves is a sign of prosperity and the making of many new friends; to the married it denotes a large family; if the leaves are dry and withered it means that you will be driven well-nigh to despair by the troubles and trials which will come upon you; if you gather up the leaves it shows that you add to your trouble by anticipating it; if you gather up the leaves and throw them away it means that you will bravely face worry and overcome obstacles ; to wear green leaves is a pleasant omen of good luck and success ; to wear withered leaves is a sign of destroyed hope ; to hold a green leaf in your hand means peace and the solving of a difficulty ; a withered leaf denotes a temporary indisposition.

Leech.—To see leeches in a dream is a bad sign, meaning treachery, deception, and debased behaviour from someone in whom you trusted ; a leech in a jar shows illness.

Leeks.—To dream of a quantity of leeks signifies labour and irksome duties ; to eat them means estrangement and a refusal ; to pull them out of the ground shows that you are likely to come to a wrong decision unless you take advice.

Legacy.—To dream of a legacy coming to you means that you may certainly hope to receive one ; if figures are seen it will show the probable value of the legacy ; if flowers are seen it would indicate the time of year at which you may expect it : spring, summer, autumn, winter, being shown by the flowers appearing in those seasons.

Legs.—To dream of your legs being fat and thick is a bad omen of an illness which will cause swelling ; lean legs denote a successful race with fortune ; very thin legs, anxiety and delicacy ; to dream that your legs are so lithesome in walking that you can scarcely keep on the ground signifies buoyant spirits and an unpractical nature ; if they feel heavy in walking it means weariness of mind and body.

Lemons.—Dreaming of lemons shows a probability of a bilious attack ; to see them growing on a tree means a visit to a foreign country.

Lemon Verbena.—If given to you in a dried and withered condition it shows death for an old person ; it is an emblem of the fragrance of a long well-spent life ; if you are picking lemon verbena it denotes that you have made a mistake in a love affair : you have been much attracted by outward appearance but now have doubts and misgivings as to the reality of your love.

Lending.—To dream of lending money means that you will be asked to help a friend out of a pecuniary difficulty.

Leopard.—To see this animal advancing towards you denotes a variety of bewildering events which will cause you much anxiety ; if you surprise a leopard it shows that someone in whom you feel great pride is likely to cause you much humiliation ; to pursue one indicates triumph over adverse circumstances or an evil report ; to see more than one leopard signifies fortune and misfortune following each other in succession.

Letters.—To write letters in red ink shows daring and good business capacity ; in purple ink, mourning, possibly for an elderly relative ; in blue ink, achievement ; in black ink, a large correspondence ; to receive a letter with a black edge denotes news of a death ; a letter with a large crest and seal upon it means the offer of a good promotion ; a letter which is folded small shows an invitation ; a large letter indicates important news ; a letter which appears to have pinpricks upon it signifies correspondence with the blind ; many letters mean congratulations on an engagement or other happy event ; to be writing a letter on a large sheet of paper shows that you will be in some difficulty and doubt as to the answering of a letter which you will shortly receive.

Lettuce.—To pick it shows solicitude for the welfare of those whom you love ; to cut it up denotes perturbing news ; to plant it means financial worry ; to eat it indicates sleeplessness.

Libel.—To dream of libel is a warning to exercise caution in your speech or you may find yourself accused of it ; to dream that you have been libelled indicates unpleasant communication with those who are at variance with you.

Liberty.—To dream of taking liberties with anyone warns you to be on your guard or you may be considered presumptuous by those whose good opinion you esteem ; to dream of others taking a liberty with you indicates that this may happen unless you are more discreet.

Lice.—Signify degradation.

Licence.—To dream of obtaining a marriage licence shows that your wedding will take place quietly and unknown to those around you ; to dream of taking out a license to sell various goods indicates a desire to seek your fortune in a new direction.

Lieutenant.—For a man this dream shows that he will be hindered in his profession by a series of misfortunes ; for a woman it denotes ambition which is unlikely to be realised.

Life Boat.—Dreaming of a life boat is a bad sign to those who are associated with the sea, meaning peril and severe storms which will cause many anxious hours to some who are at sea and to those in suspense on shore.

Light.—A brightly burning light signifies recovery to the sick and fortune and honour to the healthy.

Lighthouse.—This is a good sign showing a powerful element of success around you, security, increasing knowledge, widened outlook, and a love of travel and exploration ; to see it looking crooked or broken predicts disaster at sea.

Lightning.—To dream of lightning is a sign of mental energy and ready wit ; to see it forked foreshows a severe storm ; to see it strike the earth means an earthquake ; if it appears to strike your eyes a danger to your eyesight is predicted ; to see it strike your house indicates sickness and possibly death ; to see it fall into a room signifies the death of a relation.

Lilac.—Seeing a tree of white lilac means radiant happiness and joys shared with another with whom there is perfect oneness of purpose and love : the more luxuriant the blossom the greater the happiness ; it is an emblem of peace and perfection ; a spray of white lilac in each hand symbolises marriage with the man you truly love and the fulfilment of your heart's desire ; to pick this flower in small sprays shows that you are now enjoying much which is blissful, but that as as result of it there will be pain and tears in the future ; purple lilac seen in a large bunch on a bed shows an attack of illness which will probably disfigure the victim for the time being but will be followed by a good recovery ; to see lilac growing in profusion on a tree denotes a contented state of mind, satisfaction and pleasures.

Lily-of-the-Valley.—To see these growing indicates an event which means much to you occurring in the spring ; to pick them shows a wish about to be realised ; if you are given a large bunch of them by one of the opposite sex it denotes a happy love affair and marriage ; to be given a dead bunch means unrequited affection ; to buy them shows sympathy with those who are ill ; to see lilies-of-the-valley beside or upon a bed signifies death.

Limp.—To limp in your walk indicates that you will suffer a discomfort or injury which will cause this ; to limp on one foot means inability to come to a decision : you make up your mind as to a certain course of action only to change it almost immediately and decide on a totally different plan.

Limpets.—Dreaming of limpets denotes much tenacity of purpose, and a determination to hold on to all matters which you consider of personal importance ; to be pulling limpets off a rock shows that you endeavour to wrest from others some valuable secret which they possess but without success ; to be eating limpets is a sign of good luck to a fisherman, promising a big haul of fish.

Linen.—To dream of purchasing quantities of fine white linen shows marriage to a man of wealth ; to be wrapped in linen is a sign of bad illness, possibly death ; to be tearing linen means friction and disagreeables in the home.

Linseed.—If you are touching the linseed it shows an attack of illness necessitating poultices ; if you are eating linseed it shows pecuniary distress.

Lion.—To see a lion denotes admittance to the society of distinguished persons ; to sit or ride upon a lion shows the protection of some powerful personage and the possession of many influential friends ; to fight with a lion means a serious struggle with a dangerous person : if you overthrow him it shows that you will triumph over enemies, obstacles, and trials ; to see several lions in a forest indicates travel in the East ; to see a lion run away predicts that your folly will be apparent to everyone ; to see a lioness means good luck to your family ; to dream of eating the flesh of a lion foretells that some high office is in store for you ; to see the skin of this animal augurs wealth.

Liquorice.—To dream of chewing liquorice suggests that you will be unpleasantly reminded of a past incident, the memory of which is now inconvenient ; to be buying it shows a cautious nature unwilling to run any risks.

Liver.—To dream of your liver as large or painful shows an attack of illness which will leave you weak and depressed ; to dream of it as dried or small indicates serious misfortune ; to dream of eating calves' liver means that you will gain satisfaction from small pleasures.

Lizard.—To see one near you foreshows disagreeable events which are slowly advancing towards you ; to see several of them denotes treachery and a plot laid against you by enemies ; to see them in the distance shows misfortune through false and deceitful friends.

Lock.—To dream of locking a cupboard which is empty is a sign that you are too hesitating in your actions and often take elaborate precautions when it is too late.

Lockjaw.—Dreaming of lockjaw as attacking yourself warns you to be most careful of any cut or injury.

London Pride.—This flower indicates a clinging to habits and ideas which have long since become old-fashioned and a dislike to those things to which you are unaccustomed ; to pick it denotes steadfast affection and delight in the achievements of those whom you love ; if a bunch of it is given you by one of the opposite sex it shows the ripening of a friendship into love, and marriage late in life.

Lonely.—To dream of feeling very lonely, although numbers of people seem to be around you shows unpopularity resulting from your brusque and unattractive manner.

Looking Glass.—To be gazing into a looking-glass shows a desire to know the truth even if it be unpleasant to you. To dream that you are admiring yourself in the glass signifies immoderate vanity which may lead you into difficulties unless you are more careful ; to see a broken looking glass means illness, possibly death ; a cracked one indicates treachery.

Loss.—If you dream of losing a piece of jewellery look upon your dream as a warning and take precautions against this loss.

Lottery.—Dreaming of a lottery in which you draw the lucky number shows that you will meet with good fortune in competitions, lotteries and racing.

Love.—To dream of feeling love towards those who are mere acquaintances, and for all people whether strangers or otherwise, shows that you will spend a useful life doing valuable work in the world, but possibly leading a solitary existence and making but few friends ; for a girl to dream that she loves several men denotes that her affection is likely to be bestowed on those who are not desirous of it and that probably she will never marry ; if she dreams of loving one man she may expect much joy ending in a happy marriage ; to dream of loving someone who is very old signifies that whatever happiness comes to you in life will be after a long time of waiting and when much of your capacity for pleasure has vanished.

Love-in-a-Mist.—To see this beautiful little flower is a symbol of hope and of obtaining your heart's desire ; to pick it means joy ; to hold a bouquet of it denotes fulfilment, and happiness in love and marriage.

Luck.—To dream that you meet with a stroke of luck is an omen of good fortune ; to dream that you have just missed the opportunity of something lucky denotes that you leave too much to chance and are too haphazard ; to dream of bad luck warns you against undertaking a doubtful venture.

Luggage.—If you see a small amount only it means that you will go on a visit ; if you see a large quantity of all kinds of luggage it denotes a house removal ; luggage being carried towards you means a visitor ; if it is seen with water or a ship it shows a voyage, or that you will cross the Channel.

Lumber.—To see lumber piled up in quantities shows a house removal ; if you see a small amount in a lumber room it means that you will make a pleasant discovery among those things which you had looked upon as rubbish.

Lupin.—To see sprays of blue lupin is a pleasing sign of happiness and coming joy : you may hope in confidence that

Lute.—Hearing this is a sign of a secret sadness of which those around you know nothing ; to be playing on a lute shows grief bravely borne and concealed.

Luxury.—To dream of luxuries which you do not possess is a hopeful sign that your worldy prospects are improving and that eventually you may live in luxury ; to dream of it when you already live in much comfort shows that it would be well for you to think more of those who are in need.

Lynx.—To the married this is an unpleasant sign of quarrels and possibly separation ; to others it denotes treachery or episodes of a painful nature.

M.

Macaroni.—To dream of holding sticks of macaroni in your hand shows an endeavour to make sixpence do the work of a shilling ; to break it means distress ; to eat it signifies monotony and a mind which is content to take things as they come, and possessing no decided tastes or ideas.

Mace.—To see this carried shows that someone in whom you are interested will be offered a position of authority and honour ; to hold it indicates a personal promotion.

Machinery.—To be looking at machinery without handling it would show a taste for mechanism and success in the study of it ; to be near machinery in motion which seems to be drawing you towards it foretells a danger of an accident to you or yours caused by machinery.

Mackerel.—To eat this fish indicates that you fail to obtain something which you had regarded as a certainty ; to eat pickled mackerel means frustration and annoyance ; to see them alive shows discussion over a matter which leaves you bewildered ; to see them dead means that you will hear of a robbery on a big scale ; to catch them denotes a pleasant outing on the sea with congenial friends.

Mad Dog.—To meet one who avoids you shows that you will escape a danger of which you are unaware until the risk is over ; if it attacks you beware of touching any strange dogs for a while ; if you pursue one it denotes that you recklessly allow yourself to be drawn into dangerous undertakings which lead to no useful purpose.

Madman.—To dream of being attacked by a madman is a warning to avoid wandering in lonely places for a while ; to dream of trying to restrain a madman shows that there is a danger of someone known to you losing his reason.

Madness.—See "**Insanity.**"

Madonna Lily.—To see this flower growing denotes perfection and peace ; to pick them indicates an assurance of love, docility, and truth ; to hold a large bouquet of them indicates the attainment of an ideal ; if they are seen beside a bed it denotes the death of a young girl or child ; to see clusters of them in a church foreshows a wedding.

Magazine.—If you see several of these piled up near you it shows a reluctance to exert yourself, a love of sensation, and a craving for excitement.

Maggots.—To see food which is covered with maggots signifies that some horrible sight is brought to your notice, of which the memory will haunt you for a while ; to see them on an animal shows illness and the probable death of a favourite dog, cat, or bird.

Magic.—To dream that you are a magician and have power to work marvels indicates that there is a trace of roguery about you which will possibly lead you into a catastrophe ; to dream that you are under the spell of magic signifies that you are mistaken in your ideas as to a great friend, whom you will one day find to be far from what you imagined.

Magistrate.—To dream of more than one magistrate shows that you will appear as a witness before them.

Magnet.—If you are holding a magnet it shows a great desire to attract others to you and to claim attention and admiration from everyone you meet ; if you see the magnet at some distance and you try to reach it but cannot grasp it, you will fail in your endeavours ; if the magnet is above you and just out of reach it shows that you will be drawn by a magnetic influence to someone in a higher rank of life than yourself, but this attraction will only be transitory and will cause you to feel more of unrest than pleasure.

Magpie.—" One for sorrow, two for mirth,
        Three for a wedding, four for a birth."
This ancient saying well illustrates the meaning of a dream in which magpies appear.

Maid.—For a married woman to dream of her maids being close beside her denotes that she may expect to have trouble with them ; if they turn their backs it means that they will probably leave her without due notice ; if they put out their hands it shows that they will demand more wages ; to dream of meeting with a pleasant maid foreshows that a nice girl will attach herself and her services to you and will prove to be a treasure ; to dream of a maid in tears means serious disturbance in the house.

Maize.—To eat maize shows a determination to overcome a dislike which you feel is unreasonable.

Mallet.—This shows much influence with others, power of organisation, firmness, and courage ; if you are holding the mallet as though about to strike it means that you will be called upon to make a momentous decision and that your judgement will be wise.

Mallow.—To see clusters of them shows good business,

and freedom from care ; to dig them means deliverance from a threaten trouble or unpleasant episode.

Man.—For a girl to dream of receiving attention from a handsome man who is a stranger to her is an omen of success for her future happiness and marriage ; if the man is very old it means that she will not marry until she has experienced a broken engagement or unfortunate love affair ; to dream of a tall handsome man who advances towards her denotes newly awakened love ; an ugly man signifies domestic quarrels ; to see two men of rough visage denotes evil speaking.

Manacles.—To dream that you are held fast by heavy manacles denotes that unless someone comes to your assistance you will be in a most awkward predicament ; if the manacles fall off it means that you escape a threatened accident or injury to your hands.

Manager.—To dream of being a manager of a flourishing concern means success through your own ability ; to dream of managing a business affair which is in low water shows that you must put your whole energy into whatever you may undertake or you will bring upon yourself utter failure.

Manna.—To eat manna signifies the necessity for striving to put up with such things as you have although they are but substitutes for those you desire ; to see it denotes that you will be delivered from an unpleasant situation at a critical moment.

Manners.—If you dream of awkward ill-mannered people who annoy you by their habits it indicates an outing on pleasure, or a journey, during which you will be disconcerted by the rude behaviour of those around you ; to dream that you are considered ill-mannered warns you against mistaking rudeness for wit.

Manufactory.—To dream of being in a manufactory in which there are no signs of work or life predicts a strike ; to be in a factory in which the machinery is working and there is great activity indicates that you acquire a fortune through manufactured goods.

Map.—To study a map with a feeling of pleasure predicts an agreeable surprise in the arrival of someone dear to you from a distance ; for a girl to dream of studying a map whilst her lover is far away shows that she may hope for his speedy return.

Marble.—To see slabs of uncut marble shows success and triumph in your work ; broken marble denotes that reckless expenditure brings you to the brink of poverty ; a marble cross predicts death ; a marble floor indicates wealth.

Marbles.—To dream of playing with marbles denotes that

you are persuaded by your friends to take up some unaccustomed game which you find difficulty in learning; if the marbles roll away and disappear it shows that you will finally give up the attempt in despair.

Mare.—To see one with her foal indicates success and domestic peace.

Marigolds.—These flowers show a sunny nature seeing the best in everyone and everything ; the pleasures of life will be simple but very real.

Market.—To dream that you are in a market where all kinds of meat and vegetables are sold is a sign that in spite of economy and the effort to live within your income you will go through a time of much distress through lack of money.

Marmalade.—To make marmalade denotes a fortunate enterprise or a successful stroke of business, gratification and achievement through your own endeavours ; to eat it means pleasure with your friends ; to see jars of marmalade shows a need for guarding against extravagance.

Marriage.—To dream of being present at a wedding ceremony with flowers, palms, or the sun to be seen signifies a happy marriage for someone dear to you ; to dream of it with bad symbols, such as dark clouds or an owl, would foretell disaster as a result of the marriage ; to dream of being present at a wedding at which the bride is weeping predicts unexpected dangers and troubled happiness for her ; to dream of your own marriage when you are not engaged foretells an unfortunate love affair probably not ending in marriage : it also denotes anxieties, a poor state of health, and many disappointments ; to go to a wedding in rags shows misfortune mingled with pleasure ; to go to one dressed in black denotes the postponement of a wedding through mourning ; to go with an umbrella indicates pleasure marred, and vexation.

Marsh.—To dream of being hemmed in on all sides by a marsh signifies a liability to an attack of illness caused through chill or damp, bringing on lameness and crippling your hands.

Mask.—For a lover to dream of removing a mask predicts that unpleasant facts will come to light of which at present there is no suspicion, but which will lead to an abrupt ending of the love affair ; to put on a mask shows hypocrisy ; to see one in the distance is a warning of deception.

Mass.—To dream of seeing masses of people in a small space means that you find considerable difficulty in attending to the various claims upon you—it may be on your charity or the demands made upon your time by those who are exacting.

Mastiff.—For those who do not own a mastiff to see one

near by, warns them of a coming unexpected emergency in which there is danger of their being over-powered by the arguments of those who are masterful ; if the mastiff walks away it means that the controversy will cause a small disturbance only ; if it runs it shows that good and powerful friends will allay the anxiety.

Match.—To strike numbers of matches all of which go out at once shows a feckless nature and a jack of all trades, never making a success at the various things attempted ; to strike many matches which remain alight denotes that something that you undertake will prove to be a brilliant success; if the matches break as you try to strike them it means failure through unfortunate circumstances but through no fault of your own.

Mauve.—To dream of seeing this colour signifies deep feeling and conditions when bliss and sadness are often hand in hand ; it shows artistic taste and much power of affection, but love is governed by the head and not by the emotions ; to dream that you are wrapped in mauve from head to foot denotes the attainment of an ideal.

Maypole.—To dream that you are dancing round a maypole denotes gaiety and amusements which you find unsatisfying : whilst you enter into them in a light-hearted manner you are craving for further excitement ; to see a maypole in the distance shows that you enter enthusiastically into a scheme for providing amusement for young people.

Meadow.—To dream of being in a meadow through which a sparkling brook runs in which you see fish denotes a time of pleasure which is coming for you through some agreeable news from the country.

Meals.—To dream of setting the table for meals indicates that new tasks will fall upon you through the slackness or inability of others ; to be eating a meal in gloomy silence, whilst those around you are merry, indicates a disagreeable episode with your relatives ; to dream of eating alone shows greed, but with a large company, gaiety and pleasure.

Measles.—To dream that you have this illness prepares you for a probable attack of it ; if you dream of it in connection with a number of people an epidemic of measles is predicted.

Meat.—This is an unfortunate sign of financial worries ; if a large quantity is seen the complete failure of your source of income is predicted.

Medicine.—To see many bottles full of medicine indicates that you have a curious taste for experimenting with advertised medicines and quack remedies ; to drink it foreshows indisposition ; to give it to another denotes coming illness for someone dear to you.

Medlars.—To see a tree laden with medlars shows a series of unusual happenings bringing you to a new condition of life ; if the medlars drop off the tree upon you it denotes that the events will be to your advantage and that the new arrangement of your life will lead to prosperity ; if the medlars remain on the tree and are out of your reach it means that you will encounter obstacles and difficulty ; to eat them indicates transient happiness.

Melons.—To see melons growing signifies hope and success ; to eat them shows gratification and good news ; if a melon is given to you it predicts that you will derive much pleasure from the appreciation of those whose good opinion is of value to you.

Menagerie.—To dream of visiting a menagerie of wild beasts shows a love of natural history and a desire to travel in foreign countries ; if the cages are empty and no animals are to be seen it shows that your ambition will not be realised ; if there are many animals who fight and snarl it warns you of the thwarting of your purpose by those who will do their best to oppose you in your scheme.

Mermaid.—To those associated with the sea this is a warning of shipwreck or other peril.

Mesmerism.—If you are being mesmerised by a stranger it shows that you come under the spell of someone of the opposite sex who will have a powerful influence over you ; if you watch another being mesmerised it indicates that you desire to become a medium but fail.

Meteor.—To dream that you see a meteor denotes that you will soon hear of a wonderful discovery either in astronomy or in the development of wireless telegraphy.

Mice.—Dreaming of mice shows domestic difficulties ; it also shows a need for setting traps as this dream invariably indicates that there are mice in the house.

Michaelmas Daisy.—To see large groups of these growing signifies that you may expect an event to occur about September which will lead to changes in your life ; to pick them shows pleasure through renewed friendship and a meeting with those from whom you have been separated ; a piece of withered Michaelmas daisy in your hand means poverty.

Microscope.—If looking into one it shows a love of studying insect and plant life and that your knowledge will one day bring you fame.

Midwife.—To see a midwife signifies future trouble.

Mignonette.—Dreaming of this flower brings an assurance that what you hope for will come to pass probably at the time of year in which mignonette flowers.

Mildew.—To see this on objects around you shows that there is more need of energy in your life and that there is too much putting off till to-morrow what might be done to-day.

Milk.—To dream of milk shows that the love affair about which you have felt some anxiety will now proceed smoothly ; to see large pans of rich milk denotes prosperity and success in agricultural enterprise.

Milk Can.—To see many milk cans shows an agricultural enterprise which will be to your advantage ; if you handle them it means that you will take an active part in helping to finance a new scheme.

Milk Churn.—If you are churning with a feeling of discomfort and toil it shows the failure of a project ; if with a sensation of ease and pleasure it signifies that hoped-for plans will succeed giving much satisfaction and a prosperous outlook.

Mill.—To see this at work denotes a happy and eventful existence, if not working it indicates a single and somewhat dreary one.

Millionaire.—To dream of becoming a millionaire denotes that you attain a position of wealth through a sudden and unexpected stroke of good fortune.

Mimic.—If you dream of being a mimic with people around who applaud, it shows that you may have success as an entertainer ; if you hear yourself being mimicked it means that you need a candid friend to tell you of a bad trick.

Mincepies.—To be eating these shows happy meetings at Christmas time with those who are now far away ; many mincepies around you denote a festivity and a joyous gathering at that season.

Minister.—To meet one who greets you cordially denotes a benevolent friend who will do you a good turn when you are most in need of it.

Mint.—If you pick it and throw it away you may expect a snubbing from someone whose opinion you respect ; to eat it means curiosity ; to pull it up by the root shows an impetuous nature.

Miser.—If you are possessed of wealth and dream of being a miser it shows that you are considered very mean by those who know you ; if you are poor and dream of being a miser it means that you will one day enjoy riches but will be in danger of hoarding your worldly goods.

Mistletoe.—To see this growing signifies that a cherished hope is unlikely to be fulfilled or at any rate only after many months have passed and when you are weary of waiting; to pick it shows a budding affection which will develop into true love for someone whom you have known since childhood ; to carry a large bunch of it indicates happiness with those whom you love, meetings with those now far away, and social enjoyment at Christmas time.

Mitre.—This shows honour and promotion for a clergyman ; if a Cathedral appears also it would indicate the offer of a Bishopric.

Moat.—To dream of seeing a moat in which the water is muddy and has weed growing upon it indicates calamity and serious losses ; to boat on it shows domestic quarrels and disturbance in the home, sadness and unrest ; to cross it means that you break away from hindrances and make a new start in life ; to see it full of dead fish shows a danger of famine ; if the moat is clean and sparkling and fishes are swimming in it, very pleasant news awaits you.

Moles.—To see these animals warns you of deceit : be careful in whom you confide or you may find that mischief has been made of your confidences ; to see moles burrowing shows that you spare yourself no trouble to get to the root of a matter about which you are over-curious ; to see them dead signifies the destroying of a faint hope.

Money.—To see sums of money in a dream is hopeful of prosperity or to see figures representing sums of money is equally promising : the more you see the larger will be the amount coming to you ; the exact sum to be received through a legacy, presents, or earnings, is often shown by figures seen in a dream ; if you dream of losing money regard it as a warning and take sepcial care not to do so ; to find it shows that you will experience an undoubted piece of good luck ; to hold small coins in each hand denotes quarrelling over money matters ; to hide it means deceit ; to count large sums of money indicates wealth ; to give it away shows generosity but also a somewhat extravagant nature unable to resist the pleasure of spending money ; to see many hands grabbing at it indicates robbery.

Money-Lender.—This dream is an unpleasant sign of financial distress ; to dream that you are a money-lender shows that your methods of business are not above suspicion and that with the smallest chance you would make money by dishonest means and recklessly bring misery upon those whom you defraud ; to speak to a money-lender means persecution.

Monk.—To converse with one shows that somebody in whom you are interested becomes a monk ; if you see one pacing up and down it shows a disturbance from the apparition of a monk.

Monkey.—To dream of a monkey being near you is an unpleasant sign of ugly rumours around you and yours and also numerous troubles which are largely brought about by the injudicious words of others : be on your guard in speaking of the affairs of your friends, for probably those whom you least suspect are secret enemies.

Moon.—A crescent moon denotes good news and fortune and for a man public recognition and honour ; when gibbous it indicates sickness, misfortune and dismay ; to see it rising signifies dawning love and a new hope ; to see it setting indicates the withering of what was no more than sentiment, and the abrupt ending of a love affair ; to see a full moon signifies attainment and joy.

Moon Daisies.—If these are seen in a field or garden it foreshows pleasure and happiness coming in the early summer ; to be holding a moon daisy in your hand is not so pleasant as it may be a warning of illness to yourself ; a large bunch signifies the reaping of your due reward.

Moonstone.—To those born in February or July this is a most fortunate stone of which to dream as it is one of the birth stones for those months ; for all dreamers it is a pleasant symbol of love, placidity, and success.

Moss.—To pick it denotes remorse for the past and good intentions for the future ; to see a moss-covered heap predicts a funeral ; a moss-covered bank indicates that indolence hinders your progress ; a moss-covered gate shows decay ; to walk upon moss foreshows a shadow upon your happiness at present : in the future this will vanish and unclouded peace will be yours.

Mother.—To dream of your mother when separated from her indicates that you will shortly hear that she is particularly anxious to see you, or, if that is impossible, to have news of you : if she speaks to you it shows that she is troubled and wishes to consult with you : to dream of seeing her in distress is a warning of her coming illness.

Moths.—If moths are flying about you it is a sign of distress and disturbing incidents causing a feeling of helplessness ; moths settling upon you mean illness, nerves, and restlessness ; large beautifully-coloured moths seen at a distance show a journey to a foreign land where such moths are to be seen.

Mountain.—To see a great mountain at which you gaze with a feeling of wonder denotes travel in countries of grandeur and vast expanse ; to see mountains covered with snow indicates the realisation of a great ambition ; to climb a mountain shows that you will have opportunity for rising to fame and honour : if you fall it means a severe disappointment in your career ; to pick a flower on a mountain signifies the granting of a favour ; to see mountains obscured by dark clouds portends tragic events, great upheavals and sorrow

Mourning.—If you are buying mourning it is a sign of personal bereavement ; if you see large numbers of people in black in a street or thoroughfare it shows death for a member of the royal family.

Mouth.—To see it of normal size indicates that you will receive a verbal message of some importance ; if it appears large or distorted it means that you will be shocked by some piece of scandal concerning someone in a high position or by the abuse of those whom you esteem as worthy of honour ; a small tightly compressed mouth denotes meanness and acidity of speech ; a mouth slightly open indicates illness ; a smiling mouth signifies good news and a crooked mouth indecision.

Mowing.—If you are mowing with a machine it shows that your difficulties and hindrances will speedily be removed from your path.

Mud.—To dream of deep mud through which you try to walk shows an outing entirely spoiled by the weather which will certainly be very unpleasant ; to throw mud denotes that you are a danger to society through your love of gossip and the spreading of scandal.

Muff.—To carry a muff shows comforts ; to buy a large one means a prosperous undertaking ; to swing one denotes caprice and ostentation.

Mulatto.—To see a mulatto signifies misfortune ; to see a female mulatto means treachery, and if she bends over you it shows illness.

Mulberries.—To be eating these is a sign of passing pleasures : your wishes are gratified for the present but it will not prove to be lasting, there will always be failure in obtaining the things most hoped-for ; to be picking them shows great power of loving and much force in disliking : there is no middle course.

Mule.—To drive one indicates that you spend much time over arduous duties for which you receive but a small amount of recompense ; to see a mule near you shows that you had better change your poiut of view and own that you were in the wrong ; if you follow a mule it signifies that you will become obstinate and perverse ; to catch one means that against the advice of your relations and friends you take up a hobby which will cause inconvenience to those with whom you live.

Murder.—To dream of committing murder gives an urgent warning against the harbouring of malicious feelings and hatred ; to see a murder is an ominous warning of the violent death of someone near to you ; to dream of being murdered indicates a bad state of health and is also a caution to keep away from unfrequented places and to avoid arousing those whom you know to possess an ungovernable temper.

Mushrooms.—To pick them in a marshy field denotes sadness, tears, and troubles which will come upon you in the mushroom season ; to the lover it means quarrels, disagreeables, and possibly a broken engagement ; to eat them signifies that you take a small risk and achieve a great success ; to cook them shows gratification and health.

Music.—Signifies consolation.

Mustard.—To see mustard spread on a table denotes an illness necessitating poultices ; to see it in a large tin shows that you forget an important duty or message, for which you are sharply reprimanded ; to make it means quarrels ; to eat it indicates a capacity for the repeating of good stories.

Myrrh.—To dream of drinking myrrh foreshows a sorrow which you endeavour to conceal and alleviate by attaching yourself to undesirable people and pleasures ; to smell it denotes a necessity for bracing yourself to face a trial.

Myrtle.—To see this growing speaks of affection and peace ; to pick it predicts a declaration of love ; to carry a bunch of it shows a happy marriage.

N.

Nails.—To dream of cutting your nails shows that you will meet with many vexations in the course of the day ; to bite them indicates sourness and a gloomy outlook ; to file them denotes irritation ; to see them very long foreshows trouble or illness ; very short nails indicate an attack on your character; to dream of knocking heavy carpentering nails into a wall signifies that you must rely on your own efforts to make any success of your life ; if the nails are small and bend as you hammer them, you must recognise the need of further energy and perseverance.

Naked.—To dream that you are naked is a bad omen of distress and poverty.

Name.—To hear or see the name of a person or place in a dream signifies events occurring in connection with such person or place ; if good symbols appear pleasant events may be expected, if gloomy signs then trouble will arise associated with the name seen ; if you see a name unknown to you it usually indicates quite unlooked-for developments bringing you into contact with someone of the name shown to you in the dream ; to hear your name spoken and yet see no form shows that someone you love is thinking much about you and is in need of your sympathy and possibly of your presence.

Napkin.—To see several clean napkins laid on a table signifies hospitality and invitations ; to see them crumpled and soiled shows disorderly behaviour ; to dream of a pile of new napkins means prosperity and sometimes a wedding present.

Narcissus.—To dream of the scent of these flowers shows sentiment and coming joy which will be yours ere long ; to see them growing indicates that some new idea will unfold itself to you in the spring and will prove to be of much advantage ; to pick them means that you make the most of such things as you have knowing full well that they are far from what you desire.

Nasturtiums.—To see them in blossom denotes that an unexpected turn of fortune brings you much success ; to see clusters of the seed means that you develop a taste for curious foods which are difficult to obtain ; to eat them pickled shows perverseness.

Naval Battle.—To dream of witnessing this certainly indicates that a naval battle is to be expected.

Navigate a Vessel.—To dream that you are steering a ship through troubled water denotes that you will be obliged to take a journey on account of some worrying matter which needs your personal attention.

Neck.—If this is swollen and large it gives warning of illness affecting the throat ; if you see it looking slender and white it signifies admiration and attention from one of the opposite sex.   ʋ

Necklace.—To dream of this being placed upon you by another means that you receive a handsome present of a neck-lace ; if you are fastening one around the neck of someone it denotes that you will give away something which you treasure ; if you tear one off your neck and destroy it, you will break a bond which you have grown to feel is unendurable.

Nectarines.—To eat nectarines signifies the development of love ; to pick them denotes a happy event to which you may look forward in the summer ; to see them growing indicates that you will live in luxury.

Needles.—To see many needles shows disappointment in love ; to find them denotes deceit and mischief ; to use them signifies that you will one day reap a good reward from your industry ; if you are pricked you may expect trivial annoy-ances.

Negro.—To dream of a negro being near you means that you are likely to receive a shock through news which you will hear ; to shake hands with one warns you against the evil influence of a dark man with whom you will become acquainted in the future ; if a negro grins at you it shows robbery and deception.

Neigh.—To hear a horse neighing predicts calamity for someone dear to you ; to a business man it denotes a temporary embarrassment.

Neighbours.—To dream of your neighbours being gathered together denotes gossip which is detrimental to you ; to see them smiling around you shows that you are highly esteemed by those who know you best and that in the future you will have good cause to be grateful to your neighbours.

Nest.—To find a hen's nest means a birth ; to see a nest of snakes, a bad reputation.

Nettles.—To see and avoid them warns you to beware of meddling with things likely to be dangerous for you and to shun doubtful amusements or companions ; to pick them shows a headstrong   nature determined to seek personal experience even in disagreeable matters ; to pull them up by the root signifies that you hold strong views and are not backward in proclaiming them.

Newspaper.—To be reading it portends that news of public events will be of such interest that, becoming absorbed in it, you will forget an important appointment ; to see in your dream a newspaper which has a black edge indicates the death of a celebrity ; to hold one upside down denotes that you are so much engrossed in your own affairs that you pay no attention to matters of greater importance ; to be wrapping goods in newspaper means a poor outlook for your work or business.

Niagara.—To dream of gazing at the falls of Niagara or of hearing the rushing of this mighty torrent portends momentous events bringing about unlooked-for changes in your life : it may possibly mean that you will travel largely and see Niagara in reality.

Nickname.—If you hear yourself spoken of by an unpleasant nickname, be sure that you have earned it through your own folly or lack of graciousness when in society.

Night.—To dream of the night as black and dreary denotes a time of sorrow and distress ; if it appears full of peace and brightness it foretells joy ; to walk alone in the night signifies melancholy and solitude ; to dream of making a speech in the night warns you that you are likely to weary those with whom you converse by your prosy and incessant talk.

Nightcap.—To dream of walking out in a nightcap shows that you will be led into some foolish escapade with those of your companions who have strange ideas with regard to a joke ; to be wearing it in company would signify that you will meet with a foolish youth who imagines that he makes himself agreeable by foolish talk and the paying of cheap compliments ; for a married woman to dream of this indicates jealousy and perhaps not without cause.

Nightingale.—To dream of this bird denotes true love and happiness in marriage ; to hear it sing means mutual affection and joyful news.

Nightjar.—To dream of this strange bird denotes that you are more heroic in theory than in practice ; to hear it signifies an evening of happy memories spent with one whom you love.

Ninepins.—To be playing with these shows a mind determined to gain success whatever the cost in drudgery ; if the ninepins fall down time after time it means the failure of your plans ; if some remain standing, partial success ; if all stand up, gratification of your hope.

Nobility.—To dream that the rank of duke or earl has been conferred upon you indicates that through vain imagination and idle hope you lose your best opportunity of making any success in life ; to dream that you are offered a title of high rank shows that you have power to rise to fame through your own ability ; for a girl of lowly position to dream that someone of high rank is in love with her denotes that she has far too good an opinion of her own charm.

Nodding.—To dream of being so sleepy in company that you nod your head to one of the guests means that you will meet with such an insufferable bore that your pleasure will be entirely spoiled and you will only wish to escape ; for a youth to dream that a girl who is a stranger nods to him signifies that he will be so much attracted to some one whom he meets by chance in a crowd that he busies himself in finding the means of becoming acquainted with her.

Noise.—To dream that you hear loud and noisy people shows that you will be vexed by disturbances in your home ; to dream that you make a noise denotes that your vanity will meet with a rebuff ; to dream of being described as noisy warns you to avoid being so emphatic in your speech.

Nose.—To dream of your nose as very large denotes dissipation ; a crooked nose shows a wayward and untrustworthy character ; a nose eaten away is a bad omen of disease affecting the face ; to dream of it as thin and long denotes that you change your ideas on various subjects and alter your mode of life in accordance with your new notions.

Nose Bleeding.—Dreaming of this means that you will be vexed by an attack of it at a most inconvenient moment.

Nosegay.—To see a large nosegay of various brightly coloured flowers is a pleasing symbol of much happiness ; if you pull it to pieces it means that you will mar the joy in the life of another by your coldness and indifference.

Nougat.—To dream of eating this sweetmeat signifies that a prospective pleasure to which you are eagerly looking forward will be very disappointing, for you will be feeling dejected and peevish and will not appear at your best ; to see a box of nougat means a present of sweets.

● **Novel.**—To see a collection of these means a desire to become an authoress ; to be idly turning the pages of several novels shows that you take all your ideas from the novels you read and endeavour to imitate the heroine of each one as you read it, thereby succeeding in making yourself ridiculous in the eyes of your friends.

Nuisance.—To dream that you regard people as a nuisance when they invite you to join them in some social plan indicates that unless you are careful you may become so disagreeable that no one will wish to associate with you.

Numbers.—These are often seen in dreams as indicating events in the future : whether these events will be pleasant or the reverse can usually be decided by other signs, or by a feeling of pleasure or sadness accompanying the dream.

Nun.—For a young girl to dream of becoming a nun shows that she will desire to follow this vocation, but will meet with much opposition from her relatives and friends ; to dream of speaking with one shows that she may expect to remain unmarried through her own choice ; if a young man dreams of a nun it portends that he will become suspicious of his be-trothed and will probably discard her.

Nurse.—To dream that you see a hospital nurse beside you predicts coming illness for yourself or for someone dear to you ; if you dream that you have become a nurse and attain to a post of honour in your work it indicates that you will take up this profession and rise to distinction.

Nursing.—To dream of nursing a sick friend denotes that you will be of use and comfort to a friend in sudden illness ; if your patient is a stranger you may find that you have unconsciously been a good friend to someone who is alone in the world and who in a bad illness would be unable to afford a nurse ; to dream that your soldier lover has been wounded in battle and that you are nursing him back to health signifies that he will be promoted for a deed of bravery performed to save the life of a comrade.

Nutcrackers.—To dream of a pair of nutcrackers shows that you are striving to solve a difficult problem ; if you grasp the crackers all will be well, for you will successfully settle the matter which is troubling you.

Nutmeg.—To grate nutmeg denotes an annoying incident which will ruffle your temper for the rest of the day ; to eat it shows strongly developed likes and dislikes and a mind which is rapidly made up on any point ; to sift it means that you wish to avoid controversy with some one whose opinions are opposed to your own.

Nuts.—To see a quantity of trees laden with nuts foretells gratified ambition and wealth ; to eat them indicates good health and abundance ; if the nuts are dry and without kernels it shows reverses and embarrassment ; to dream of being surrounded by nut trees on which there is no fruit signifies tragedy, sorrow and parting.

O.

Oak.—To dream of a large oak tree in leaf is a hopeful sign of wealth, strength, and achievement; for a lover it predicts much happiness and prosperity in marriage; if the tree is bare, patience will be necessary before your hope or ambition will be realised; if the tree is withered or partly cut down, losses and grief are indicated; to climb an oak tree shows a rise in position.

Oar.—For a youth to dream of an oar shows that much of his success in life will come through his popularity and efficiency in sport; if you dream of losing one or more oars whilst rowing it is a sign of danger and distress; to break one means recklessness for which you will pay dearly: for a lover or husband to dream this foreshows affliction and sorrow.

Oats.—To dream of a field of green oats signifies that before long you will reap the reward of your patient waiting; wealth and a long life are foreshown by seeing it ripe; misfortune if you see it wind swept.

Obellak.—This is a sign of fame and wealth; if you mount it, great honour will be conferred upon you.

Obituary.—To dream of reading your own obituary notice foreshows a severe illness through which you will not be expected to live but you will take everyone by surprise and make a good recovery; to see the obituary notice of a friend or relative is usually an omen of death for him or her.

Observatory.—To dream that you visit an observatory for the purpose of viewing the stars or for astronomical study is a sign that you will wish to devote your life to these subjects and live in retirement and solitude, too deeply engrossed in your studies to pay heed to your fellow-creatures.

Ocean.—To dream that you see a large vessel sailing across the ocean shows that a vast distance separates you from someone you love; if you see a steamer a voyage is predicted.

Offence.—To dream that you have given offence to someone with whom you much desire to be friendly signifies that you overdo your amiability and run the risk of being considered gushing.

Office.—If you dream of being at unaccustomed work in a large office, the offer of new and interesting employment is shown ; if the office is in disorder and you see ink marks and papers scattered on the floor, it means that you will forfeit a good post through your own fault. ,

Officer.—If you dream that you are an officer of high rank you may hope to succeed in your profession whatever it may be ; if you dream of being an officer unable to exercise authority you may expect to work hard and receive but scanty payment.

Oil.—To see oil flowing signifies abundant crops and profitable transactions ; to spill it shows extravagant habits ; to discover it, wealth.

Ointment.—To make it shows that the many schemes which you have in mind for benefiting others will tax your strength and your means to carry them into effect ; to use it denotes an irritable state of mind and indisposition ; to smell it means a desire to investigate and arrive at your own conclusions in all matters.

Old.—To dream of old buildings as falling is a warning of danger ; to see them in the distance would foreshow loss of income through depreciation of property ; old clothes signify that your income is likely to diminish as you advance in years ; old letters or books mean that you have a dislike to throwing away anything even when it has become useless to you.

Old Man.—To see an aged man near you who holds up his hand as if to admonish, tells you to pay attention to the advice of those of greater experience than yourself ; an aged man in the distance suggests a caution to be prudent.

Old Woman.—If her countenance is unpleasant you are warned of a woman who will seek to harm you by evil speaking and gossip ; an aged woman in the distance shows the possession of a faithful friend and wise counsellor.

Olive Oil.—To drink olive oil shows that your expectations are exceeded and that there will be no lack of such things as you desire ; to pour it upon yourself denotes gladness.

Olives.—To dream that you see olives growing is a prediction of honour and dignity being conferred upon you ; to eat them indicates that you must undertake a disagreeable matter from a sense of duty ; to carry them means peace and contentment.

Onions.—If you eat onions you may expect that something which you supposed was a secret will be discovered ; to cut them up means disputes with your inferiors ; to cook them

E

shows that the cares of a household will become a burden ; to pull them from the ground signifies toil and perplexity.

Onyx.—If you hold these gems in your hand it assures you of satisfaction and the happy ending to a matter about which you have had misgivings.

Opal.—For those born in October this is a specially fortunate gem of which to dream as it is one of the birth stones for that month ; for all persons this dream would portend pleasure and realised wishes ; to the lover it promises happiness in marriage.

Opera.—To dream of attending the opera in company with one of the opposite sex denotes gaiety followed by pain and displeasure ; to the married it is a danger signal of severance through jealousy.

Opera Glasses.—If you look through them and perceive nothing it means that you will lose the confidence of your friends because of your inquisitive questions ; to look into them and see a number of people shows popularity and social pleasure ; if you gaze at an empty buliding you will fail in an attempt to become famous as a singer or actor ; to level them at a stranger means an introduction, to level them at someone whom you know is a sign of contempt ; if you break them you will make yourself ridiculous in the eyes of your friends by your pride.

Orange.—This colour displayed to you in a dream signifies that you are unconventional and possessed of a vivid personality and original ideas ; if you appear to be clothed in orange colour it denotes that fluency of speech will largely assist in your progress.

Orange Blossom.—For the betrothed to dream of being decked in orange-blossom proclaims a speedy marriage ; to those who are not engaged it is an omen of shattered hope and a troubled love affair ; to see it growing speaks of happiness and affection and the dawning of love ; to pick it indicates the fulfilment of a cherished hope bringing you peace and joy.

Orange Lily.—If you see a cluster of these flowers you may expect to hear surprising news ; to pick them means determination and courage, and the mastery of those who oppose you ; to carry a spray of them promises you attainment to honour through the success of a new scheme.

Oranges.—To see them growing proclaims good news from someone abroad who is dear to you ; to pick them means fulfilment and probably new interests and travels ; to see them in a dish shows amusement ; on a bed, illness ; in a churchyard, the death of a relation in the winter ; to eat a sweet orange speaks of pleasant events ; a sour one, discontent with your lot and endeavours to change it ; to drink the juice of an orange predicts a feverish attack to peel one neatly indicates that you balance the pros and cons in all you do and seldom err in your decision ; to peel one clumsily signifies a blunder which may bring unpleasant results upon you.

Orchard.—To dream that you are in an orchard in which there are trees in blossom speaks of coming joy and love ; if the trees are bare it shows that you must wait for that which will eventually bring you satisfaction ; to see an orchard of fruit trees in the distance is a sign that although you may have trifling vexations nothing serious will occur to mar your happiness : to the married this dream predicts domestic peace and healthy children.

Orchestra.—To dream of hearing beautiful music from an orchestra denotes good news already on its way ; if you hear mistakes and confused sounds it foretells disturbing news ; to see the orchestra playing but not to hear it indicates a doubtful pleasure.

Orchids.—To see numbers of these growing in a variety of beautiful colours is a sign of wealth and a life of ease and pleasure ; to pick them shows generosity ; to wear them means association with the rich and powerful ; to plant them denotes coming good fortune.

Organ.—To hear an organ giving forth loud and joyous music proclaims a wedding ; if the music is slow and solemn it foreshows serious illness, sometimes death ; to play it indicates that in spite of obstacles your ambition will be realised ; should you see the organ without hearing music it denotes that you weary of a subject before you have given yourself sufficient time in which to master it.

Ornaments.—If you see a number of ornaments around you be sure that your habit of frittering away your money on totally useless articles will lead you into debt, and that as a result of your fecklessness penury and want will be your lot ; if the ornaments are broken it means that you will suffer through the extravagance of another.

Orrisroot.—To dream of this signifies that you make yourself agreeable and appear sweetness itself to those whose appreciation you desire ; but that in reality you are hard and unyielding and far from being what you appear to be on the surface.

Ostrioh.—If the ostrich runs towards you expect to hear startling news and rumours of public upheavals ; to touch it denotes a tendency to conceit and self-praise ; to ride upon one means that you carry your eccentricity to excess ; to chase one indicates an attempt to disguise disagreeable facts ; if the ostrich chases you swift retribution will overtake you.

Otter.—If an otter comes near, you may expect to receive a disagreeable shock through some unpleasant spite on the part of those of whom you have always thought highly and regarded as loyal and affectionate friends ; to chase one shows cunning and a dislike to interference in any personal matter.

Oven.—For a married women this dream foretells strife and disagreeable incidents ; to the single it is an omen of daily difficulties and lack of comfort ; to heat it shows feasting and satisfaction.

Overcoat.—If you are struggling into an overcoat which is too small for you, you may expect to have changes in your life and to become of much importance ; if you put one on which is too large you will suffer loss and illness ; if it is so long that it envelops you from head to foot it shows that unless you reform a time may come when you will feel remorse and shame, and will endeavour to hide yourself from relatives and friends.

Owl.—This bird is an omen of misfortune and poverty ; if it flies you will receive tidings of grief ; if it alights upon you illness or sorrow is predicted ; to lovers this bird is a symbol of bad news and unpleasant rumours ; for those who are contemplating new work or enterprise to dream of the owl should be a warning to proceed with caution.

Ox.—To see a team of oxen at work brings gain and good fortune; to see one drinking means theft; a mad one, personal danger ; without horns, reconciliation with a former enemy ; fighting with another, family quarrels ; to see one running shows a secret divulged ; a lean one signifies poverty ; a white one, honour and favours ; a black one, a risky undertaking ; to see one jump shows obstacles ; to see one walk on the hind legs, money troubles ; to see one eat, hospitality and domestic peace.

Oyster.—Dreaming of a dish of oysters foreshows that you will enjoy this delicacy in company with your friends ; to eat them is a sign of good health ; to open them and experience much difficulty in so doing is an indication that you will appreciate the pleasures of life much more in your later years than in your youthful days.

P.

Packing.—If you pack in confusion and disorder and with the feeling that you will not be ready to start for the train it foreshows disarranged plans and the postponement of a prospective journey ; if you pack an array of new clothes, you may expect a visit of gaiety and pleasure ; shabby clothes indicate a journey taken on distasteful business or duty ; to pack a variety of objects signifies charitable inclinations.

Padlock.—To open it means a surprise ; to close it precaution ; to find one is a warning to use a lock on your valuables and on private papers or letters ; to break one denotes dishonesty ; to put one on a door cautions you that someone in whom you trust is unworthy of your confidence.

Page.—If the page bows low to you be sure that someone in whom you confide will criticise you in a treacherous manner to those who are of an inferior position ; if he shakes his head it denotes the betrayal of a secret.

Pain.—To suffer this in a dream invariably denotes that you will awake in pain ; to dream of pain without feeling it predicts domestic trouble or disturbance in family matters ; to a lover a disquieting omen of misfortune is predicted by this dream.

Paint.—To paint your face shows a need for disguising unfortunate facts ; to a lover it denotes deceit and the concealing of secrets ; to see a painted woman warns you not to trust her ; a painted man, coarseness ; to be painting your house means a stroke of good luck ; to smell paint foreshows illness.

Palace.—To see one portends good fortune and favours ; to live in one, advancement and honour ; if you see it burn or fall, you will run the risk of losing your fortune through recklessness.

Palm Tree.—This is a symbol of power, honour, and victory ; to dream that you are under a large palm promises you the comforts of life, many friends, and beautiful surroundings ; to the single it predicts happiness in marriage ; fame and triumph are foreshown by the carrying of a palm leaf.

Pampas Grass.—A large plant of this will mean a somewhat monotonous though useful life ; to carry a branch of it shows a pathetic endeavour to hide your sadness or poverty under cover of a cheerful countenance.

Pancakes.—If the pancakes are light and crisp you may expect a pleasant surprise ; if they are heavy you will spend the day in a doleful condition ; to cook them brings an assurance of success and shows that you will have but few troubles to contend with.

Pansy.—To see a variety of these flowers signifies placidity, modesty, contentment, and the possession of many advantages to pick them shows the attainment of your heart's desire.

Pantaloons.—A surprising incident.

Panther.—If it approaches near you may expect to be shocked at the treacherous behaviour of a friend whom you have always regarded as honourable ; if it springs upon you it shows a severe shock or mental breakdown ; if you dream of a tame panther which you caress it foretells that you have some ungrateful person in your household or possibly a disloyal friend ; to chase one means the discovery of a scandalous story of which you are able to prove the falseness ; to be chased by one denotes that you will some day be found out in a dishonourable action.

Pantomime.—This dream should caution you to beware of one of your friends who is of a particularly jovial nature, for a remark of yours made to that friend is likely to be misconstrued and will lead to mischief-making, causing you much annoyance.

Pantry.—For a young woman to dream of being at work in a pantry means that some man who will desire to marry her will be of an unreliable character, working only when it pleases him or when it is particularly inconvenient to be short of cash : he will borrow without scruple, knowing full well that he cannot repay the debt and by plausible stories will extract sums of money from those who are easily imposed upon ; the dream should be regarded as a warning to avoid the advances of such a man ; if a youth dreams of being at work in a pantry it declares that he will never have much¹ success in life as he is careless and throws away good opportunities.

Paper.—To dream that you see much paper of the same size and shape shows that you will receive money, either a present or an unexpected payment of a debt which you had given up hope of receiving ; if the paper is soiled and crumpled you will squander it and perhaps commit some indiscretion, the results of which you will have cause to remember for a long while.

Parade.—To dream of a parade of soldiers and that you are delighted with the military display foretells unexpected pleasure leading to new interests in your life ; to a business man it denotes success in trade through his enterprise in some dealing with the military authorities ; to the youth it shows an ambitious career as a soldier ; to a young girl it would point to a gay lover who will possibly forsake her ; to a married woman it means a kindhearted, but somewhat disloyal husband.

Paradise.—To dream of paradise signifies that your ideal in life is probably too exalted for realisation in this world.

Parasol.—To dream of possessing a new, gaily-coloured parasol predicts flirtations, gaiety and admiration ; to break it means the refusal of an ardent suitor and, in the future, regretting it ; to carry one shut shows that you will be placed at some disadvantage by a jealous woman ; for a married woman to dream of breaking her parasol is a bad omen of misfortune for her husband.

Parcel.—To receive one means a present ; to carry a minute one denotes that you will soon hear a piece of news bringing much interest and delight to yourself and happiness to another ; to carry a large one shows the transaction of troublesome business.

Pardon.—To ask pardon of someone towards whom you feel dislike indicates that it is you who are in the wrong and that you should take the first opportunity of making amends ; to ask pardon of a stranger shows humiliation and sometimes disgrace.

Parents.—To dream of your parents cautions you to regard their wishes or you may have cause to regret your indifference ; to see them in comfort and happiness in their old age assures you of health, peace, and affection in your home ; to have a serious quarrel with them and leave them in anger indicates that unless you use self-control you may one day commit a serious crime ; if your parents are dead and they appear to you in a dream regard it as a warning to be careful in the avoidance of such things as you know they would not approve ; or if you are contemplating new work or enterprise be on your guard and do nothing rashly ; if you have a guilty conscience as to your behaviour to another and your parents appear to you in a dream, be sure that it is meant as a rebuke and an entreaty to you to make such reparation to that person as is possible ; if a young woman about to be married has this dream and her parents appear with smiling countenances she may feel assured of happiness in her marriage ; if they appear sad or vexed it indicates that she would do well to break off her engagement for nothing but misfortune will come of it.

Park.—If you dream of being in a large park with many people around you it foretells a visit to a country house where you will make new and influential friends ; to dream of walking in a park in which you are counting the trees predicts an inheritance.

Parliament.—For a young woman to dream that her chief interest in life is centred in parliamentary news denotes that she will become acquainted with a member of parliament with whom she will fall in love at first sight ; for those who dream that they listen to a parliamentary debate on a personal matter displays the fact that they are too fond of discussing private affairs in public and that they are noted for their garrulous talk.

Parrot.—To see this bird signifies mental energy, travel, and many interests and friends ; if it alights upon you and chatters it warns you to beware of flattery and a dangerous neighbour.

Parsnips.—To eat them means that you are likely to be deceived by appearances ; to cook them shows thrift ; to dig them denotes toil and poor circumstances.

Parting.—To dream of parting from those whom you love is the event casting its shadow before it and you must prepare for separation from someone dear to you.

Partridge.—To see them flying signifies good news of your lover or friends ; to see them dead means a present ; to eat them shows profit and the gaining of a wish ; to carry them denotes prosperity.

Party.—To dream that you receive an invitation to a party which you decline means that if you go you will regret it ; to dream of being present at a large evening party at which all the guests are strangers to you indicates your removal to a new neighbourhood and the making of many friends ; to dream of giving a large party for which you make sumptuous arrangements predicts an unexpected turn of good fortune ; to dream of it and see bare tables and dingy rooms foretells that your pleasures must be curtailed through lack of means.

Passing Bell.—To hear this in a dream predicts death though not necessarily for someone near and dear to you ; if you see the bell and hear it toll, it would undoubtedly mean a personal sorrow.

Passion Flower.—To dream of this flower is a sign of tribulation followed by joy.

Pastry.—To eat it shows that your desires are limited to those things which are within your reach ; to make it means that you will have your wits about you in an emergency.

Path.—A narrow path which is rough and steep foreshows tribulation and anxiety ; if it is wide and green you may hope for joy ; if it is stony and painful to walk upon you may be sure that some of the hindrances and obstacles in your life will be difficult to surmount.

Pawnbroker.—To dream that you have been forced to visit a pawnbroker indicates financial worry and inability to pay a pressing claim ; to dream that you become a pawnbroker shows that through boldness and indifference to consequences you hit upon a lucky and lucrative enterprise.

Peaches.—To eat them signifies pleasure and content ; to pick them shows graciousness, and happiness with someone you love ; to see them on a dish shows prosperity and satisfaction.

Peacock.—If you see it in a garden it is a sign of prosperity, possibly of an inheritance of property ; if very near you it is an omen of misfortune and your troubles are likely to be as numerous as the colours seen in the peacock ; if you follow one it denotes vanity and unbounded ambition ; if it spreads its tail, ostentation ; for an unmarried man to dream of a peacock signifies that he will marry a beautiful woman ; for a girl to dream of this bird denotes that she will have a handsome husband and a grand wedding ; to hear the peacock scream predicts a severe storm, probably causing considerable damage.

Pearls.—A dream of pearls is a most fortunate one for those born in January, July or September, as a pearl is one of the birth stones for those months ; for others it is not considered a favourable dream, but much depends upon the way in which the pearls are seen ; if you see large and beautiful pearls it foretells riches ; a ring of pearls, a death and a probable legacy ; to wear a ring of pearls, solitude and tears ; a bracelet of pearls which appears too large for you denotes an unhappy love affair and possibly a broken engagement.

Pears.—To eat them ripe and mellow brings joy and the fulfilment of a wish ; sleepy pears mean misery and tears ; hard pears, treachery ; to gather them, approaching festivities ; to see them growing, cheerfulness and pleasure.

Peas.—To see these growing shows that an experiment about which you had misgivings will turn out an unqualified success ; to eat them brings good fortune and favourable business prospects.

Pelican.—This bird is a symbol of loneliness, separation, and yearning for the unattainable ; if it is flying you will receive news from those who are far away in isolated parts of the world.

Penguins.—To see many of these strange birds indicates interesting news of expeditions and discoveries in the northern regions ; to catch one shows that you may become famous through your investigations in natural history.

Penknife.—To hold one signifies enemies and hatred ; to find one, jealousy and disloyalty.

Pension.—If you dream that you have a pension from a friend it denotes that you will be dependent upon your own savings and the help of your friends in later years ; to dream of receiving a pension is a sign that you should avoid extravagance and endeavour to save for your old age or a pension may be your only source of income.

Peonies.—Coloured peonies growing in masses predict that you will be called upon to make a decision of much importance to you before another summer is past ; if the peonies are broken and lie on the ground you will probably throw away your chance of happiness by coming to a wrong conclusion ; if they are erect you will decide wisely ; if the petals are scattered and the ground appears to be carpeted with red you will hear of bad news, possibly of an operation or sudden illness for a relative or friend ; to hold a bunch of these flowers shows a determined excitable nature attracting many of the opposite sex, but probably not marrying until late in life ; white peonies growing in masses speak of tranquility, the pleasures of youth, an appreciation of beauty ; if they lie broken on the ground it would indicate the shattering of hope or of an ideal ; to carry a bunch of them means virtue and steadfast love.

Pepper.—To smell it means vexation ; to eat it, avarice ; to buy it, an irksome task.

Perfume.—To dream of using a variety of perfumes shows vulgarity and possibly immodesty ; to buy it denotes display and folly ; to break a bottle of it means that you enter recklessly into any amusement which provides you with excitement.

Perjury.—If you dream of committing perjury it warns you to be less untruthful or this bad habit may one day bring upon you serious consequences and public disgrace.

Phantom.—To see a phantom in your dream who beckons to you foreshows personal sorrow or illness ; if it covers its face you are warned against continuing your present mode of life, or you may bring disgrace upon yourself.

Pheasants.—To see them near you means good fortune, flying, speedy and propitious news ; to carry one shows honour ; to kill one, danger ; to eat one, hospitality and good friends.

Phlox.—If you dream of the scent of these flowers you may hope for happiness in love and marriage ; if you see them growing in a variety of colours you will enjoy that for which you have hoped and waited in patience ; to gather them means love and peace.

Piano.—To dream of hearing pleasant and cheerful tunes played on the piano is a sign of domestic happiness and concord ; to buy one shows an ambition not easily gratified ; to play one means that you make the most of your opportunities ; to dream that you receive a present of a handsome piano indicates that you will gain that for which you have aimed.

Pickaxe.—If you see pickaxes laid upon the ground, difficulties with labour and strikes are foreshown.

Pickles.—For a man to dream of eating pickles denotes that he will be somewhat exacting in his demands upon those around him and lacking in consideration for their comfort and pleasure ; for a woman this dream signifies that she is apt to put the worst construction upon the motives of others and to imagine offence where none is intended ; for a young man to dream of eating pickled cucumber predicts that he will be loved by a woman older than himself and probably of a sour disposition.

Picnic.—For a young woman to dream of going to a picnic with strangers denotes that she will meet with a youth who is not considered very sharp in his wits and who will vex her by his persistent attention.

Pictures.—To dream that you see beautiful pictures denotes a keen appreciation of Art in all forms and a desire to attain to a high standard of perfection.

Piebald.—To see a piebald pony near signifies amazement at some startling piece of news ; to ride upon it means that you will make many attempts in fresh interests but will always tire of each one before you have made a success of it ; to chase one denotes love of excitement and variety ; to catch it fore-tells that a curious coincidence leads to a renewal of a youthful love affair.

Pigeons.—If they alight upon you it promises reconcilia-tion with someone dear to you from whom you have been estranged ; if they fly towards you good and happy news is on its way ; if with wings far outspread, news from a great dis-tance ; to see them dead shows grief ; to feed them means contentment and generosity.

Pigs.—To see them assures you of gain and success in agricultural interests ; to chase them means that you will earn a reputation for cowardice if you do not amend your behaviour towards those who cannot defend themselves ; to feed them shows that there may be sluggards who will wish to live at your expense ; if a pig pursues you in a savage manner prepare for bad news from someone in the country.

Pillar.—To see a tall unbroken pillar is a symbol of strength and protection from danger ; to rest upon it shows that you possess good and powerful friends and the love of an honour-able man ; to see one broken predicts loss, sorrow, and despair.

Pillow.—If you dream that your pillow is covered with blood it is a bad omen of a severe accident to the head ; if you see it much torn it foreshows the possibility of mental derange-ment either for yourself or for one near and dear to you ; to see it white and clean denotes that happiness and peace will be yours ; to dream that you throw it at an invisible object indicates an imaginary grievance.

Pinafore.—For the mature to dream of wearing a pinafore foretells loss of memory.

Pincushion.—To make one shows thrift and order ; to unpick one and prick your fingers, an unpleasant discovery ; to see one without pins, a visitor ; to see one with many pins indicates a need for method and energy to remedy your lack of neatness.

Pineapple.—To see an abundance of pineapples is a sign of wealth ; to eat them denotes the affection of a rich man who will bestow many gifts upon you ; to carry one means that a faint hope is developing into a delightful fact.

Pinetrees.—To be in the midst of these trees and to hear them sighing in the wind is an omen of sadness foretelling a secret sorrow and an aching heart ; to carry a branch of pine shows danger.

Pink.—To dream of this colour foretells hope and joy ; to dream that you are surrounded by diaphanous pink material promises you the fulfilment of your dearest wish and blissful happiness.

Pinks.—If you pick these sweet-scented flowers you may expect a delightful meeting with someone dear to you in the summer ; to dream of their scent means contentment and happiness.

Pins.—If you dream of picking them up you may expect to have bickering and disputes over petty affairs during the day ; if you prick yourself it means that you will be the aggressor.

Pipe.—To smoke one means satisfaction and the completion of a troublesome matter ; to see several pipes foreshows news from a man who is much in your thoughts ; to break one denotes displeasure and quarrels.

Pistol.—To see this near is an ominous warning of personal danger and, with other bad signs, of a violent death ; to fire a pistol predicts tragedy ; to see one at a distance indicates sad news of those dear to you from whom you are separated ; for a girl to dream that her lover carries a pistol discloses the fact that he may at some time use violence to her and that she would do well to be careful not to arouse his temper.

Pitcher.—To break one means that you will bring misfortune upon yourself through your own carelessness ; to carry one shows an endeavour to relieve a dull and monotonous life by throwing your energy into somewhat unnecessary work.

Pitch Fork.—To handle one shows that you stir up feud and make peace and quiet impossible ; to see one means danger of accident.

Plains.—To dream of being on a beautiful plain, happiness.

Play.—To dream of playing at childish games signifies a pleasant condition of life when all is well and contentment and peace are around you ; to play at ball predicts the receipt of money ; if the ball rolls away you must expect delay in receiving it ; to see others play at ball without taking part yourself denotes that faintheartedness has been your stumbling-block.

Plough.—If it comes towards you you may hope for success in what you undertake ; if it is going from you embarrassment in business is shown ; if you are ploughing expect to go through much toil and frustration before you conquer your difficulties.

Plum Pudding.—To make a plum pudding is a symbol of friendship and generosity ; to eat it in company with strangers foreshows new events and interests ; to eat it alone means solitude ; to see it uncut denotes festivity and cheerfulness at Christmas-time.

Plums.—To see an abundance of ripe plums on their trees foreshows a new development of plans leading to happiness ; to see them green means unchanging friendship ; to eat them shows gratification and an happy experience in the summer.

Poison.—If you dream of drinking poison it warns you to be most careful to avoid any carelessness which might lead to this accident ; if you see a bottle of poison beside you it is an ominous sign of danger showing that unless you use self-control you may some day be tempted to take it.

Policeman.—If you see one near it prepares you for coming trouble probably caused by those with whom you are most closely associated ; if he walks away the matter will be satisfactorily cleared up and your anxiety will soon be allayed ; if he holds up his hand it shows danger of accident ; if he carries a burning torch it gives warning of fire ; if he rides on a horse it denotes power and display ; if you see him at a distance it tells you to beware of theft and underhand practices.

Pomegranate.—To see these growing brings assurance of love, peace, and abundance ; to eat them means power.

Pond.—To dream of a pond of clear water foretells friendship and wealth ; if the water be muddy, poverty and distress ; filled with large fish, important and pleasant news from afar ; filled with dead fish, theft and dismay.

Pope.—Unexpected gain and happiness in the future are shown by this dream.

Poppy.—Scarlet poppies seen growing are significant of a pleasant occurrence in the early summer ; if they are broken and their petals scattered you may be sure that you will experience or will hear of, some tribulation when poppies are in flower ; to pick them shows relief from pain or trouble ; pink poppies are a symbol of gaiety, hope and love ; yellow poppies, asceticism and steadfast love ; white poppies, innocence and joy.

Porcupine.—If you meet one you must prepare to encounter a powerful obstacle in your career ; if it follows you it means that you will need much ingenuity in order to avoid a trap laid for you by an enemy ; if you carry one it shows that you will come triumphantly through all difficulties and will rise to fame.

Port.—To dream of a sea-port in which there are numbers of people foreshows a voyage to a new country where you will discover some relatives of whose existence you had not heard ; if a bird hovers over the port you may expect glad tidings from afar.

Porter or Porteress.—If you dream that a porter or porteress hands you a piece of paper or a handkerchief it signifies scandal coming to light in a most unlooked-for manner.

Portrait.—Long life to one who dreams of his own portrait, but treachery to one who dreams of receiving it.

Post.—If near you it signifies a formidable obstacle ; a broken post means that you will encounter a storm of opposition to your plan.

Postman.—If you dream of meeting him a clandestine correspondence is shown ; if he delivers letters at your house it denotes important and profitable news ; if you see him delivering letters at other houses and missing your own you must expect to have to wait for the desired tidings.

Potatoes.—If you plant them it shows that you will have need of patience in your daily life ; if you dig them you will see a good result of a doubtful matter ; if you carry them it means burdens and difficulty ; to eat old potatoes signifies poverty ; to eat new ones, amiability ; to cook them, monotony.

Praise.—To dream of giving praise to a stranger indicates that you will seek to gain your own ends by falsehood ; to receive praise from a stranger means impudent flattery.

Precipice.—To see one denotes snares and danger ; to fall into one, a crushing blow, loss and undoing ; to rise from a precipice brings you mastery and a reward.

Presents.—To receive them from a distinguished person denotes a fortunate change in you life ; from a man, a trustworthy friend and good advice ; from a woman, love ; from a boy, misgivings and doubt ; to give a present means that you desire to give pleasure to others but are sometimes at a loss as to the best method of doing so.

Preserved Fruits.—To see these shows that your anticipation of a pleasure will prove to be the most enjoyable part of it ; to eat them means feasting and family gatherings.

Preserves.—To make or eat them foretells the acquisition of money.

Priest.—If he is beside you in his robes, illness is foreshown ; if he speaks it means that you will be influenced by a priest to change your mode of life and possibly your religion.

Primroses.—To see these growing signifies that after a time of sadness you will experience joy ; to pick them shows simplicity, gentleness, and the fulfilment of a desire in the spring ; to carry a bunch of them foretells a meeting with someone you love.

Primulas.—To see them growing in masses is a sign of artistic tastes and a love of nature with but little thought for material comforts ; to pick them shows congenial friends and placidity.

Prison.—If you enter one it denotes sorrow and trials ; to remain in it, desolation ; to leave it, disgrace.

Privet.—To dream that you are beside a privet bush is a sign of mourning ; to gather it discloses the fact that unless you endeavour to conquer your morbid ideas and gloomy manner you will become a sore trial to those around you.

Procession.—To join in a procession denotes constancy in love ; to see one means triumph and exhaltation.

Promenade.—To be promenading signifies joy followed by sorrow.

Provisions.—If you dream of buying a quantity of provisions you may be sure that you will go to a strange place where you will experience difficulty in your shopping.

Prude.—To dream that you are considered prudish suggests that you are too much inclined to dictate to others as to what you consider to be suitable behaviour.

Prunes.—To see these predicts obstacles in the way of your wishes ; to eat them shows a lack of imagination and vivacity.

Psalms.—To sing psalms denotes courage in a time of danger.

Purple.—This is a colour of various meanings depending to some extent on other signs accompanying it ; seen draping a chair or bed or associated with a church it would be an ominous sign of approaching death, probably for a man ; to hold a roll of purple velvet in you hand signifies clear judgement, a love of justice and profound respect for detail ; purple cloth denotes intellect and distinction and honour for a clergy man.

Purple Clematis.—If it is seen growing in profusion upon a house you may expect to hear eventful news of a member of that household ; if you see it withered and falling it means sorrow or pain ; if you gather it you will soothe the anxieties of those who may be in trouble ; to wear a spray of it foreshows association with dignitaries and the probable development of a romantic love affair late in life.

Purse.—To dream of losing it is most unlucky, although if you regard the dream as a warning and take precautions you may avert this misfortune ; to hide it signifies theft and that someone may try to cheat you out of a sum of money; to find a purse means that you are too much inclined to depend on the generosity of others and that one day they may weary of your helplessness ; to dream that your purse is stolen foretells money worries.

Pyramids.—To see them denotes attainment to honour and wealth ; to stand upon one proclaims victory and fame.

Q.

Quadrangle.—To dream that you walk in a quadrangle denotes that you object to even a small alteration in your daily life and that you become unreasonably vexed if one hour only has to be spent in an unaccustomed manner ;to dream that you see a quadrangle means perplexity.

Quail.—If this bird flies towards you expect bad tidings during the day ; to pursue one shows melancholy.

Quarantine.—To dream of being in quarantine denotes an epidemic of which you will probably be one of the victims ; if you dream of it in connection with your friends it displays the fact that some of them are disloyal and will ignore you when it happens to be convenient to them.

Quarrel.—To dream of a quarrel with a relative or friend usually means that some unpleasantness is near ; to quarrel with a stranger denotes an awkward mistake which places you in a trying position ; to dream of a quarrel and see a cat shows that the cause of it will be money affairs ; if you see a key it will be the question of your liberty which causes the contention ; to dream that you quarrel with a man usually foreshows a much more serious matter than when it is with a woman.

Quarry.—To dream of a quarry in which you see the stone being hewn foretells a time of tribulation and hard circumstances ; to be working in a quarry denotes dreariness and that the obstacles in your life will have jagged edges ; to fall into one predicts that a sudden death will probably take place before many months are over among your relatives or friends.

Quartette.—For those without musical talent to dream that they take part in a quartette indicates that they will not be easily daunted by rebuffs ; to hear beautiful music from a quartette signifies unselfishness and the faculty of seeing brightness beneath each cloud.

Quay.—To dream that you stand upon a quay by which you see ships unloading their goods foretells that you may expect a valuable present from abroad ; to dream of fishing from a quay is a sign of hopefulness even when there appears to be little to hope for.

Queen.—To dream that you speak with a queen foretells riches and honour ; to follow her means that you gain a high position through influential friends ; to see a queen upon her throne indicates security and peace ; to see her on foot denotes anarchy and shameful disloyalty.

Queue.—If you dream that you stand at the head of a long queue you may feel certain that you will not lose good opportunities through lack of self-confidence ; to stand at the end of it cautions you not to be so timid and hesitating, for whilst you pause and consider, another has seized upon a fortunate chance which might have been yours.

Quicksands.—To dream of walking on quicksands is a warning that your health needs care or you may have a serious breakdown ; to dream that you are sinking in the quicksand indicates mental distress caused by the strange behaviour of someone near and dear to you.

Quill Pen.—To write with one shows that you may expect before long to sign your maiden name for the last time in a marriage register ; to carry one shows impatience and intolerance ; to break one means an upsetting interview.

Quince.—To see these trees in blossom is a pleasing sign of unusual occurrences taking place of deep interest to you ; to gather quinces indicates creature comforts, pleasures, and appreciation of the good things of life, but it also gives warning that it would be wise not to become too dependent upon them, for circumstances may arise which will deprive you of much that makes life so agreeable ; to eat quince jam indicates joy mingled with memories which cause you sadness.

Quoits.—To dream of watching a game of quoits foretells a visit to the country on pleasure ; to play quoits denotes that in a most unexpected manner you meet an old friend whom you have not seen for many years and a happy friendship is renewed.

R.

Rabbit.—To see dead rabbits means domestic duties, shopping, and feelings of boredom ; to see many of them alive denotes expensive pleasures ; to eat them shows good health, but warns you that you must depend upon your own efforts for your amusements and must be content with simple ones ; to see a black rabbit signifies an accident ; a white one, friendship.

Race.—To the lover a dream of winning a race foreshows completed happiness ; to lose a race is a bad omen in all love affairs ; for the man of business to dream of winning a race promises good success and fortune through his own efforts ; to lose it means many disappointments and a doubt of his ever reaching the top of the tree ; to a married woman this dream indicates daily struggle and need for endurance ; if she dreams of winning a race, she may hope for peace and comfort after a time of anxiety.

Racehorse.—If you see it galloping you may expect good luck and the winning of a large sum of money ; if it walks and appears weary, beware of any speculation for a time.

Raffle.—To dream of raffling warns you not to allow the habit of gambling to grow upon you, or it may be your ruin.

Raft.—To see this floating foretells a journey, the longer the raft the more extensive the line of journey ; to sail on a raft shows travel in distant countries and adventures through which you come successfully.

Rag Doll.—To see this near indicates simplicity that sometimes verges on folly ; to hold it denotes that you will mourn for someone dear to you, but unworthy of your trust.

Rage.—If you dream of being in a great rage for no apparent cause warns you of the fact that you are becoming so bad-tempered that you will soon make your own life and the lives of others unbearable ; to dream that your rage is aroused by a child proclaims a scoundrel ; if by one of the opposite sex it means that you have cause and provocation for your rage.

Rags.—To see a heap of these denotes misery and disgrace ;

to see a few rags cautions you against frivolity and the need for taking life more seriously.

Railroad.—To dream of travelling by railroad foretells to those who keep house that they will break up their establishment ; to young persons it indicates the loss of their home ; to lovers it is a sign that if they marry they will lead a roving life without possessing a settled home.

Rain.—If the rain is light and unaccompanied by wind this is a good dream for workers, indicating advancement and profit; if the rain is heavy and causes you discomfort it is a sign of coming misfortune ; if you see rain falling whilst the sun shines, it shows that whatever trouble you may have will soon disappear, and happier days will dawn for you.

Rainbow.—It is an excellent dream to see a rainbow, the brighter the colours the more abundant will your happiness be ; it is a symbol of health and general prosperity ; to lovers it foretells a happy and wealthy marriage ; if the rainbow appears broken it denotes separation ; if at a distance you may expect to hear good news from a distant friend ; seen in the west it is a good omen for the poor and sick ; in the east, a pleasant sign to the rich ; if it is overheard you may prepare for misery and the death of someone you love.

Rake.—To dream that you are using this implement indicates a persevering nature which should bring you pleasing success in the future ; to rake newly-mown hay forehows the awakening of love ; to rake gravel shows a nervous and irritable condition ; to rake straw shows a meagre existence.

Ram.—To see it near denotes an unpleasant person whom you would do well to avoid ; if it butts you it signifies pain, agitation, and troublesome circumstances.

Rat.—To see one near shows impending troubles, domestic annoyance, bad health, and general discomfort ; if it attacks you it means that there are designing and treacherous persons around you ; if you see several rats you are warned of the fact that you will be troubled by these creatures unless you take precautions to prevent it.

Raven.—If this bird is near it is an omen of misfortune.

gloom and despondency ; to see it fly shows tidings of a death ; to hear it croak signifies mourning and sadness ; to see several of them denotes poverty, a bad harvest, and calamity.

Rays.—To dream that you have rays of light around your head is a favourable sign of coming joy ; if you see rays around the head of an enemy he will defeat you ; for a man to see rays around the head of a woman shows that his love will be reciprocated and that he may hope for happiness in marriage.

Razor.—This is a symbol of disagreement and should warn those who dream of it not to interfere in any quarrel among their friends or relatives, for if they attempt to smooth matters over they will only increase the mischief and cause offence to both parties.

Reading.—To dream of reading romances shows dangerous inclinations or brief pleasures ; to read serious books indicates rapid advancement.

Reaping.—To dream that you are reaping is not a good omen for your present condition as it signifies anxiety, tedious occupations, and sorrow, but if you reap with ease you may hope for improvement and prosperity in the future.

Red Hot Poker.—If you carry this flower be sure that you will bring yourself within the range of unpleasant criticism by your flaunting manner.

Repairing.—If you dream of repairing a house it foretells illness ; but if you dream of finding some needed repairs already done it is a sign that you will have a piece of good luck in connection with your work or business ; to dream of some house being pulled to pieces for repairs is an omen of severe illness or death for the master of it.

Reprieve.—To dream that you are reprieved from a disagreeable duty or from anything to which you had been looking forward with dismay tells you that you will probably be fortunate enough to avoid it ; to dream of a reprieve from the consequences of what you have done denotes that you will escape punishment through the influence of a good friend.

Reptile.—To dream of any animals which are known as reptiles such as toads, snakes, alligators, and their like, is a bad omen of coming misfortune, treachery, or illness.

Rescue.—If you dream of rescuing anyone from peril it is a sign that your presence of mind and bravery will one day be put to a severe test ; to dream that you rescue yourself from a small danger denotes that you will rise in the world either by means of increased wealth or new honours ; to dream that you are rescued from drowning or other danger foretells a serious accident in which you have a narrow escape from death.

Resign.—For those who hold any official position to dream of resigning warns them that it would be well to make the most of their present opportunities and to save their money, for the day may not be far distant when they will be forced to resign on account of ill-health or other necessity ; for those who are not in a position to resign any employment to dream of doing so shows that they will take up some unexpected work of which they will rapidly tire.

Resuscitate.—To dream of resuscitating a drowned person usually foretells that you will one day be called upon to do this and will receive an ovation of thanks and public recognition of your bravery ; to dream of resuscitating someone who at once recovers denotes that you will engage in some enterprise which attracts public attention.

Return.—If a person who is travelling or sojourning abroad dreams of an immediate return it signifies the arrival of bad news ; to dream of returning from a journey before you have started to go on it denotes that you will meet with a serious accident should you go.

Rhinoceros.—To see it near shows a risky proceeding into which you plunge without hesitation : your friends and relations will do much to persuade you to give up your scheme, but your indifference to the opinion of others prevents any chance of their persuasions being successful ; to chase it predicts a calamity which you bring upon yourself by your obstinacy ; to confront it indicates callousness.

Rhododendrons.—If you dream of a variety of these shrubs in flower eventful changes bringing much happiness will occur in the spring or early summer ; to plant them denotes a happy surprise.

Ribbon.—To dream of purchasing gaily-coloured ribbons

foretells that although you expect gaiety and enjoyment you will be disappointed, for things will occur to frustrate your pleasure ; for the lover to dream of a quantity of yellow ribbon shows that there will probably be strife caused by jealousy.

Ribs.—For the married to dream of broken ribs usually means a quarrel between husband and wife.

Rice.—This is a sign of plenty ; to dream of eating it means increased happiness and that you will one day become very wealthy.

Riches.—To dream of great riches probably denotes that you will one day unexpectedly come into a fortune, but it also warns you against the reckless spending of it ; to dream of snatching riches from another shows that you will increase your income by fraud.

Rider.—To one who never rides on horseback to dream of doing so with a sensation of pleasure indicates unforeseen events bringing good luck ; to fall from the horse or to ride with a feeling of fear denotes loss or trouble.

Ring.—For a married woman to dream of a gold ring foretells that she will soon receive an invitation to a wedding ; it is not considered a good omen for a girl who is engaged to be married to dream that she is wearing a wedding ring, as it announces the fact that she will not have all the happiness she desires in her love affair, and that probably if she marries early in life the match will be an unfortunate one ; to dream that a pearl ring is given to you indicates that you will receive a hasty summons to take an immediate journey on account of the sudden illness of a friend or relation ; to dream of losing a ring which does not belong to you signifies that you will have many troubles, but will be able to surmount them by the help of someone who is dear to you.

Riot.—To dream of a tumult or riot foretells scarcity and bad crops to farmers and a poor business outlook to tradesmen or mechanics ; if you take part in the riot and are injured, it foretells serious personal loss ; if you appear successful and pacify the crowd, it indicates triumph.

Rival.—For a lover to dream that he has a rival is a sign that jealousy is likely to be a cause of friction between him and his betrothed and that he had better curb these jealous feelings, or he may regret it.

River.—To see a deep and dark looking river is not a cheerful sign as it foreshows trouble and illness for yourself or for those who are dear to you ; if the river appears very wide you may expect some time to elapse before your anxieties will be over ; a small river flowing quickly denotes confusion in your affairs ; to cross a large and wide river without effort foretells a splendid fortune ; if you experience difficulty or if the water is rough you may expect obstacles, but these will be overcome if you finally reach the bank in safety ; for a girl to dream of this predicts that she will travel and meet with a man in good circumstances who will become her husband.

Road.—Fortunate circumstances are predicted by dreaming of a good and straight road ; if you walk upon an uneven and muddy road you must expect to meet with many hindrances ; if it be full of ruts some of those with whom you deal will cheat you ; to dream that you see several roads or stand at cross roads denotes that before long you will have to make a momentous decision which will affect your whole future ; if you see signs of movement on the roads it portends that you will not remain long in one neighbourhood.

Robbers.—To dream of being attacked by robbers foretells loss of money or a calamity which deprives you of valuable property ; to a lover this dream is a warning that there is a rival who will strive to gain the affections of his beloved.

Robin.—This is a symbol of affection and good friends who will help you through any trouble or difficulties in which you may find yourself ; to see robins around your house is an omen of good fortune and abundance ; if you hear them singing but do not see them you may expect illness and perhaps death.

Rockets.—To see these flying in the air foretells joy and gladness at some event about to happen ; to the married it announces the birth of a child, or to those who have daughters it may signify the marriage of one of them ; to the unmarried it denotes that they may soon expect to become engaged, which event will be followed shortly by a happy marriage.

Rocking Chair.—To sit in one shows contemplation of a new idea or scheme about which you are a little doubtful ; to see one means that you will obtain a good post or gain some other advantage.

Rocks.—If you are upon them prepare for alarms and agitation ; if you come down from them and do not stumble you will find a smooth path through your life.

Rolling Pin.—To dream of using this indicates that you will be capable of smoothing out your difficulties and will usually find an easy path in which to tread as the result of your own ingenuity ; if you see one but do not use it you will know that you will need the help of others to untie your knots.

Rooster.—If a girl hears the crowing of a cock it denotes that she will speedily meet with some man to whom she will become engaged ; if a lover has this dream it is a sign that he has a formidable rival ; to the married it shows quarrels or jealousy.

Ropes.—To dream that you are tied with rope is a sign that you will undergo some unpleasant experience from which you will have much difficulty in extricating yourself ; if the rope is round your feet only it shows that you have brought misfortune upon yourself through your own folly ; to see it upon your hands only means that you consider that another is responsible for the mess in which you find yourself and that you will be very angry with that person; to see large coils of rope is a bad sign of a serious accident happening to you.

Rosemary.—To see this growing signifies a good reputation; to smell it foreshows mourning ; to pick it indicates an endeavour to find a remedy to soothe your sorrow.

Roses.—To dream of their scent brings an assurance of happiness in love ; to see them growing is a sign of contentment and fulfilled desire ; to pick them foretells a joyous event which will take place in the summer ; to hold a large bunch of white roses means marriage ; yellow roses denote enjoyment ; red roses, delight ; if you see red rose petals scattered in quantities upon the ground it indicates illness, probably an operation or, to those engaged to be married, that some unfortunate event will postpone the wedding ; if you see roses in the form of a cross it would foreshow a death probably occurring in the summer.

Rouge.—See " **Paint.**"

Rowing.—To dream that you are rowing upon a clear and sparkling river gives hope that your dearest wish will be fulfilled ; if in company with one of the opposite sex it means that your happiness will be dependent upon that person ; if the river is dark or rough you must expect trial and tribulation before the attainment of your wish ; to be rowing on the sea denotes an experience in which you must take a certain amount of risk ; if the sea is very rough and you row with exertion you are likely to go through a time of suspense which will leave you enfeebled in health.

Ruby.—This is a fortunate stone of which to dream for those born in August or November as it is one of the birth stones for those months ; to all dreamers it would be a sign of costly presents and riches.

Rue.—If you pick it you may anticipate a day of family annoyance ; to smell it shows remorse ; to carry it means that you will bear the burdens of others.

Ruins.—To see them denotes repentance and an abhorrence of the past ; to wander among them shows that although you are aware of the danger into which you are running you will persist in following the path which leads down hill.

Run.—It is a good sign to dream of running with a feeling of pleasure for it speaks of good health and ability to carry out such things as you most desire to do ; if you run from a relentless pursuer it warns you that you will need to have all your wits about you in a coming emergency ; if you stumble as you run it shows that you must expect to fail in your endeavour to escape from an unpleasant episode ; to see many people running is a sign of quarrels ; to run after an enemy means victory ; to run naked is a sign of infidelity ; to dream that you are running aimlessly or in pursuit of an object which you cannot see proclaims the fact that you depend too much upon your own judgement and that you would do better to listen to the advice of others.

Rust.—If you see rust upon yourself you may certainly take it to mean that you had better exert yourself a little more and sharpen your wits, or you will become such a bore that your friends will desert you ; if you see rust upon any bright object it indicates that a great disappointment is in store for you ; to see it upon a door shows a friendless condition ; upon a hat, a weak mentality.

S.

Sacks.—To see a quantity of sacks indicates an unlooked-for event which will cause you some uneasiness.

Sailing.—To sail on a smooth blue sea promises pleasure and tranquility ; on a rough sea, that you will venture upon a doubtful experiment and encounter many difficulties, but will surmount them ; to sail on a dark angry-looking sea denotes a turmol from which you cannot escape.

Sailor.—To see him near shows that you may expect news from abroad of an interesting nature ; to shake hands with one foreshows that you will shortly be introduced to a sailor who will probably become dear to you.

Salad.—To see a salad which is decorated with various good things and a rich sauce foretells a picnic ; to see it without sauce or decoration means that you pay far too much attention to your diet ; to eat it denotes sleeplessness, sometimes illness ; to help yourself to it shows embarrassments.

Salmon.—If you see it on a dish you may expect a very pleasant outing with someone dear to you at the time of year when salmon is in season ; if you eat it you will receive a good present or have a cheering piece of news.

Salt.—If the salt appears moist and sticky it signifies a miserable experience causing you to shed tears in secret ; to see salt in a block denotes solid worth and usefulness but of a somewhat uninteresting character ; to eat it shows wisdom and discernment.

Sand.—To dream of walking on a large expanse of sand indicates restlessness, a longing for the unattainable, and a searching for those things which you cannot find, causing an unsettled state of mind ; if a starfish or beautiful sea anemone were found on the sand, it would be a hopeful sign that after a time of waiting your desires would be fulfilled ; to dig in the sand shows an optimist who is always on the lookout for the next best when the best has failed ; to let sand sift through your fingers means instability.

Sapphire.—For those born in February, March, or June this beautiful stone is a particularly fortunate one to see in a dream, being one of the birth stones for those months ; if you dream of a sapphire ring you may expect a proposal ; a cluster of these gems means hope fulfilled and riches.

Sauce.—To make it shows a desire to achieve some striking success in a new idea or in the working out of a patent ; if the sauce becomes lumpy you will not succeed in your endeavour ; to eat bread sauce denotes an insipid character ; onion sauce, churlishness ; tomatoe sauce, amiability ; apple sauce, satisfaction.

Saucepans.—To see several of these is an omen of misfortune : many troubles will befall you and your courage will be tested in meeting them ; to clean a saucepan foreshows domestic tribulation.

Sausages.—To see them predicts affliction ; to cut them apart shows quarrels ; to make them, complaints ; to eat them, joyousness to the young, good health to the old.

Saw.—Interference which will bring upon you much trouble is signified by dreaming of a saw.

Sawing.—To dream of sawing wood is a sign that you are always ready in a good-natured way to help another out of a difficulty ; to saw stout logs of wood is an omen of a prosperous undertaking ; for a lover to dream of sawing wood which is very hard foretells that he will offend his sweetheart, and will find it difficult to persuade her to overlook the trouble.

Scaffold.—This means that you will enter into a rash speculation.

Scales.—If you are using them it warns you to be more accurate in what you say or you will find your word is doubted on some occasion when it is important to you to be accounted truthful ; if you see large scales it denotes justice and the law ; if a policeman or judge were also seen it would be a bad omen of possible arrest and appearance before a court.

Scarecrow.—This warns you to avoid interfering in the private affairs of those around you or you will be likely to find that you will receive the cold shoulder from them ; to erect a scarecrow means that you are too fond of drawing attention to small failings and faults in others.

Sceptre.—This is a fortunate symbol of distinction and honour.

School.—To dream of being in one foretells increasing knowledge ; to go into one, modesty ; to bring your children into school shows that you will set them a good example.

Scissors.—These signify quarrels between lovers, disputes and disagreeables with married couples, friction with friends, and trouble in business.

Scorpion.—To see it near signifies loss by secret enemies.

Screaming.—This is an unfortunate sign in a dream, denoting a serious accident for a relative or friend ; if the screams are incessant it is a sign that there is a doubt of that person recovering from the injuries received ; if you yourself are screaming it foretells a severe attack of pain or mental shock.

Screw.—To see a small screw is a pleasant omen of success but a large screw indicates that you will encounter much trouble through a love affair.

Sculptor.—This dream signifies profit ; to see a sculptor at work foreshows development of your work or plans.

Scythe.—To use it foreshows that you will bring innumerable troubles upon yourself by your unreasonable self-will ; to see it near indicates brief and pain.

Sea.—To see it very rough and with large waves breaking means a bad stormcausing serious damage and possibly loss of life ; if you see it dark and sullen, it foreshows trouble ahead which you cannot sceape to see it calm and blue means happiness coming for you, probably in connection with some-one associated with the sea ; to dream of swimming in it with the waves breaking over you and with a feeling that you make no progress against them foretells an illness for someone very dear to you ; if the waves are small and the water shallow the illness will be slight ; if the waves break fiercely and you are in deep water the illness will be more severe and the convalescence tedious ; to be walking in the sea which suddenly becomes so deep that it engulfs you signifies separation, and a struggle against existing circumstances.

Sea Kale.—To pick it denotes curiosity ; to eat it, fascination ; to see it growing, a satisfactory conclusion to a vexed question.

Seal.—This animal seen near is a symbol of patience which will be well rewarded eventually ; if it comes towards you it is a good sign of increasing wealth.

Sealing Wax.—To use it shows a well-kept secret ; if the wax breaks the secret will be divulged in a mysterious manner ; to see sticks of sealing wax indicates that you are wise theoretically but seldom bring your wisdom to bear on practical matters.

Seaweed.—To dream of seaweed denotes a joy of which only the memory remains.

Sermon.—To dream that you listen to a sermon shows weariness and sleeplessness ; if you are in a church and hear a sermon from a stranger, it means that you will have new and somewhat startling theories propounded to you which will puzzle and possibly embarrass you.

Serpent.—See " **Snake.**"

Sewing.—To dream that you are at work on a tedious piece of sewing of which there seems no ending means that you will have innumerable little vexations to encounter ; to dream that you are at work on a diminutive piece of white work foreshows a birth.

Shadow.—To dream of your own shadow is a sign that you will commit a folly or some fault of which you will be much ashamed.

Shark.—If near you it is an ominous sign of death ; seen at a distance it foretells grief and pain.

Shawl.—To dream that you wrap yourself in a shawl denotes that you will become fidgetty and of so cranky a nature that you will find yourself ignored.

Shaving.—To dream of shaving indicates that you are apt to make molehills into mountains.

Sheaves.—To see sheaves of corn indicates illness or sorrow; if you stand amidst the sheaves, loss of a dear one.

Sheep.—To see a flock of these promises prosperity to land-owners or those who have any interest in agriculture ; to others this dream shows that they have a tendency to follow in any direction which appears easiest and to give least resistance and that they will always fail in taking a decisive step forward ; to follow a flock of sheep means that there will be things in life intensely irritating to you which are caused by sheer stupidity ; to meet a flock foreshows that you will constantly find yourself driven into an uncomfortable corner from which there seems no apparent escape ; to see them sleeping or dead shows sorrow ; to see one sheep alone promises an easy but somewhat dull existence ; to hear them bleat means grief and parting.

Shell.—Loss of time and money is shown by the finding of an empty shell : good luck if you find one which is full.

Shepherd.—The appearance of one cautions you against taking unnecessary risks in all matters.

Ship.—To see a ship tossing upon a rough sea and pieces of wood floating around it foretells a shipwreck and loss of life : to see a ship crowded with human beings steaming out of harbour shows that you will encounter many strange and mysterious events in your life and will be baffled in your contact with them ; to dream of being in a large vessel which is stationary denotes that if you take a long journey by sea there will be hindrances in the way of your departure ; to see a ship in full sail under calm conditions indicates that com- munication with the spirit world is about to be facilitated ; also that news of great interest from distant lands will come and that trade and prosperity will be increased ; if a black flag flies on the ship, distress and possibly death are shown ; if the sail is slack and flaps in the breeze, a time of misfortune and much delayed or bad news must be expected.

Shipwreck.—To dream that you are on a sinking ship foreshows peril or overwhelming sorrow ; to see a shipwreck means that you will be dismayed by some sad news.

Shirt.—To dream of a shirt is considered an omen of good fortune to all who dream of it, but if the shirt is torn you will meet with disappointment.

Shoes.—To dream of possessing many new shoes is a sign of good fortune ; to lose your shoes, poverty.

Shoot.—To see a person shooting denotes some disagreeable event about to take place ; if you shoot at a target you may expect misfortune.

Shop.—To dream of many shops, among which you are unable to find one of the kind you are seeking, means that you will forget some important business of which you will be unpleasantly reminded before long.

Shoulder.—To see it large shows wealth and strength ; dislocated, bad news ; fleshy, a grasping and greedy nature.

Showbills.—To dream of placing one upon a wall predicts that some injury will befall you ; to read one means that you will fail to receive the reward of your labours.

Shrimps.—To eat them is a sign of pleasures or amusements that you desire to keep secret ; to catch them shows cheerfulness ; to see them swimming denotes a tendency to defective eyesight.

Sickle.—To see it near but without holding it signifies that you will experience sorrow and pain caused by the callous behaviour of some one you love ; if you grasp it you will take decisive measures in some matter which may seem at first sight to be hard but in the end will prove to have been for the best.

Sickness.—To dream of this foretells illness and loneliness, sometimes privation.

Signpost.—If near it denotes doubt and perplexity over some important decision on which possibly your whole future

F

happiness depends ; a broken signpost shows that you take a wrong turning in your life, and afterwards have much cause to regret it.

Silk.—This dream means abundance and gain.

Silver Ware.—To sell it means dismay and difficulty ; to buy it, good fortune and luck in what you undertake.

Singing.—For a man to dream of singing brings hope ; to a woman, distress.

Skeleton.—To dream of this means a feeling of disgust at some information which is told to you and which you are asked not to reveal.

Sky.—A clear blue sky denotes hope and love ; a red sky, increase of wealth ; if you ascend into the sky you may expect honour ; a cloudy sky is an omen of misfortune.

Slaughter House.—To dream of this shows that you are in danger but can avoid it by precaution ; to see animals slaughtered foretells horror at some news of which you will hear or will read.

Sleep.—To dream that you sleep with a babe shows illness for someone you love ; with one of the opposite sex, hindrance in your projects ; with a person of the same sex, perplexing and disagreable events ; for a woman to dream of sleeping with her absent husband foreshows bad news ; with her daughter, family discomfort and turmoil; with her sister, an unexpected departure ; with a melancholy-looking woman, illness.

Sleeplessness.—To dream that you cannot sleep is a sign of coming sorrow.

Smoke.—To see puffs of smoke denotes a brief joy ; a cloud of smoke, false hope ; smoke which is blown aside means fickleness and vanity.

Snail.—To see several snails near denotes that mischief is going on around you of which you are unaware ; if you see them moving it means bad weather ; if one is upon you it indicates dissipation.

Snake.—To dream of this shows treachery, disloyalty, and hidden dangers caused by those whom you least suspect ; if the snake is near or advancing towards you it is an ominous sign of bad illness, possibly caused by poisoning ; if it raises its head injury by the malice of a man is predicted ; if it twines around you it is a sign that your life is in danger ; to kill one brings triumph over what appears to be a terrible disaster.

Sneeze.—To dream of sneezing once means astonishment ; if you sneeze several times you may expect to feel irritable and disappointed during the day.

Snow.—To dream of it at a time of year in which it could not be expected predicts a spell of unusually cold weather ; seen with bare trees it would foreshow an event which will closely concern you taking place in the winter : the nature of the event can generally be discerned by other signs in the dream, for instance, a brilliantly-lighted house would foretell an enjoyable visit in the winter ; if you see snow falling fast and thickly disaster and tragedy caused by severe weather are indicated ; snow falling heavily upon you is a sign of grief which numbs you into despair ; snow seen with red patches upon it means that you will hear of crime and horrible doings ; to walk in it denotes obstacles.

Snowdrops.—These are a symbol of youth and innocency ; to see them growing signifies an event affecting you or yours which will take place about February ; if you see them in a wreath or cross it probably foretells the death of an infant or young child ; if you pick them it signifies sorrow for the past but hope in the future.

Soap.—To see much soap signifies temporary trouble in business ; to use it means a pleasant relief to your mind.

Society.—To dream of being in the company of many distinguished persons foretells honour and happiness.

Soldier.—To dream of a soldier means that you may count upon the loyalty and affection of your friends for they will always be faithful to you ; for a girl engaged to be married, to dream of talking with a soldier shows that she will probably go abroad shortly after her marriage.

Solomon's Seal.—To dream of this plant shows understanding, devotion, and joyousness ; to pick it means deliberation in all you do, and vexation with those who may try to hurry you in your decision.

Somnambulist.—Illness and sorrow are foreshown by dreaming that you walk in your sleep.

Sores.—To dream of your arm as having sores means unfortunate business ; sores in the mouth signify unwise words which you afterwards regret.

Sorrow.—To dream that you experience this is a forecast of what will shortly come upon you.

Spade.—To use it means toil and care ; to see it, disappointment and failure.

Sparrows.—If they fly you may look for disturbing news if they alight near you it is an omen of poverty.

Spanish Iris.—To dream of these flowers in a variety of colours speaks of peace and beauty ; to pick them means the fulfilment of your hope.

Spectre.—White, brings joy, pleasure, and good fortune ; black, pain and trouble.

Sphinx.—To dream of the Sphinx indicates that your hopes will be set on things far beyond your reach and that as nothing but the very best in life has any attraction for you, you will probably never attain complete happiness ; if you dream of one of the opposite sex in connection with the Sphinx you may be sure that much of your happiness or lack of it will be dependent upon that person who at present is a complete stranger to you and will come into your life in an unlooked-for manner.

Spice.—To dream of this means that your statements are not always to be relied upon, and that the good stories which you are fond of repeating are considerably decorated or exaggerated.

Spider.—If it looks at you, expect to be triumphant in a disputed will or money settlement ; to dream of many spiders in the morning denotes a probable law suit ; if they run over you it foretells good fortune, sometimes an inheritance of much wealth ; to see one at work means patience, industry, and mental attainment ; to kill one brings loss.

Sponge.—If you see several sponges it means avarice and bad faith ; if you hold one you may expect to hear or see something which will cause you to shudder.

Spring.—A spring of gushing water is a pleasant omen of wealth and honour ; a dried-up spring shows poverty or illness.

Spy.—To dream of a spy means servitude and bondage ; to dream that you are spying denotes dangerous curiosity.

Squirrel.—This is a symbol of contentment and cheerfulness : although you may never be wealthy you will be loved by those around you, and on the whole you will lead a smooth life ; to a girl this dream signifies that someone of a timid nature has fallen in love with her, but hesitates to approach her through shyness.

Stable.—To dream of a stable is a sign that you will enjoy hospitality and pleasant entertainments.

Stage Coach.—To ride in one denotes loss through delays ; to run after one means that you will be out of employment for a long while ; to see one pass will rid you of troublesome friends ; if you are in a stage coach which turns over without injuring you, it signifies good luck in speculation ; if you are hurt, you must expect misfortune.

Star.—To see them shining brightly brings happiness and success ; to see them pale or dim means affliction ; seen in numbers over a house foretells danger of death in the family ; a falling star signifies a quarrel with someone dear to you ; if shooting over a house, danger of fire.

Steel.—To break it in your dream is a sign of triumph over obstacles or enemies ; if you touch it only, your position in life is secure ; if you try to bend it and cannot, there is risk of your meeting with serious accidents.

Steeple.—To dream of a church steeple is not a good omen, showing troubled conditions in your life and the realization that those things at which you are aiming can seldon be reached ; if the steeple is crooked or bending, it foreshows coming disaster or crushing blow to your hope.

Steps.—To dream that you carry wooden steps which do not belong to you foretells the fact that unaccustomed duties will fall to your lot through the illness of someone with whom you are associated ; if you mount the steps you will shortly afterwards improve your position.

Stick.—To hold a long stick foretells investigation ; a walking stick denotes absentmindedness or a bad memory ; to lean upon it, illness or injury ; to lose it, fluctuation in money matters ; to beat with it shows a grudge which you are slow to forgive ; to receive a beating with one predicts serious trouble and possibly a law suit.

Stilts.—To walk upon them shows a desire to appear different in the eyes of your friends from that which you really are, and you will often feel it an effort to keep up this subterfuge ; if you slip off, your pride and vain glory will have a fall.

Stirrup.—To dream of this signifies a short journey or expedition by road.

Stock.—To dream of the scent of these flowers means gratified wishes and pleasures ; to see them growing, visits and enjoyment with friends in the summer ; to pick them, an unexpected happiness with someone whom you have not seen for a long while.

Stockings.—Moderate happiness tinged with regrets is shown by dreaming of cotton stockings ; silk ones predict gain ; to take them off means that you seize upon your first opportunity for paying off an old score ; stockings with many holes in them signify loss through neglect.

Stones.—To break them denotes poverty and monotony ; to pick them up, anger and quarrels ; to gather them into a heap, precaution ; to see many stones shows hardship and vexation.

Stool.—A large stool is a symbol of honour ; a small one indicates that your success in life will be meagre.

Storks.—To dream of these in summer tells you to beware of robbery or fraud ; in the winter, bad weather and a great misfortune are shown by this dream ; a stork near means that whilst you hesitate in a decision a profitable chance is lost.

Storm.—To dream of a great storm signifies peril or

outrageous doings ; to a sailor or those associated with the sea it is a bad omen of coming disaster.

Stove.—If it is alight it is a sign of wealth, but if it is cold, poverty is predicted.

Strangle.—To dream that you strangle someone gives warning that unless you curb your bitterness and malice, you may become a danger to yourself and to others.

Straw.—A bundle of straw is a sign of gain through industry ; scattered about it indicates poverty.

Strawberries.—To see them growing denotes pleasure and gratification of your wishes ; to see them or their leaves upon a person predicts an attack of scarlet fever for that person ; dishes of strawberries near mean eventful changes bringing much that is delightful to you ; for a girl to dream of eating them tells her that she will receive a proposal of marriage from a wealthy man ; to plant them shows unexpected good fortune.

Straw Hat.—To wear one means modesty and simple pleasures ; to carry one, self-assurance.

Street.—To dream of a narrow cobbled street of empty houses with a necklace of pearls seen lying in the roadside foretells war and devastation in all directions, tragedy and suffering for those in high positions ; to be walking in a street in which there is no sign of life and the houses appear gloomy, indicates the approach of a bad epidemic.

Street Lamps.—To see them brilliantly lighted means enjoyment and excitement ; to see them extinguished, a dismal failure of a project ; to dream of lighting one shows a foolish desire to draw attention to yourself.

Struggle.—To dream that you struggle to free yourself from an unseen foe denotes that you will be tempted to injure someone towards whom you feel a strong animosity ; to struggle in pain predicts serious illness ; to struggle with a man, danger ; with a woman, daily difficulties ; with a child, an emergency in which you prove a failure.

Study.—To dream of study means that you will find

tranquility and lasting happiness chiefly through your own resources.

Stutter.—To dream that you stutter denotes that when you most desire to appear at your best your wits forsake you and you are speechless through shyness.

Suicide.—To dream of committing suicide is a grave warning that you should seek medical advice without delay, for serious mental disorder is shown by this dream.

Sun.—To dream of the sun " shining in his strength " promises happiness, health, and success in love ; to see it rise, good news, prosperity, and the discovery of secrets ; the setting sun shows sadness or misfortune ; the sun being rayless or appearing in a haze denotes illness : for a man it means discredit, failure, or undoing ; seen with brilliant face, glory and fame ; a red sun means alarm or amazing news ; the conjunction of the sun and moon portends a great war ; to see it shining upon a house foreshows happiness and good fortune for those who live in it.

Sunbonnet.—To wear it means originality, personal charm and attraction ; to carry one shows coquetry ; to see it means ambition.

Sun Dial.—If you see this in a dream you are warned to take heed how you spend your time.

Sunflower.—To see these growing indicates learning and a satisfactory conclusion in matters which you desire to investigate ; if you dream of them in a garden known to you it foretells that you will hear good news of someone in whom you are much interested ; if you plant them you may expect a scheme to work out greatly to your advantage ; if you pick them your lover or husband will rise to fame ; if you see them broken or bending, it foretells failure and disappointment.

Surgeon.—To dream of a surgeon is ominous of an unexpected event of an unpleasant nature.

Suspenders.—To wear them means precaution ; to take them off, a disagreeable surprise.

Swallows.—If you appear to follow them it shows a voyage to a warm climate under happy conditions ; if they alight upon you it predicts that your riches will have increased when you return; to see one swallow near indicates complete success; happiness and good fortune are foretold by seeing its nest ; if it enters your house it brings joyful tidings for someone you love.

Swamp.—To fall into one means a catastrophe bringing you to poverty.

Swan.—A white swan is signif can of riches ; a black one of troublesome conditions in your home and possible separations ; the cry of a swan sometimes denotes death.

Swearing.—To dream that you hear bad language is a sign that unless you reform your habits you will rapidly go down hill.

Sweeping.—To sweep the room of a stranger denotes well merited confidence ; to sweep your own room means that you perform your daily duties with energy and good-will ; to sweep a cellar brings misfortune and the discovery of unpleasant facts.

Sweetbriar.—To dream of its scent means satisfied longing; to pick it, implicit trust in someone dear to you.

Sweetheart.—To dream of your sweetheart is a foretaste of the joy you will experience in a meeting which will shortly take place.

Sweet Peas.—Happiness in love and marriage are shown by dreaming of the scent of these flowers ; to see them growing brings peace and confidence ; to pick them, simplicity and affection.

Sweet William.—This flower signifies that your happiness in the past has tinged your future with sadness ; to pick them shews regret for youthful follies.

Sword.—To dream of this means that you may expect danger, or sudden illness, or even death ; to grasp it warns you that slander and dangerous gossip are around you ; to wear it signifies the possession of power ; to see a sword in its sheath lying upon a table predicts honour and glory for someone dear to you.

T.

Tableau.—-For a girl to dream that she takes the chief part in a tableau in which she is a failure, portends that if she marries her husband will spend most of his substance upon dress and will be a feckless fellow.

Tablecloth.—To see it soiled warns you of domestic annoyance ; snowy white, comfort.

Tailor.—To dream of a tailor signifies that you are somewhat unreliable and indiscreet and will bring criticiam and snubbing upon yourself by your foolish behaviour.

Talking.—If you dream that you talk volubly it shows that you will be exposed to some malicious plans ; if you hear much talking around you be careful with regard to your neighbours.

Tea.— To dream of drinking it indicates that your pleasure in life will be mingled with anxiety, and that from time to time you will experience an undue share of worry ; to make it signifies that you will be stirred up to do something unpleasant or irksome task which you have been putting off continually ; for a girl to dream of taking tea with her sweetheart means that she will not be received with open arms by his family and that there will be many small vexations and disputes for her to encounter ; to see it growing foretells that you will probably become wealthy through tea plantations.

Tea Pot.—If the handle is towards you, hospitality ; if the spout, invitations and social enjoyments ; if it is broken, gossip and scandal at a tea party.

Tears.—To dream of tears foreshows a coming dispute with someone dear to you.

Teeth.—To dream of your teeth as sound and white is a sign of health and good luck ; if they are loose, distress or misfortune ; if they fall out, death of a relation or friend ; if you see them long and yellow you will live to a good old age without experiencing much trouble with your teeth ; if they ache, a visit to the dentist is suggested by your dream.

Telegram.—To send one means that you will shortly be

forwarding serious news to a relative or friend ; to see an unopened telegram shows that you may expect one imme-diately ; if a hand holds it out to you, it predicts an unexpected arrival or meeting ; if the telegram has a cross or black upon it bad news or a death is indicated ; an open telegram in your hand with colour or other good signs to be seen, would fore-show a very happy unexpected event causing much delight and excitement.

Telephone.—To dream that you talk on the telephone prepares you for the fact that someone for whom you have much regard will shortly be saying unkind things behind your back.

Telescope.—To look into one foretells the probability of your having trouble with your eyesight.

Tempest.—To dream of this indicates that you will meet with abuse and opposition.

Temptation.—To dream of being tempted to commit an act of folly or disgrace warns you that some of those with whom you associate are undesirable companions, and that if you do not take heed you may be led into serious mischief.

Tennis.—To play it shows dexterity and calm self-assur-ance which enables you to master most difficulties ; to see it played means pleasure and social entertainments.

Theatre.—To dream that you are in a theatre in which you see no audience foretells that you will shed tears of remorse for some action, the result of which cannot be undone.

Thieves.—To see them forewarns you of robbery ; to dream that you associate with them means that you are fascinated by an offer from some unscrupulous man who professes to be able to show you a method by which money can be made easily and rapidly : but this dream must certainly warn you not to listen to such a proposal.

Thigh.—To dream of a broken thigh denotes loss of goods sent to distant parts ; for a girl to dream of it means that she is likely to marry a stranger and live far away from her rela-tives ; this dream predicts widowhood for a woman ; to dream of your thigh being injured or painful foreshows an accident, probably a fall.

Thimble.—For a girl to dream that she receives a thimble as a present predicts that she will never marry ; to find one indicates change of employment ; to lose one, indignation over a small matter.

Thirst.—It is considered most unfortunate to dream of suffering from thirst as it denotes loss of income and ill-fortune; if however the thirst is quenched, you will surmount a temporary difficulty and will become rich.

Thistle.—This is a pleasant symbol of strength, endurance, and affection ; to cut them signifies a desire to reform those who are astray and to remove obstacles from the path of those in difficulty ; if you grasp a thistle you will receive an injury whilst assisting another.

Thorn.—If you have a thorn in your foot you may expect to move to a new neighbourhood and to dislike those with whom you most associate ; a thorn in your hand means that you will meet with pain and disappointment ; in your head, grief ; in your arm, a distressing incident with friend or lover.

Thrashing.—To dream of thrashing corn is a hopeful sign of your rising to an important position through your own ability.

Threads.—To see them tangled means intrigue ; to dismantle them, confusion in affairs which with patience you will remedy ; to split them means the betrayal of a secret ; to break them, failure through your own impetuosity.

Throat.—To dream of discomfort or pain in your throat usually foreshows that you will have some ailment affecting it ; if you dream of it as strong and powerful, it indicates that you will become a good singer if you persevere in the culture of your voice.

Throne.—To see an empty throne denotes public misfortune ; to see it broken foreshows an accident to the head of your family.

Thrush.—To hear it sing betokens an unthought-of joy ;

to see it in a cage, despair ; to see it fly, news of someone dear to you.

Thumb.—To dream of your thumb as large and powerful foretells an opportunity in which you will prove yourself superior to those who have hitherto somewhat despised you ; if it appears withered or small you will experience defeat by an opponent ; if it is long and turns outwards you will enter recklessly into a speculation and possibly lose a large sum of money ; if you see it hanging limply it foretells an accident to your hand or thumb.

Thunder.—To dream that you are out in a thunder storm foretells the approach of a bad storm ; to hear it is a warning of danger ; to see a thunderbolt fall is a signal of calamity or death for a friend.

Tiger.—If it is near, aud you endeavour to evade it, you may expect to be harassed and perplexed ; it at a distance and it springs, disturbing news from India ; a tiger upon its hind legs indicates that you will be in danger through some-one who is in a position of authority.

Timber.—To see piles of timber is a sign of well-being and prosperity in your affairs.

Time.—Time is dreamed of in various ways, sometimes in symbols only, or figures, days, or months may be shown ; for instance, you much desire the return of your lover or great friend : in a dream you see a bunch of daffodils or other spring flowers and a happy sensation accompanies the dream, you would therefore be assured of a joyful meeting in the spring ; or there may be something which you particularly wish to do and are anxious to shoose a propitious day for it : a dream is quite likely to come to your assistance by showing you a date such as Tuesday, July 1st ; if this is seen without any ominous signs choose that day for your plan, for it would certainly be a fortunate one ; the date of a bad illness or a death is often indicated in dreams as are happy events ; time may also be predicted by flowers or trees only, without any figures appearing.

Tits.—To dream of these beautiful birds is a happy omen

of coming pleasure ; if one alights upon you it shows the near presence of someone you love in whom you may feel complete confidence ; to see them fly means joyous news.

Toads.—To see them near is a sign of much that is unpleasant being around you and of disagreeable discoveries ; this dream cautions you to be on your guard for malicious talking causes much discomfort and may separate the best of friends ; it is also a bad omen of worry and money difficulties, and of coming into contact with the sordid side of life ; to dream of toads crawling over you signifies severe illness and much mental distress.

Tobacco.—To dream of seeing piles of tobacco is a sign of bad luck in a speculation or business transaction ; to smoke it means that you depend upon creature comforts to keep you good-tempered ; to take snuff is a sign of giving in to bad habits ; and is also an unfortunate omen of disagreements in a love affair.

Tomato.—An increase of worldly goods is signified by dreaming of tomatoes ; to see them in numbers around you indicates success in an enterprise such as tomato growing; to eat them means health and geniality ; to pick them brings a time of leisure after much labour.

Tombs.—To dream of large important-looking tombs signifies that you will visit a cathedral or old church where you will be much interested in the discovery of the tomb of an ancestor ; to dream of many small tombs indicates an epidemic causing much loss of life.

Tongs.—A pair of fire tongs is a symbol of anxiety and disturbance in the home ; to use them shows distaste for those things which fall to your lot.

Tongue.—A sore tongue denotes that you will make mischief by your indiscreet or unkind words ; to dream of it as large and swollen signifies illness.

Tortoise.—To see one near indicates that you will experience delay in trying to adjust a troublesome piece of business and will find difficulty in arriving at a satisfactory conclusion upon the matter, as information which would throw light upon it is not forthcoming ; to pursue one means an attempt to do that of which you have no knowledge.

Tow.—To dream that you have tow upon you is a danger signal of fire caused through carelessness ; to see large quantities of tow shows that you will try various kinds of work but will become tired of each one ; to handle tow means that you remain engrossed in your friends for a while but it is a passing affection only and when you become weary of them they are discarded and others take their place.

Tower.—To see this predicts your rising to a good and prosperous position in life ; if the tower is broken or crooked you must expect to meet with many hindrances.

Train.—To dream of a train into which you endeavour to step but always fail shows that a journey of which you feel no doubt about taking will unexpectedly have to be given up at the last moment ; to see many trains passing means unlooked for changes and new plans ; if you are in a train with a feeling of pleasure you may expect a happy meeting with someone dear to you in connection with a journey ; if you dream of a train rushing past you it warns you not to venture upon a journey for a time, or you may be in danger of a serious accident.

Train.—To dream that you bear the train of a bride is a sign that you will meet with a man at a wedding who will fall in love with you but will be in no hurry to marry until he has ascertained whether you are likely to inherit a fortune ; you will find out in an unexpected way that, unless there is a prospect of money, his devotion to you may be expected to cease.

Travel.—On foot denotes embarrassment and delay in what you undertake or hope for ; on horseback, good fortune.

Treacle.—To eat it, amusement ; to see it flow from a cask, increase of fortune ; to cook it, a doubtful experiment.

Treasure.—If you dream of seeking treasure, you may expect to travel in foreign countries and collect many interesting objects and possibly make your home abroad ; to dream that you have found a treasure of great value denotes that unexpected good fortune will be yours.

Trees.—To dream of green trees is a sign of hope ; shattered by a storm, agitation and disagreements ; withered, disappointments or sorrow ; leafless, an event to be expected in the winter ; in bud, happiness ; cut down, misfortune ; to dream of planting them promises you success in life ; a large cedar tree indicates the possession of much that is pleasant and increasing prosperity ; it is a symbol of calmness, courage, and endurance ; an almond tree in flower proclaims love and joy ; a plane tree foreshows a time of uncertainty and possibly vexation ; a Judas tree tells you of treachery.

Tricks.—To dream that one of the opposite sex plays tricks upon you proclaims that you will lose your love.

Triumphal Arch.—To see this erected near is a fortunate omen of your future honour and high position ; to see it decorated denotes a wedding.

Trout.—To see them means a ray of hope ; to eat them, entire satisfaction.

True Lover's Knot.—To dream of seeing a true lover's knot is a happy omen foreshadowing faithfulness in love and enduring friendship.

Trumpets.—To see them denotes that you will be the leader in some scheme which is to benefit many, and that you will become famous through this work ; to blow a trumpet means that you will be called upon to break a piece of bad news or unpleasant facts to some friends or relations ; to blow a trumpet with an assembly of people around you signifies that your name will one day become known to all the world ; a broken trumpet signifies conceit ; to hear trumpets is an omen of illness or death.

Trunk.—If you see it full you may expect a generous present ; empty predicts a loss.

Tub.—If it be filled with water you have evil to fear ; empty signifies trouble caused through forgetfulness ; to run against one means calamity.

Tulips.—These are a sign of radiancy, health, and success ;

to pick them shows advancement and constancy in love and friendship ; to hold a large bunch of them signifies that many cheerful events may be anticipated.

Tumour.—To dream of a tumour portends news of serious illness ; to dream of tumours means the coming bankruptcy of someone who owes you money.

Tunnel.—To dream that you are in a tunnel with a feeling of dismay foretells that you will make a wrong decision in an important matter ; for the lover it is a sign that there may be cause for distrust, but if light is visible at the end of the tunnel the doubt will pass away and happiness be assured.

Turkey.—To see a turkey cock strutting signifies that your pride is unseemly ; to chase one means that you are committing injurious follies ; to see the hens predicts illness ; to eat turkey, enjoyment and hospitality.

Turnip.—To eat them signifies vexation at the result of some plan which you had imagined would work remarkably well ; to pull them from the ground predicts the discovery of secrets and domestic quarrels.

Turnpike.—To dream of this denotes that the reminiscences which you relate of the past are of more interest than your topics of the present.

Turnstile.—To walk through one means that you cleverly evade a disagreeable incident or unpleasant discussion without offending anyone ; to see it shows that you must endeavour to come to a decision but that you dislike finality and so continue to waver as to your opinion ; to stand beside a turnstile indicates that you will be doubtful as to your reply to a proposal of marriage which you are likely to receive in the near future.

Turquoise.—This is a fortunate dream for those born in May, Spetember, or October, being one of the birth stones for those months ; to others it would be a symbol of hope and pleasure.

Turtle.—To see them signifies good fortune ; to eat them, refinement and luxury ; the lover who dreams of eating turtle may expect to marry someone of good birth.

Turtle Dove.—To see one near is an assurance of fidelity and love ; if it alights upon you there will be happy news of your lover ; to the married it would signify peace, gentleness, and happiness in the home.

Twins.—To dream of seeing twins is a sign of sympathy, and the perfection of happiness.

U.

Ugly.—To dream of ugly people around you shows that you will be worried by your own personal appearance which seems to you to have become unusually plain ; to dream that you receive a proposal of marriage from an ugly suitor denotes that your future husband will have many excellent points but good looks will not be among them.

Umbrella.—To see it open foretells bad weather and grumbling ; closed and rolled means that you will receive a good present ; to break or tear it is a sign that you will be blamed unjustly for some misdeed and will find it a difficult matter to prove your innocence ; to lose it cautions you against doing so.

Undertaker.—To dream of conversing with an undertaker is an omen of coming sorrow and mourning.

Undress.—To dream of undressing signifies that through absentmindedness you will appear before your friends in ridiculous attire and will be covered with confusion when you discover your mistake ; to dream of undressing in the presence of others denotes slander ; to see others undress means that you are addicted to unpleasant stories and unseemly jokes.

Unfaithful.—To dream that you have been unfaithful to

someone who has implicit trust in you is a warning to avoid this coming to pass at all costs.

Unusual.—If you dream that you are considered unusual, you may expect to receive congratulations from your friends on your brilliant achievement in some piece of work or talent.

V,

Vaccinate.—To dream of being vaccinated foretells that you will probably take up work abroad in which you may run some risk to your health and that as a precaution you will be vaccinated.

Vain.—To dream that you wish to be considered vain means that you have little cause for vanity ; to accuse others of being vain indicates jealousy.

Valentine.—To receive one which has a seal upon it indicates a joyful surprise of a sum of money or good present from an unknown source ; to receive a large valentine denotes a diffident lover ; to send one shows unrequited love.

Valet.—To dream of a valet who comes bowing towards you warns you that you have an unsuspected enemy.

Vampire.—To see it near brings a message of gloom and sorrow ; to see it hovering means that you await the expected news of a death.

Van.—To dream of a black van denotes disgrace ; a red van, news or presents ; a grey van, illness ; to drive a van means an interesting experiment in which you succeed ; to see one upset, misfortune and losses.

Variegated Holly.—This shows gaiety, the making of new friends, and pleasant events in the holly season ; to pick it means a sharp encounter with one of the opposite sex in which you are victorious.

Vault.—An unexpected inheritance is foreshown by dreaming of a vault.

Vegetable Marrow.—To dream of this means sadness or monetary losses through bad crops either at home or abroad ; to eat it shows propriety and the observance of rules ; to cut it, a new hope ; to cook it, contentment and sagacity.

Vegetables.—To see quantities of these means wearisome oil ; to gather them, disputes ; to eat them, misfortune.

Veil.—To wear a black one predicts mourning ; a white one, approaching marriage ; a grey one, a useful life ; a pink one, pretended modesty ; a blue one, precaution.

Velvet.—To wear it gives promise that you will enjoy wealth and power ; to see scarlet velvet signifies pomp and splendour ; purple, honour and profit ; black, dignity and advancement.

Vengeance.—To dream of taking vengeance upon someone to whom you owe no grudge is a warning that an attack of unreasonable jealousy will lead you into committing a disgraceful act for which you will be despised by your friends.

Venison.—To eat it brings prosperity and enjoyment with congenial friends ; to see it uncooked indicates lack of wisdom in an undertaking.

Vermicelli.—To cook it shows an attempt to disguise some new idea or plans from those around you ; to eat it means the revival of a happy memory ; to break it, a vexatious occurrence.

Vermilion.—To dream of this striking colour means that you will be told some vivid story probably of a somewhat unpleasant nature, the memory of which will haunt you.

Vermin.—This dream portends deceit and treachery on the part of someone who will appear to be seeking to please you in every way.

Vicar.—To dream of calling upon your Vicar on business portends that you will shortly ask him to officiate at a wedding or baptism ; to see him advancing towards you shows reconciliation in a long standing feud.

Vice.—To dream that you are held by a carpenter's vice means that you will need powerful assistance to extricate you from the mess into which you get yourself by your folly ; to dream of a condition of vice or that you are considered vicious is a serious warning that there is heed for much reformation in your life.

Village.—To see one which appears poor means loss of office or work ; to see one which is prosperous is a fortunate on en of wealth and peaceful conditions ; to see one burning shows misery and danger.

Villain.—To dream that you associate with one is an indication that someone with whom you will become acquainted will turn out to be an undesirable character ; to dream that you have become a villain warns you to walk more warily.

Vine.—This is a fortunate dream and predicts that things will go well with you, and that you may expect peace, joy, and abundance.

Vinegar.—Red vinegar denotes that someone will insult you ; white vinegar, that your friends will be injured ; to drink it foretells labour in vain ; to a lover it shows falseness.

Vineyard.—This dream proclaims the attainment of your heart's desire to walk in it, the possession of wealth and honour.

Violet.—To dream of purple violets is a recognised sign of spirituality ; to see three large single violets is a mark of reaching to perfection ; this dream would also show much that is beautiful in love ; if you see purple violets growing beside water and you pick them, it foreshows the death of a man, either a relative or dear friend ; or to see them upon a bed or in a cross would also predict the death of a man ; to see them growing luxuriantly in a garden signifies that your happiness is dependent upon a man, and that there is much to which you may look forward in the future ; to pick them beans the finding of happiness in its fullest sense ; white violets are symbols of innocence, peace, and gentleness ; those who constantly dream of white violets are usually child lovers, though they are seldom demonstrative in their affection ; to pick white violets from beside water indicates the death of a woman whose death will much affect your life; or if the violets were seen upon a bed or in a wreath it would also foretell death for a woman; to see them growing in masses denotes love and joy; to pick them, the fulfilment of your hope.

Viper.—See "**Snake.**"

Virginia Creeper.—To see this growing in profusion upon a house foreshows something of much interest to you occurring in the early autumn; if the creeper is withered and falling, depressing news of a friend is shown; to see it upon a bed predicts illness or death for an old person.

Vision.—To dream that a wonderful vision appears to you in sleep is an omen of peace and joy.

Visit.—The visit of a stranger denotes that you will undertake some enterprise at present unthought of; to pay a visit with a feeling of gloom indicates a misfortune or loss; to be visited by a physician predicts illness.

Visitor.—To dream that you are a visitor in an unknown house and amongst strangers means that before long you will be placed in an awkward position through the upsetting of your plans and that you must live in an hotel for the time being; if you receive an unexpected visitor it shows that you will soon hear of a birth.

Vitriol.—To dream of vitriol is a grave warning to use self-control, or some day you may commit some terrible act of violence.

Vixen.—If you dream that you are spoken of as a vixen it denotes that there is risk of your growing to resemble this unless you heed the warning of your dream.

Voices.—To hear voices of horror or dismay denotes that some of your friends or relations will be taken suddenly ill or meet with an accident; to hear angelic voices foretells the passing on of someone known to you who is ill; to hear voices of harmony is a sign of peaceful conditions in your life.

Volcano.—To dream of this foretells serious danger of

accident or explosion ; to dream that you witness an eruption warns you of fire.

Volume.—To dream of searching for a volume which cannot be found shows that your relations and friends will object to the books which you read and will either hide or destroy them.

Volunteer.—If you volunteer to do some piece of work which no one will undertake, it signifies that charity will be a conspicuous trait in your character.

Votes.—If you dream of soliciting votes you may be sure that your position in life will largely depend upon the influence of others ; if you dream of receiving a number of votes it would be a good omen for your success in a contest.

Vulgar.—To dream of this is a hint that a trace of it is to be found in yourself ; to dream that you have horror of anything approaching vulgarity warns you not to become self-complacent.

Vulture.—To dream of this bird is a foreboding of evil and unrest in various quarters of the globe ; to see them in numbers on the ground predicts a famine ; seen in or over a house they denote death ; two vultures seen circling in the air foreshow distress and war ; if one flies towards you, it is an omen of tears, tragedy, and sorrow.

W.

Wadding.—If a woman sees a quantity of wadding in a dream it foretells the fact that she will become so thin that those who are unkind will describe her as scraggy ; to wear it means a danger of scalds or burns.

Wading.—In clear still water with a feeling of pleasure is a good omen in a love affair ; if the water is muddy, a short time of bliss followed by strife and worry ; to dream of wading against your will indicates intrigue probably ending in a law suit.

Wages.—To dream of paying them denotes bad temper and disappointment ; to receive them, grumbling.

Waggon.—To see one loaded denotes a prosperous outlook ; if some of the load falls off, partial success only ; to ride in it, change of fortune for the better.

Walter.—An unsettled condition in your domestic affairs.

Walking.—To feel fatigue in walking foreshows a time of anxiety as to ways and means ; to be walking in muddy places shows an unpleasant character ; to walk with a swagger denotes that you make yourself ridiculous by your arrogance ; if you walk under a house and a sparrow's nest falls and the dirt from it scatters upon your face an attack of shingles is predicted ; if you walk under a ladder which slips, an accident in or near your house is foretold.

Wall.—To dream of being between high walls denotes many difficulties in your life and that much courage will be necessary to overcome them ; if the walls are moss covered it shows that some of your misfortunes are due to lack of energy and initiative on your part and could be remedied ; if the walls are crumbling it indicates the approach of a catastrophe about to overtake you ; to walk upon the edge of a narrow wall is a sign of impending danger and personal risk ; to walk upon a high and wide wall indicates the undertaking of some enterprise requiring courage ; if you go to the end of the wall without stumbling your scheme will be successfully carried out.

Wall Flower.—To dream of its scent brings the revival of happy memories ; to see it growing means the serious consideration of a new plan ; to pick it shows that you pride yourself upon being sensible, but have no regard for appearances.

Walnuts.—To eat these foretells the fulfilment of your most sanguine hopes ; to see them green, doubt and delay ; to gather them, calculation and good sense.

Wandering.—To dream of wandering about in an aimless manner indicates loss of goods through fire ; to dream of a wanderer denotes disgrace.

Want.—To dream that you are in want when in reality you are in comfort speaks to you of those who may be in need of your generosity.

War.—To dream of war portends news which will cause general consternation ; it is also a forecast of trouble, disturbed conditions, and harassing events ; for a family it predicts partings, and loss of money or health.

Warehouse.—To dream that you are in an empty warehouse signifies misery and desolation ; if it is packed with goods, a well merited success in life.

Warming Pan.—To see one polished and shining denotes comfort and domestic peace ; to use it, indisposition.

Warts.—To dream that your hands are covered with these warns you to be careful in conducting your business, and to avoid bad company.

Washing.—To dream of washing clothes means that you will shortly be striving to defend the character of a friend ; to wash lace means pleasant news ; stockings, thrift ; handkerchiefs, expectations.

Wasps,—To dream of a swarm of wasps is significant of distress caused by the sharp tongues of those around you ; to see them in a room means strife, petty thefts, and domestic disturbances ; to be stung foreshows pain and trouble.

Waste Places.—These are a symbol of some risky enterprise.

Watch.—To dream of having a watch is a warning to be careful how you spend your time.

Watchman.—If you call him in it betokens alarm and danger of robbery ; to see anyone taken to prison by a watchman means that you must be careful as to your methods of business ; to see several watchmen together indicates loss of money.

Water.—To see a rushing torrent of muddy water gives warning of danger through drowning or other accident with water ; to see a wide stretch of calm water foreshows a voyage.

Water-lily.—To see them growing brings affection and peace ; to gather them, a declaration of love.

Waves.—To dream of watching great waves in the company of one of the opposite sex foretells a troubled love affair ; if the waves subside and the sea becomes calm, after a time of suspense your love will end in a happy marriage ; to watch small waves lightly flecked with foam means that there will be no obstacles in the way of your happiness ; to count them shows the undertaking of a thankless task.

Wax.—To dream of this signifies a weak character.

Wax Candle.—To dream of seeing a wax candle alight is an omen of happiness in the home ; many wax candles burning and suddenly becoming dim predicts sudden death for a relative or friend.

Weasel.—This animal denotes cunning, and the sly behaviour of someone with whom you associate.

Weather Cock.—To dream of this is a sign that you feel incapable of making up your mind definitely on any matter without first consulting each one with whom you come in contact : in the end you settle upon an entirely different course of action.

Wedding.—To dream of a wedding at which you are a spectator only and at which you see bunches of holly or corn instead of the flowers which you would expect to see, foretells the fact that you will be distressed at some news of an unhappy marriage ; to dream of being present at a wedding at which you see beautiful flowers and other good symbols, predicts much pleasure at a forthcoming marriage ; if you hold flowers in your hand, it means that you will be one of the bridesmaids.

Wedding Cake.—To see this predicts a prosperous and speedy marriage ; to eat it means good luck and happy news.

Weeds.—To see them growing in profusion is a sign of blighted hopes ; to pull them up means family vexation and trials ; to burn them indicates that you refuse any responsibility in the affairs of those around you.

Weeping.—This is a sign of coming tribulation ; to see others weep shows sorrow affecting many.

Weighing.—To dream of weighing is a sign that your accuracy and care will greatly assist towards your final success ; to see a weighing machine denotes deliberation and good judgement.

Well.—A well full of clear sparkling water, denotes successful speculation ; an overflowing well, losses.

Whale.—To see it swinming towards you is a warning of personal danger which may be averted if you use caution if it swims away the danger is passing ; to pursue it shows a desire to become notorious.

Wheat.—To see large quantities of wheat in store signifies money.

Wheel.—To dream of seeing this is symbolic of the wheel of fortune being near you ; if it turns rapidly, prosperity and happiness are at hand ; if the wheel is still, delay is indicated and further patience will be needed ; a broken wheel is a bad sign of disappointment as to an expected inheritance ; the fortune which should have been yours will be squandered by those from whom you would have received it, and a small legacy is all that you may now expect ; if you see two wheels revolving it signifies mysterious happenings, remarkable achievements in the air, and power and success for those who are dear to you ; to turn a wheel up a hill shows that you have difficult burdens to bear and much monotony in your life ; if it seems to bound out of your hand and turn rapidly it predicts that the burdens will be removed and your life be full of energy and pleasure ; to follow a rapidly moving wheel shows an enterprising mind, untiring energy, and love of travel ; to be dragged down hill by it is ominous of evil and of rapidly occurring events over which you are powerless ; to see a piece of black cloth upon it signifies a calamity caused through an accident ; with white, a wedding.

Wheelwright.—Sorrow followed by joy is the meaning of this dream.

Whip.—For a woman to dream of a whip is an unpleasant omen of trials and vexation in her marriage ; for a man it has much the same meaning, for he will marry a slovenly woman who will make his home comfortless and miserable,

Whirlwind.—To dream of being caught in a whirlwind is a sign of scandal.

White.—This is a colour of placidity, calm, and self-control ; white seen with red upon it or a bunch of scarlet flowers predicts a coming tragedy possibly through a love affair ; white seen with lilies or other beautiful flowers foretells a wedding or festivity.

White Clematis.—A forecast of peace and love is shown by dreaming of this flower.

White Lead.—Denotes quarrels.

White Wax.—This is an indication of coming grief ; to mariners it means security and safety in voyaging.

Widow.—To dream of widowhood is a sad omen of that which will be your lot in the future.

Widower.—For a girl to dream of marrying one indicates that someone whom she has known since childhood and who has recently become a widower will desire to marry her and although he will be many years her senior she will have a good and considerate husband ; for a man to dream of becoming a widower foretells the serious illness and possible death of his wife.

Wife.—To dream that your wife is calling to you when away from her foreshows bad news of sudden illness or some other misfortune having come upon her.

Wig.—To wear one foretells an injury or illness affecting your hair ; to see it means ambition.

Wild Beasts.—To dream of many wild beasts denotes mental anxiety caused by your present circumstances ; if they lie down the protection and favour of the powerful is shown.

Will.—To dream that you make it signifies bad news about your health ; to see a will near predicts a good legacy.

Willow.—To be under a weeping willow tree is a sign of misfortune or bereavement ; if the willow is bending down and touches you the trouble is very near ; this tree is a symbol of sadness and of nature's sympathy.

Wind.—To hear a great wind is a sign of terror ; to battle against it means that you will have a hard struggle in life but, providing you can endure, comfort and happiness will follow ; to feel a gentle breeze blowing upon you foreshows happiness in love.

Windmill.—To see it moving is a sign of unsettled conditions and of changes and chances in your life ; to see it in sunshine means great success in a venturous enterprise.

Windows.—To dream that you throw yourself out warns you to avoid the harbouring of morbid thoughts ; to fall from a window predicts an accident ; if you step through it someone will injure you ; an open widnow means that you are regarded with favour by many ; a closed one shows embarrassment.

Wine.—To drink champagne in company with others denotes wealth and festivity ; alone, a slow recovery from illness or sorrow ; to see bottles of white wine shows that you will enjoy the friendship of great personages ; red, doubtful or risky pleasures ; to see it flow, bloodshed ; to pour it away, a disaster in the family.

Winter Jessamine.—This flower is a symbol of brightness and of making the best of a bad business when such befalls you ; to pick it means good fellowship and enjoyment.

Wistaria.—This beautiful creeper is a sign of affection and peace in the home.

Witch.—This dream signifies that you will leave your home and wander in strange places ; if you dream that a witch has cast an evil spell about you it is a warning that if you are not careful you will come under the bad influence of some woman.

Witness.—To dream of being called as witness against someone known to you is an ominous sign of a serious dispute which will be settled in the law courts ; to witness against a stranger means that you will be compelled much against your will to bear witness in a court of law.

Wolf.—To see one means that you have an avaricious and hard-hearted neighbour ; to conquer it means that you will be victorious over someone who has all the bad qualities of a wolf ; if you pursue it, a danger will be averted.

Woodoutter.—This dream signifies a condition of profitless toil.

Woods.—To hide yourself in them indicates a danger of disgrace.

Woodyard.—To be in one brings a happy change of fortune; to own one, good luck and abundance.

Wool.—To see piles of wool brings comforts and riches ; to buy it means that you will marry your present lover ; to sell it foretells illness ; a wool dealer denotes affluence.

Workman.—To speak with one means a trifling but vexing incident ; to see one, success in an undertaking.

Worms.—To see them crawling upon a house indicates contagious disease ; crawling upon a man or woman gives warning against such persons, for they will be a danger in your life and should be regarded with horror ; if worms crawl towards you, beware of treachery and dishonour ; to kill them means that you take steps to prevent the spreading of a scandal or lie ; to pick them up proves your guilt of disloyalty to your lover or friends.

Wormwood.—Grief and pain are foretold by dreaming of this.

Wound.—To dream that you are wounded by a dagger signifies a danger of an attack of violence or an operation ; a wound made by an unknown person foretells much trouble in unexpected ways ; by a wolf, infidelity ; if the wound heals you will emerge in triumph through an attack made upon your character ; to wound another means that through your lack of frankness unjust suspicion will fall upon a friend.

Wreath.—This is a symbol of marriage and much happiness in store for you.

Wren.—This bird seen near foreshows an unusual occurrence bringing you joy ; to see it flying means pleasant news from someone whom you thought to have forgotten you.

Write.—To write with difficulty or displeasure means a false accusation.

Y.

Yacht.—To see it sailing upon a calm sea is a sign of vigour, congenial friends and pleasure; to sail in it, health and success; to build one, an unexpected turn of good fortune.

Yard.—An empty yard denotes loss of business.

Yarn.—Seen in abundance portends a busy but cheerful life; to waste it is ominous of disgrace.

Yawn.—To dream of yawning foretells discontent with your present conditions of which you will become heartily tired, and you will make up your mind to seek your fortune abroad; for a married woman to dream this means that she will spend anxious days and nights through illness in the family.

Yeast.—To eat it denotes illness; to see it rise, improvement.

Yellow.—This colour indicates a sunny nature capable of seeing the best in everyone and everything; to dream that you are draped in yellow material signifies that the happiness which will be yours in the future will be brought about by an entirely unforeseen event through meeting with one of the opposite sex.

Yellow Topaz.—This is a most fortunate dream to those born in July or August being one of the birth stones for those months; to all dreamers it is an omen of good fortune and health.

Yeoman.—If he comes towards you it is a prediction of evil; if he walks away, a misfortune is avoided.

Yew Tree.—To dream of a large and spreading yew tree is significant of your attaining to a prominent position in life, and of an inheritance from a relative; to stand beneath a drooping yew tree means that there are shadows over you and much that seems hard; if you see sunlight through the tree you may hope for a speedy lifting of your clouds.

Yoke.—For a girl to dream that she drives a yoke of oxen signifies that she will marry an industrious man who will by hard work gain success and greatly improve his position.

Young.—To dream of being extremely juvenile denotes that you will receive some unexpected news.

Young Men.—To dream of several young men augurs but little good to the dreamer.

Youth.—For a woman to dream that her youth is restored signifies that she will live in happiness with a loving and true husband.

Z.

Zebra.—To see it near signifies that something for which you have long waited is now within sight, but you will be much disappointed for you will find that it was not worth waiting for after all ; to ride upon one means changes and travel ; if it pursues you, a treacherous friend will harm you.

Zig Zag.—To dream that you see an object in the form of a zig-zag foretells the rapid advance of a striking event which will be difficult to deal with ; a zig zag upon a wall denotes forked lightning.

Zino.—To see a large quantity of this means that you will be persuaded to join some old friends who have settled in one of the colonies : you will throw in your lot with them and make a good success of this new venture.

Zino Ointment.—This dream foretells that you will be troubled about a disfigurement, and will spend much money in your endeavours to cure it.

Zodiac.—To dream of the twelve signs of the Zodiac foretells a terrific storm over land and sea, so violent that its damaging traces will be seen in all directions ; for a man this dream denotes that he will become very popular and will travel to all parts of the globe.

Zoo.—To dream that you are at the Zoo denotes prosperity and pleasant events ; it also predicts your paying a visit to it within a short time ; for a young woman to dream that she sees the Zoo shows that she will meet with some man whilst visiting it, to whom she will eventually become engaged ; he will prove to be an excellent match, as he will rise to fame through his ability and learning in the study of natural history ; for a young man to dream of the Zoo portends that he will marry a woman of means who will be a good deal his senior and to whom he will be in complete servitude.

FORTUNE-TELLING

HOW TO TELL FORTUNES BY DOMINOES.

L AY them with their faces on the table and shuffle them ; then draw one and see the number, which has its meaning as follows :—

Double-six.—Receiving a handsome sum of money.

Six-five.—Going to a place of public amusement.

Six-four.—Lawsuits and trouble, which can only be avoided by great care.

Six-three.—A ride in a carriage.

Six-two.—A present of clothing.

Six-one.—You will soon perform a friendly action.

Six-blank.—Guard against scandal, or you will suffer by your inattention.

Double-five.—A new abode to your advantage.

Five-four.—A fortunate speculation in business.

Five-three.—A visit from a superior.

Five-two.—A pleasant excursion on the water.

Five-one.—A love intrigue.

Five-blank.—A funeral, but not of a relation.

Double-four.—Drinking liquor at a distance.

Four-three.—A false alarm at your house.

Four-two.—Beware of thieves and swindlers.

Four-one.—Expect trouble from creditors.

Four-blank.—You will receive a letter from an angry friend.

Double-three.—A sudden wedding, at which you will be vexed, and by which you will lose a friend.

Three-two.—Buy no lottery tickets, nor enter into any game of chance, or you will assuredly lose.

Three-one.—A great discovery is at hand.

Three-blank.—A child.

Double-two.—You will have a jealous partner.

Two-one.—You will soon find something to your advantage in the street or road.

Two-blank.—You will lose money or some article of value.

Double-one.—The loss of a friend, whom you will very much miss.

One-blank.—You are being closely watched by one whom you little expect.

Double-blank.—The worst presage in all the set; you will meet trouble from a quarter for which you are quite unprepared.

It is useless for persons to draw more than three dominoes at one time of trial, or in one and the same week, as they will only deceive themselves. Shuffle the dominoes each time of choosing.

HOW TO TELL FORTUNES BY DICE.

TAKE three dice, shake them well in the box with your left hand, and then cast them out on a board or table, on which you have previously drawn a circle with chalk.

Three.—A pleasing surprise.

Four.—A disagreeable one.

Five.—A stranger who will prove a friend.

Six.—Loss of property.

Seven.—Undeserved scandal.

Eight.—Merited reproach.

Nine.—A wedding.

Ten.—A christening.

Eleven.—A death that concerns you.

Twelve.—A letter speedily.

Thirteen.—Tears and sighs.

Fourteen.—Beware that you are not drawn into some trouble or plot by a secret enemy.

Fifteen.—Immediate prosperity and happiness.

Sixteen.—A pleasant journey.

Seventeen.—You will either be on the water, or have dealings with those belonging to it, to your advantage.

Eighteen.—A great profit, rise in life, or some most desirable good will happen almost immediately.

To show the same number twice at one trial, portends news from abroad, be the number what it may. If the dice roll over the circle, the number thrown goes for nothing, but the occurrence shows sharp words; and if they fall to the floor it is blows. In throwing out the dice, if one remains on the top of the other, it is an omen of which I would have them take care.

HOW TO TELL FORTUNES FROM THE HAND.

I SHALL now say something of palmistry, which is a judgment of the conditions, inclinations, and fortunes of men and women, from the various lines and characters which nature has imprinted in the hand, which are almost as various as the hands that have them. And to render what I shall say more plain, I will in the first place present the scheme or figures of the hand, and explain the various lines therein.

1. *Line of Life.*   4. *Girdle of Venus.*
2. *Table Line.*   5. *Line of Death.*
3. *Natural Line.*   6. *Mount of Venus.*

By this figure the reader will see that one of these lines, and which indeed is reckoned the principal, is called the line of life ; this line encloses the thumb, separating it from the hollow of the hand. The next to it, which is called the natural line, takes its beginning from the rising of the fore-finger, near the line of life, and reaches to the table line, and generally makes a triangle. The table line, commonly called the line of fortune, begins under the little finger, and ends near the middle finger. The girdle of Venus, which is another line so called, begins near the joint of the little finger, and ends between the forefinger and the middle finger. The line of death is that which plainly appears in a counter line to that of life, and is by some called the sister line, ending usually at the other end ; for when the line of life is ending, death comes, and it can go no farther. There are also lines in the fleshy parts, as in the ball of the thumb, which is called the mount of Venus, under each of the fingers, are called mounts, which are each one governed by a several planet ; and the hollow of the hand is called the plain of Mars.

I now proceed to give judgment of these several lines. And in the first place take notice, that in palmistry the left hand is chiefly to be regarded ; because therein the lines are most visible, and have the strictest communication with the heart and brain.   Now, having premised these, in the next place observe the line of life, and if it be fair, extended to its full length, and not broken with an intermixture of cross lines, it shows long life and health ; and it is the same if a double line of life appears, as there sometimes does.   When the stars appear in this line it is a significator of great losses and calamities ; if on it there appear the figure of two O's, or a Y, it threatens the person with blindness.   If it wraps itself about the table line, then does it promise wealth and honour to be attained by prudence and industry ; if the line be cut or jagged at the upper end, it denotes much sickness.   If this line be cut by any line coming from the mount of Venus, it declares the person to be unfortunate in love, and business also, and threatens him with sudden death.   A cross between the line of life and the table line, shows the person to be very liberal and charitable, and of a noble spirit.   Let us now see the signification of the table line.

The table line, when broad, and of a lovely colour, shows a healthful constitution, and a quiet and contented mind, and courageous spirit.   But if it has crosses towards the little finger, it threatens the party with much affliction by sickness.   If the line be doubled, or divided in three parts, in any of the extremities, it shows the party to be of a generous temper, and of a good fortune to support it ; but if this line be forked at the end, it threatens the person shall suffer by jealousies, fears, and doubts, and with the loss of riches got by deceit.   If three points such as these . . . are found in it, they denote the person prudent and liberal, a lover of learning and of good temper.   If it spreads itself to the fore and middle fingers, and ends blunt, it denotes preferment. Let us now see what is signified by the middle finger.

The line has in it sometimes (for there is scarce one hand in which it varies not) divers significant characters.   Many, small lines between this and the table line threatens the party with sickness, and also gives him hopes of recovery. A half cross branching into this line, declares the person shall have honour, riches, and good success in all his undertakings.   A half moon denotes cold and watery distempers, but a sun or star upon this line promiseth prosperity and riches.   This line doubled in a woman, shows she will have several husbands, but without any children by them.

The line of Venus, if it happens to be cut or divided near the forefinger, threatens ruin to the party, and that it shall befall him by means of bad company. Two crosses upon this line, one being on the forefinger, and the other bending towards the little finger, shows the party to be weak and inclined to modesty and virtue ; and, indeed, it generally denotes modesty in women ; and therefore, those who desire such wives, usually choose them by this standard.

The life line, if it be straight and crossed by other lines, shows the person to be of a sound judgment, and a piercing understanding ; but if it be winding, crooked, and bending outward, it shows deceit and flattery, and that the person is not to be trusted. If it makes a triangle, or a quadrangle, it shows a person to be of a noble descent and ambitious.

The plain of Mars being in the hollow of the hand, or if the line passes through it, which renders it very plain, is fortunate : this plain being hollowed, and the lines crooked and distorted, threaten the party to fall by his ill conduct. When the lines begin at the wrist, long within the plain, reaching the crown of the hand, they show the person to be one given to quarrelling, often in broils and of a hot and fiery spirit, by which he shall suffer much damage. If deep, large crosses in the middle of the plain, it shows the party shall obtain honour by martial exploits ; but if it be a woman, that she shall have several husbands.

The line of death is fatal, when any crosses or broken lines appear in it ; for they threaten the person with sickness and short life. A bloody spot in the line denotes a violent death. A star like a comet, threatens ruin by war, and death by pestilence ; but if a bright sun appear therein, it promises long life and prosperity.

As for the lines in the wrist, being fair they denote good fortune, but if crossed and broken, the contrary.

Thus much with respect to the several lines in the hand. Now as to the judgment to be made from the hand itself : If the hand be soft and long, and lean withal, it denotes a person of good understanding, a lover of peace, and honest, discreet, serviceable, a good neighbour, and a lover of learning. He whose hands are very thick and very short, is thereby signified to be faithful, strong, and laborious, and one that cannot long retain his anger. He whose hands are full of hairs, and those hairs thick and great ones, and his fingers withal crooked, he is thereby noted to be luxurious, vain, false, of a dull understanding and disposition, and more foolish than wise. He whose hands and fingers do bend upwards, is commonly a man liberal, serviceable, a keeper of secrecy, and apt to be poor (for he is seldom fortunate), to do any man courtesy. He whose hand is stiff and will not bend at the upper joint, near his finger, is always a wretched, miserable person, covetous, obstinate, incredulous, and one that will believe nothing that contradicts his own private interest. And thus much shall suffice to be said of judgment made by palmistry.

Of the Nails of the Fingers.

Broad nails show the person to be bashful, fearful, but of gentle nature. When there is a certain white mark at the extremity of them, it shows that the person has more honesty than subtlety, and that his worldly substance will be impaired through negligence. White nails and long, denote much sickness and infirmity, especially fevers, an indication of strength and deceit by women. If upon the white anything appears at the extremity that is pale, it denotes short life by sudden death, and the person to be given to melancholy. When there appears a certain mixed redness, of divers colours, at the beginning of the nails, it shows the person to be choleric and quarrelsome. When the extremity is black, it is a sign of husbandry. Narrow nails denote the person to be inclined to mischief, and to do injury to his neighbour. Long nails show the person to be good-natured, but mistrustful, and loves reconciliation rather than differences. Oblique nails signify deceit, and want of courage. Little and round nails denote obstinate anger and hatred. If they be crooked at the extremity, they show pride and fierceness. Round nails show a choleric person, yet soon reconciled, honest, and a lover of secret sciences. Fleshy nails denote the person to be mild in his temper, idle, and lazy. Pale and black nails show the person to be very deceitful to his neighbour, and subject to many diseases. Red and marked nails signify a choleric and martial nature, given to cruelty ; and, as many little marks as there are, they speak of so many evil desires.

Several Characters or Semblances of Letters, and Lines in the Hand, as they tend to signify Riches, Honour, Long Life, Marriage, Short Life, Poverty, Loss, and Number of Wives, Children, Sickness, untimely Death, and many other things, according to the art of Palmistry, etc.

There are in this case divers letters, lines appearing in the hand, by which the wise in all ages have given judgment in the foregoing premises.

If the letter A be found on the Mount of Jupiter, or at the root of the middle finger, promises growing fortune, and perhaps considerable preferments by the favour of princes and great men.

If B be found on the Mount of the Sun, which is at the root of the finger, it signifies length of days, prosperity, and much to be beloved, as also a virtuous person.

If C, with a star over it, appears on the Mount of Venus, it gives the person early and happy life.

If the letter L be on the Mount of Saturn, which is at the root of the middle finger, and cut with cross lines, it denotes the party to be under much affliction, to be given to melancholy, and short-lived.

The letter K on the Mount of Mercury, which is at the root of the little finger, denotes the party to rise to preferment by ingenuity and marriage.

The letter D on the Mount of the Moon, denotes the party kind, good-natured, and much beloved.

The letter G in the Plain of Mars, near the Line of Life, speaks the party to be of a violent temper, given to anger, and threatens him or her with sudden untimely death ; however, to a woman it promises a husband that grows great in military affairs ; and thus much for characters of this kind.

HOW TO TELL FORTUNES BY MOLES.

THESE little marks on the skin, although they appear to be the effect of chance or accident, and might easily pass with the unthinking for things of no moment are nevertheless of the utmost consequence, since from their colour, situation, size, and figure, may be accurately gathered the temper of, and the events that will happen to, the person bearing them. As our philosopher, who was a most excellent anatomist, made these signs form a very particular branch of his studies, the result of his great labours and long experience will, we doubt not, be found very agreeable to our readers, and we shall accordingly proceed to give them a faithful translation of his observations. To enable them to turn more easily to the definitions, we have arranged them under heads.

On the Wrist or between that and the Finger ends.— Shows the person to be of an ingenious and industrious turn, faithful in his engagements, amorous and constant in his affections, rather of a saving disposition, with a great degree of sobriety and regularity in his dealings. It foreshows a comfortable acquisition of fortune, with a good partner, and beautiful children ; but some disagreeable circumstance will happen about the age of thirty, which will continue four or five years. In a man, it denotes being twice married in a woman, only once, but that she will survive her husband

Below the Elbow and the Wrist.—Shows a placid and cheerful disposition, industry, and a love of reading, particularly books of science ; it foretells much prosperity and happiness toward the middle of life, but after having undergone many hardships, if not imprisonment, it also denotes that your eldest son will rise to honours in the State, and marry a woman, not of his own country, who will bring him much riches.

Near either Elbow.—Shows a restless and unsteady disposition, with a great desire of travelling, much discontented in the married state, and of an idle turn ; it indicates no very great prosperity rather of a sinking than a rising condition, with many unpleasant adventures, much to your discredit ; marriage with a person who will make you unhappy, and children who will be disobedient and cause you much trouble.

On the Right or Left Arm.—Shows a courageous disposition, great fortitude, resolution, industry, and conjugal fidelity, it foretells that the person will fight many battles, and be successful in all ; that you will be prosperous in your undertakings, obtain a decent competency, and live very happy ; it denotes that a man will be a widower at forty, but in a woman it shows that she will be survived by her husband.

On the Left Shoulder.—Shows a person of a quarrelsome and unruly disposition, always inclined to dispute for trifles, rather indolent but much inclined to the pleasures of love, and faithful to the conjugal vows. It denotes a life not much varied either with pleasures or misfortunes ; they indicate many children, and moderate success in business, but dangers by sea.

On the Right Shoulder.—Shows a person of a prudent and discreet temper, one possessed of much wisdom, given to great secrecy, very industrious, but not very amorous, yet faithful to conjugal ties ; it indicates great prosperity and advancement in life, a good partner, and many friends, with great profit from a journey to a distant country about the age of thirty-five.

On any part from the Shoulders to the Loins.— Shows an even and mild temper given to sloth, and rather cowardly, very amorous, but unfaithful ; it denotes decay in health and wealth, with troubles and difficulties in the decline of life, and much vexation from children.

On the Loins.—Shows industry and honesty, an amorous disposition, with great vigour, courage, and fidelity ; it foretells success in business and in love, many children, acquirement of riches and honours, with much travelling ; it also indicates a great loss by lending of money, and quarrelling among friends, who will attempt to deceive you.

On either Hip.—Shows a contented disposition, given to industry, and faithful in engagements, of an abstemious turn ; it foretells moderate success in life, with many children, who will undergo many hardships with great fortitude, and arrive at ease and affluence by dint of their industry and ingenuity.

On the Right Thigh.—Shows the person to be of an agreeable temper, and very courageous; it also denotes success in life, accumulation of riches by marriage, and many fine children, chiefly girls.

On the Left Thigh.—Shows a good and benevolent disposition, a great turn for industry, and little inclined to the pleasures of love ; it indicates many sorrows in life, great poverty, unfaithful friends, and imprisonment by false swearing.

On the Left Knee.—Shows a hasty and passionate disposition, extravagant and inconsiderate turn, with no great inclination to industry and honesty, but possessed of much benevolence ; it indicates good success in undertakings, particularly in contracts, a rich marriage and an only child.

On the Right Knee.—Shows an amiable temper, honest disposition, and a turn for amorous pleasures and industry ; it foretells great success in love, and the choice of a conjugal partner, with few sorrows, many friends, and dutiful children.

On either Leg.—Shows a person to be of a thoughtless, indolent disposition, and much given to extravagance and dissipation ; it denotes many difficulties through life, but that you will surmount them all ; it shows that imprisonment will happen to you at an early age, but that in general you will be more fortunate than otherwise ; you will marry an agreeable person, who will survive you, by whom you will have four children, two of which will die young.

On either Ankle.—Shows an effeminate disposition, given to foppery in dress, and cowardice in a man ; but in a woman it denotes courage, wit and activity ; they foretell success in life, with an agreeable partner, accumulation of honours and riches, and much pleasure in the affairs of love.

On either Foot.—Shows a melancholy and inactive disposition, given to reading, and a sedentary life ; they foretell sickness and unexpected misfortunes, with many sorrows and much trouble, an unhappy choice of a partner for life, with disobedient and unfortunate children.

On the Right side of the Forehead or Right Temple. —Shows an active and industrious disposition, much given to the sports of love ; it denotes that the person will be very successful in life, marry an agreeable partner, and arrive at unexpected riches and honors, and have a son who will become a great man.

On the Right Eyebrow.—Shows a sprightly, active disposition, a great turn for gallantry, much courage, and great perseverance ; it denotes wealth, and success in love, war, and business ; that you will marry an agreeable mate, live happy, have children, and die at an advanced old age at a distance from home.

On the Left Eyebrow, Temple, or side of the Forehead.—Shows an indolent, peevish temper, a turn for debauchery and liquor, and very cowardly ; it foretells poverty, imprisonment, and disappointments in all your undertakings, with undutiful children, and a bad-tempered partner.

On the outside Corner of either Eye.—Shows a sober, honest, and steady disposition ; it foretells a violent death, after a life considerably varied by pleasures and misfortunes ; in general, it foreshadows that poverty will keep at a distance.

On either Cheek.—Shows an industrious, benevolent, and sober disposition, given to be grave and solemn, but of a steady courage and unshaken fortitude ; it denotes a moderate success in life, neither becoming rich nor falling into poverty ; it also foretells an agreeable and industrious partner, with two children, who will do better than the parents.

On the Chin.—Shows an amiable and tranquil disposition, industrious, and much inclined to travelling ; it denotes that the person will be highly successful in life, accumulating a large and splendid fortune, with many respectable and worthy friends, an agreeable conjugal partner, and fine children ; but it also denotes losses by sea and in foreign countries.

On either Lip. – Shows a delicate appetite, a sober disposition ; of an industrious and benevolent turn ; it denotes that the person will be successful in undertakings, particularly in love affairs ; that you will rise above your present condition, and be greatly respected and esteemed ; that you will endeavour to obtain some situation, in which you will at first prove unsuccessful, but afterwards prevail.

On the Nose.—Shows a hasty and passionate disposition, faithful to engagements, candid, open, and sincere in friendship, courageous and honest, but very petulant, and rather given to drink ; it denotes great success through life and in love affairs, that you will become rich, marry well, have fine children, and be much esteemed by your neighbours and acquaintances ; that you will travel much, particularly by water.

On the Throat.—Shows a friendly and generous disposition, of a sober turn, given to industry ; it denotes riches by marriage, and great success afterward in your undertakings, with fine children, who will go to a far distant country, where they will marry, grow rich, and return to their native land.

On the side of the Neck.—Shows a meek and sober disposition, but firm and steady in friendship, rather given to industry ; it denotes much sickness, and that you will be in great danger of suffocation, but that you will rise to unexpected honours and dignity, receive large legacies, and grow very rich ; but also that your children will fall into poverty and disgrace.

On the Right Breast.—Shows an intemperate and indolent disposition, rather given to drink, strongly attached to the joys of love ; it denotes much misfortune in life, with a sudden reverse from riches to poverty ; many unpleasant and disagreeable accidents, with a sober and industrious partner, many children, mostly girls, who will all marry well, and be a great comfort to your old age ; it warns you to beware of pretended friends, who will harm you much.

On the Left Breast.—Shows an industrious and sober disposition, much given to walking ; it denotes great success in life and in love, that you will accumulate riches, and have many children, mostly boys, who will make their fortunes by sea.

On the Bosom.—Shows a quarrelsome and unhappy temper, given to low debauchery, and exceedingly indolent, and unsteady ; it denotes a life neither very prosperous nor very miserable, but passed without many friends or much esteem.

Under the Left Breast, over the Heart.—Shows a rambling and unsettled disposition, given to drinking and little careful of your actions.   In a woman it indicates sincerity in love, industry, and a strict regard for character ; in life it denotes a varied mixture of good and bad fortune, the former rather prevailing ; it denotes imprisonment for debt, but not of long duration ; to a woman it denotes children who will become rich, live happy and respected, and marry well.

On the Right Side near any part of the Ribs.—Shows

an indolent, cowardly disposition, given to excessive drinking, of an inferior capacity; it denotes an easy life, rather of poverty than riches, little respected, a partner of an uneven and disagreeable temper, with undutiful children, who will fall into many difficulties.

On the Stomach.—Shows an indolent and slothful disposition, given to gluttony, very selfish, addicted to the pleasures of love and drink, negligent of dress, and cowardly; it denotes small success in life, many crosses, some imprisonment, and travelling, with losses by sea; but it foretells that you will marry an agreeable partner, of a sweet temper, have children who will be industrious and become very respectable in life.

Important Facts.—We shall remark to our readers, that it is of much importance to be particular in ascertaining the exact situation of the mole, its form, whether it be round, angular, or oblong; also its size and colour, because these variations add or diminish the degree of those qualities and events which our author's explanation has attached to each; for example, if the mole be perfectly round, then it denotes much good fortune; if of an angular form, a mixture of good and bad fortune; if oblong, then a moderate portion of good, a kind of happy medium; the deeper the colour, the more powerful will be either the good or bad fortune indicated; the lighter in colour, either will be in a less degree, as our author has uniformly spoken of a mediate colour neither dark nor light. if it be very hairy, it denotes many misfortunes, but not so if only a few long hairs grow upon it, then it shows prosperity in your undertakings; again, the larger the mole is, the more serious will be either the prosperity or adversity predicted; and the smaller it is, the less of either will fall to your share; our author has taken the middling size.

THE MOON.

JUDGMENTS DRAWN FROM THE MOON'S AGE.

1.   A child born within twenty-four hours after the new moon, will be fortunate and live to a good old age. Whatever is dreamt on that day will be fortunate and pleasing to the dreamer.

2.   The second day is very lucky for discovering things lost, or hidden treasure; the child born on this day shall thrive.

3.   The child born on the third day will be fortunate through persons in power, and whatever is dreamed will prove true.

4. The fourth day is bad; persons falling sick on this day rarely recover.

5. The fifth day is favourable to begin a good work, and the dreams will be tolerably successful; the child born on this day will be vain and deceitful.

6. The sixth day the dreams will not immediately come to pass, and the child born will not live long.

7. On the seventh day do not tell your dreams, for much depends on concealing them; if sickness befalls you on this day, you will soon recover; the child born will live long, but have many troubles.

8. On the eighth day the dreams will come to pass; whatever business a person undertakes on this day will prosper.

9. The ninth day differs very little from the former; the child born on this day will arrive at great riches and honour.

10. The tenth day is likely to be fatal; those who fall sick will rarely recover; but the child born on this day will live long and be a great traveller.

11. The child that is born on the eleventh day will be much devoted to religion, of an engaging form and manners.

12. On the twelfth day the dreams are rather fortunate, and the child born shall live long.

13. On the thirteenth day the dreams will prove true in a very short time.

14. If you ask a favour of anyone on the fourteenth day, it will be granted.

15. The sickness that befalls a person on the fifteenth day is likely to prove mortal.

16. The child that is born on the sixteenth day will be of very ill-manners and unfortunate; it is nevertheless a good day for the buying and selling all kinds of merchandise.

17. The child born on the seventeenth day will be very foolish; it is a very unfortunate day to transact any kind of business, or contract marriage.

18. The child born on the eighteenth day will be valiant but will suffer considerable hardships; if a female, she will be chaste and industrious, and live respected to a great age.

19. The nineteenth day is dangerous; the child born will be very ill-disposed and malicious.

20. On the twentieth day the dreams are true, but the child born will be dishonest.

21. The child born on the twenty-first day will grow up healthy and strong, but be of a very selfish, ungenteel turn of mind.

22. The child born on the twenty-second day will be fortunate; he or she will be of a cheerful countenance, religious, and much beloved.

23. The child that is born on the twenty-third day will be of an ungovernable temper, will forsake his friends, and choose to wander about in a foreign country, and will be very unhappy through life.

24. The child born on the twenty-fourth day will achieve many heroic actions, and will be much admired for his extraordinary abilities.

25. The child born on the twenty-fifth day will be very wicked; he will meet with many dangers, and is likely to come to an ill end.

26. On the twenty-sixth day the dreams are certain; the child then born will be rich, and much esteemed.

27. The twenty-seventh day is very favourable for dreams, and the child then born will be of a sweet and amiable disposition.

28. The child born on the twenty-eighth day will be the delight of his parents, but will not live to any great age.

29. The child born on the twenty-ninth day will experience many hardships, though in the end they may turn out happily. It is good to marry on this day; and business begun on this day will be prosperous.

30. The child that is born on the thirtieth day will be fortunate and happy, and well skilled in the arts and sciences.

A BRIEF PROGNOSTICATION CONCERNING CHILDREN BORN
ON ANY DAY OF THE WEEK.

Sunday, the child shall be of long life, and obtain riches.

Monday, weak, and of an effeminate temper, which seldom brings a man to honour.

Tuesday, worse: though he may, with extraordinary vigilance, conquer the inordinate desires to which he will be subject, still he will be in danger of dying by violence, if he uses not great precaution.

Wednesday, he shall be given to the study of learning and shall profit thereby.

Thursday, he shall arrive to great honour and dignity.

Friday, he shall be of a strong constitution.

Saturday is another bad day; notwithstanding, the child may come to good, though it be seldom; but most children born on this day are of a heavy, dull, and dogged disposition.

HOW TO TELL FORTUNES BY CARDS

A S many of those events about to happen may be easily gathered from the cards, we have here affixed the definition which each card in the pack bears separately ; by the combining them the reader must judge for himself, observing the following directions in laying them out :—First, the person whose fortune is to be told, if a man, must choose one of the four kings to represent himself—if a woman, she must select one of the queens ; the chosen card will stand for the husband or wife, or lover of the party whose fortune is to be told, and the knave of the suit for the most intimate person of their family ; you must then shuffle and cut the cards well, and let the person whose fortune is to be ascertained, cut them three times, showing the bottom card ; this must be repeated three times ; then shuffle them again, let them be cut once, and display them in rows on a table, taking care always to have an odd number in each row, nine is the right number, and to place your cards exactly under each other ; after this consult the situation in which the person stands by the definition we have here annexed to each card, and after having repeated it three times, form your conclusion, remember that every thing is within your circle as far as you can count thirteen any way from the card that represents the person, his wife, or her husband, and their intimate friend ; and also that of the thirteenth card every way is of the greatest consequence ; either the whole pack, or only the picked cards may be used.

Another mode with the picked cards is to shuffle and cut them, take three cards from the top—if there be two of a suit, take out the highest card ; if three, take all ; when you have gone through the pack, shuffle and cut the remainder, and do as before, and repeat the same a third time ; than take a general view of all the cards drawn, and next couple them, a top and bottom card, then shuffle and cut them into three heaps, laying one apart in the first round to form a fourth heap ; the first heap at the left hand relates to yourself entirely, the next to your family, and the third is the confirmation of the former two ; you must proceed a second and third time, adding each time one to the single card, then three single cards gives the connection of the operation ; observe you must add the card which represents the person whose fortune is consulted to the three, if it be not there already.

The Ace of Clubs.—Promises great wealth, much prosperity in life, and tranquillity of mind.

The King of Clubs.—Announces a man who is humane,

upright, affectionate, and faithful in all his engagements ; he will be very happy himself, and make every one with whom he has connection so, if he can.

The Queen of Clubs.—Shows a tender, mild, and rather amorous disposition.

The Knave of Clubs.—Shows a generous, sincere and zealous friend, who will exert himself warmly for your interest and welfare.

The Ten of Clubs.—Denotes great riches to come speedily from an unexpected quarter ; but it also threatens that you will at the same time lose some very dear friend.

The Nine of Clubs.—Shows that you will displease some of your friends, by too steady an adherence to your own way of thinking, nor will your success in the undertaking reconcile them to you, or procure you your own approbation.

The Eight of Clubs.—Shows the person to be covetous, and extremely fond of money ; that he will obtain it, but that it will rather prove a torment than a comfort to him, as he will not make proper use of it.

The Seven of Clubs.—Promises the most brilliant fortune, and the most exquisite bliss that this world can afford ; but beware of the opposite sex, from them alone you can experience misfortune.

The Six of Clubs.—Shows you will engage in a very lucrative partnership, and that your children will behave well.

The Five of Clubs.—Declares that you will be shortly married to a person who will mend your circumstances.

The Four of Clubs.—Shows frequent change of object.

The Trey of Clubs.—Shows that you will be three times married, and each time to a wealthy person.

The Deuce of Clubs.—Shows that there will be some unfortunate opposition to your favourite inclination, which will disturb you.

The Ace of Diamonds.—Shows a person who is fond of rural sports, a great builder, and a gardener ; one who delights in planting and laying out groves, woods, shrubberies, and other such amusements ; but that his enterprises of this nature will have success or disappointment according to the cards that are near it ; it likewise signifies a letter.

The King of Diamonds.—Shows a man of a fiery temper, preserving his anger long, seeking for opportunities of revenge, and obstinate in his resolutions.

The Queen of Diamonds.—Signifies that the woman will not be a steady and industrious housekeeper ; that she will be fond of company, be a coquette, and not overvirtuous

The Knave of Diamonds.—However nearly related, he will look more to his own interest than yours, he will be tenacious of his own opinion, and will fly off if contradicted.

The Ten of Diamonds.—Promises a country husband or a wife with great wealth and many children ; the card next to it will tell the number of children, it also signifies a purse of gold.

The Nine of Diamonds.—Declares that the person will be of a roving disposition, never contented with his lot, and forever meeting with vexations and disappointments, and risks a shameful end.

The Eight of Diamonds.—Shows that the person, in his youth, will be an enemy to marriage, and thus run the risk of dying unmarried ; but that if he does marry, it will be late in life, and then it will be with some person whose disposition is so ill-assorted to theirs, that it will be the cause of misfortunes.

The Seven of Diamonds.—Shows that you will spend your happiest days in the country, where if you remain, your happiness will be uninterrupted ; but if you come to town, you will be tormented by the infidelity of your conjugal partner, and the squandering of your substance.

The Six of Diamonds.—Shows an early marriage and premature widowhood ; but that the second marriage will probably make you worse off.

The Five of Diamonds.—Shows you a well-assorted marriage with a mate who will punctually perform the hymenial duties, and that you will have good children, who will keep you from grief.

The Four of Diamonds.—Shows the evil life of the person you will be married to, and very great vexation to yourself, through the whole course of your life.

The Trey of Diamonds.—Shows that you will be engaged in quarrels, lawsuits, and domestic disagreements ; your partner for life will be of a vixen and abusive temper, fail in the performance of the nuptial duties, and make you unhappy.

The Deuce of Diamonds.—Shows that your heart will be engaged in love, at an early period ; that your parents will not approve your choice, and that if you marry without their consent, they will hardly forgive you.

The Ace of Hearts.—Signifies merry-making, feasting, and good humour ; if the ace be attended by spades, it foretells quarrelling in your cups, and ill-temper to your family while you are in a state of intoxication ; if by hearts, it shows cordiality and affection between the parties ; if by diamonds, your feast will be from home, perhaps in the country ; if by clubs, the occasion of the meeting will be upon some bargain or agreement ; if your ace of hearts is in the neighbourhood of face cards of both sexes, with clubs near it, it will be about a match-making ; if all the face cards are kings or knaves, or both, it will concern the buying or selling of some personal property ; if all queens, it will regard conciliation between parties, and if queens and knaves, it will be about the reconciliation and reunion of a married couple.

The King of Hearts.—Shows a man of a fair complexion, of an easy and good-natured disposition, but inclined to be hasty and passionate, and rash in his undertakings.

The Queen of Hearts.—Shows a woman of a very fair complexion, or of great beauty, her temper rather fiery, verging on the termagant, one who will not make an obedient wife, nor one who will be very happy in her own reflections.

The Knave of Hearts.—Is a person of no particular sex, but always the dearest friend, or nearest relation of the consulting party, ever attractive and intruding, equally jealous of doing harm or good as the whim of the moment strikes, passionate and hard to be reconciled, but always zealous and warm in the cause of the consulting party, though probably not according to their fancy, as they will be as industrious to prevent their schemes as to forward them, if they do not accord with his own disposition.

You must pay great attention to the cards that stand next to the knave, as from them alone you can judge whether the person it represents will favour your inclination or not.

The Ten of Hearts.—Shows good nature and many children ; it is a corrective to the bad tidings of the cards, but may stand next to it ; and if its neighbouring cards are of good import, it ascertains and confirms their value.

The Nine of Hearts.—Promises wealth, grandeur, and high esteem ; if cards that are unfavourable stand near to it, you must look for disaappointment and reverse ; if favourable cards follow these last at a small distance, expect to retrieve your losses, whether of peace or of goods.

The Eight of Hearts.—Points out a strong inclination to get intoxicated ; this, if accompanied with unfavourable cards, will be attended with loss of property, decay of health, and falling off of friends ; if by favourable cards, it indicates reformation and recovery from the bad consequences of the former.

The Seven of Hearts.—Shows the person to be of a fickle and unfaithful disposition, addicted to vice and subject to the mean art of recrimination, to excuse themselves, although without foundation.

The Six of Hearts.—Shows a generous, open, and credulous disposition, easily imposed upon, and ever the dupe of flatterers, but the good-natured friend of the distressed. If this card comes before your king or queen, you will be the dupe, if after, you will have the better.

The Five of Hearts.—Shows a wavering, unsteady disposition never attached to one object, and free from any violent passion or attachment.

The Four of Hearts.—Shows that the person will not be married until very late in life, and that this will probably proceed from too great a delicacy in making a choice.

The Trey of Hearts.—Shows that your own imprudence will greatly contribute to your experiencing the ill-will of others

The Deuce of Hearts.—Shows that extraordinary success and good fortune will attend the person, though if unfavourable cards attend, this will be a long time delayed.

The Ace of Spades.—Totally relates to the affairs of love, without specifying whether lawful or unlawful.

The King of Spades.—Shows a man who is ambitious, and certainly successful at court, or with some great man who will have it in his power to advance him ; but let him beware of reverse.

The Queen of Spades.—Shows a person who will be corrupted by the great of both sexes.

The Knave of Spades.—Shows a person who, although they have your welfare at heart, will be too indolent to pursue it with zeal, unless you take frequent opportunities of rousing their attention.

The Ten of Spades.—Is a card of bad import, it will in a great measure counteract the good effect of the other cards ; but unless it be seconded by other unfortunate cards its influence may be gotten over.

The Nine of Spades.— Is the worst card in the whole pack ; it portends dangerous sickness, a total loss of fortune, cruel calamity, and endless dissension in your family.

The Eight of Spades.—Shows that you will experience strong opposition from your friends, whom you imagine to be such ; if this card comes close to you, abandon your enterprise and adopt another plan.

The Seven of Spades.—Shows the loss of a most valuable friend, whose death will plunge you into very great distress.

The Six of Spades.—Announces a mediocrity of fortune, and very great uncertainty in your undertakings.

The Five of Spades.—Will give very little interruption to your success ; it promises you good luck in the choice of a companion for life, that you will meet with one very fond of you, and immoderately attached to the joys of hymen, but shows your temper to be rather sullen.

The Four of Spades.—Shows speedy sickness, and that your friends will injure your fortune.

The Trey of Spades.—Shows that you will be unfortunate in marriage, and that you will be made happy.

The Deuce of Spades.—Always signifies a coffin, but whom it is for, must depend entirely on the other cards that are near.

HOW TO TELL FORTUNES BY TEA-LEAVES OR COFFEE-GROUNDS.

Directions to Pour out the Coffee-grounds.—Pour the grounds of coffee in a white cup, shake them well about in it, so that their particles may cover the whole surface of the cup ; then reverse it into the saucer, that all the super-fluous parts may be drained, and the figures required for fortune-telling be formed. The person that acts the fortune-teller must always bend his thoughts upon him or her that wishes to have their fortune told, and upon their rank and profession, in order to give plausibility to their predictions. It is not to be expected, upon taking up the cup, that the figures will be accurately represented as they are in the pack, and it is quite sufficient if they bear some resemblance to any of the thirty-two emblems ; and the more fertile the fancy shall be of the person that inspects the cup, the more he will discover in it. In other respects, every one who takes pleasure in this amusement, must himself be a judge, under what circumstances he is to make changes in point of time, speaking just as it suits, in the present, the past, or the future ; in the same manner their ingenuity ought to direct them when to speak, more or less pointedly and determinately, with regard to sex.

The Leaf of Clover.—Is, as well here as in common life, a lucky sign. Its different position in the cup alone makes the difference ; because, if it is on the top, it shows that the good fortune is not far distant ; but it is subject to delay, if it is in the middle or at the bottom. Should clouds surround it, it shows that many disagreeables will attend the good for-tune ; in the clear, it prognosticates serene and undisturbed happiness, as bright as and parth wishes.

The Serpent.—Always the emblem of falsehood and enmity, is likewise here a general sign of an enemy. On the top, or in the middle of the cup, it promises to the consulting party the triumph he desires over his enemy ; but he will not obtain it so easy if the serpent be in the thick or cloudy part. By the letter which frequently appears near the emblem, the enemy may be easily guessed, it makes the initial of his name.

The Letter.—By letters we communicate to our friends either pleasant or unpleasant news, and such is the case here ; if this emblem is in the clear part, it denotes the speedy arrival of welcome news ; surrounded with dots, it announces the arrival of a considerable remittance in money ; but hemmed in by clouds, it is quite the contrary and forebodes some melancholy or bad tidings, a loss or some other sinister accident. If it be in the clear, and accompanied by a heart, lovers may expect a letter, which secures to the party the possession of the beloved object ; but in the thick it denotes a refusal.

The Coffin.—The emblem of death, prognosticates the same thing here, or at least a long and tedious illness, if it be in the thick or turbid. In the clear, it denotes long life. In the thick, at the top, it signifies a considerable estate left to the party by some rich relation ; in the same manner at the bottom, it shows that the deceased is not so nearly related to the consulting party.

The Star.—Denotes happiness if in the clear, and at the top of the cup ; clouded, or in the thick, it signifies long life, though exposed to various troubles. If dots are about it, it foretells great fortune, wealth, high respectability, etc. Several stars denotes so many good and happy children ; but surrounded with dashes, shows that your children will cause you grief and vexation in your old age, and that you ought to prevent it by giving them a good education in time.

The Dog.—Being at all times the emblem of fidelity or envy, has also a two-fold meaning here. At the top, in the clear, it signifies true and faithful friends, but if his image be surrounded with clouds and dashes, it shows that those whom you take for your friends are not to be depended on ; but if the dog be at the bottom of the cup, you have to dread the effects of extreme envy or jealousy.

The Lily.—If this emblem be at the top, or in the middle of the cup, it signifies that the consulting party either has or will have a virtuous spouse ; if it be at the bottom it denotes quite the reverse. In the clear, the lily further betokens long and happy life ; if clouded or in the thick, it portends trouble and vexation, especially on the part of one's relations.

The Cross.—Be it one or more, it generally predicts

adversities. Its position varies, and so do the circumstances. If it be at the top, and in the clear, it shows that the misfortunes of the party will soon be at an end, or that he will easily get over them ; but if it appears in the middle or at the bottom in the thick, the party must expect many severe trials ; if it appears with dots, either in the clear or the thick, it promises a speedy change of one's sorrow.

The Clouds.—If they be more light than dark, you may expect a good result from your hopes ; but if they are black, you must give it up. Surrounded with dots, they imply success in trade, and in all your undertakings ; but the brighter they are, the greater will be your happiness.

The Sun.—An emblem of the greatest luck and happiness, if in the clear ; but in the thick it bodes a great deal of sadness ; surrounded by dots or dashes denotes that an alteration will easily take place.

The Moon.—If it appears in the clear, it denotes high honours ; in the dark or the thick part, it implies sadness, which will, however, pass without great prejudice. But if it be at the bottom of the cup, the consulting party will be very fortunate both by water and land.

Mountains.—If it represents only the mountain, it indicates the favour of people of high rank ; but several of them, especially in the thick, are signs of powerful enemies ; in the clear, they signify the contrary, or friends in high life, who are endeavouring to promote the consulting party.

The Tree.—One tree only, be it in the clear or thick part, points out lasting good health ; several trees denote that your wishes will be accomplished. If they are encompassed with dashes, it is a token that your fortune is in its blossom, and will require some time to bring it to maturity. If they are accompanied by dots, it is a sign that you will make your fortune in the country where you reside.

The Pedestrian.—Denotes, in general, a merchant, good business, pleasant news, and the recovery of lost things. It also signifies that the consulting party will soon enlist, or get some engagement.

The Rider.—Denotes good news from abroad in money matters, a good situation in a foreign country, or good prospects. He that doubts his fortune is promised a lasting by this emblem.

The Woman.—Signifies much joy in general. If in the clear, this emblem has a more favourable signification than in the thick ; there it shows very great happiness ; here a great deal of jealousy. If dots surround the image, it explains the lady's wealth. The different positions in the cup show at the top and in the middle that you will be in love with a virgin ; but at the bottom it marks that she is a widow.

The Mouse.—As this animal lives by stealth, it is also an emblem here of theft or robbery ; if it be in the clear, it shows that you will get again what you lost in a wonderful manner ; but if it appears in the thick, you may renounce this hope.

The Roads, or serpentine lines, indicate ways ; if they are covered with clouds and in the thick, they are marks of past or future reverses ; but if in the clear and serene, are a token of some fortunate change ; encompassed with many points or dots, they signify gain of money, likewise long life.

The Ring signifies marriage. If the ring is in the clear, it portends happiness ; surrounded with clouds denotes that the party must use precaution lest they be deceived. It is most inauspicious if the ring appear at the bottom of the cup as it forebodes separation.

The Anchor implies success in business if at the bottom ; at the top in the clear, love and constancy ; in thick or cloudy parts, love, but inconstant.

The Cross, be there one or more, predicts adversity. At the top, in the clear, denotes the party's misfortunes to be near an end.

The Heart.—If in the clear, it signifies future pleasure ; if surrounded with dots, it promises recovery of money ; if two are together, it shows the party is about marrying.

The Rod shows difference with relations about legacies ; in the thick, illness.

Flowers.—If the party be married, he may expect good children, who will be a blessing to him in his old age.

Mountains.—If only one, it indicates the favour of people of high rank ; if clouded, powerful foes.

Fish imply lucky events by water, if in the clear ; if in the thick, the consulter will fish in troubled water.

CHARMS AND CEREMONIES.

For knowing Future Events.—Any person fasting on midsummer eve, and sitting in the church porch, will, at midnight, see the spirits of persons of that parish, who will die that year, come and knock at the church door in the order and succession in which they will die. One of these watchers there being several in company, fell into a profound sleep, so that he could not be waked ; whilst in this state his ghost was seen by the rest of his companions knocking at the church door. Any unmarried woman fasting on midsummer eve, and a midnight laying a clean cloth, with bread, cheese, and ale, and sitting down as if going to eat, the street door being left open, the person whom she is afterward to marry will come into the room, and drink to her by bowing ; and afterward filling the glass, will leave it on the table, and making another bow, retire. On St. Agnes's night, the 21st of January, take a row of pins, and pull out every one, one after another, saying a paternoster, on sticking a pin in your sleeve, and you will dream of him you shall marry. Another method to see a future spouse in a dream : the party inquiring must lie in a different county from that in which he commonly resides, and on going to bed, must knit the left garter about the right-legged stocking, letting the other garter and stocking alone ; and as you rehearse the following verses, at every comma knit a knot :

This knot I knit,
To know the thing I know not yet,
That I may see
The man that shall my husband be,
How he goes and what he wears,
And what he does all days and years.

Accordingly, in a dream he will appear with the insignia of his trade or profession. Another performed by charming the moon, thus : At the first appearance of the new moon, immediately after the new year's day, go out in the evening and stand over the spears of a gate or stile, and looking on the moon, repeat the following lines :

All hail to thee moon ! all hail to thee,
I prithee, good moon, reveal to me
This night who my husband must be !

The party will then dream of her future husband. A slice of the bride-cake, thricedrawn through the wedding-ring, and laid under the head of an unmarried woman, will make them dream of their future husband. The same is practised in the north with a piece of the groaning cheese.

To discover a Thief by the Sieve and Shears.—Stick the points of the shears in the wood of the sieve, and let two persons support it, balanced upright, with their two fingers ; then read a certain chapter in the Bible, and afterward ask St. Peter and St. Paul if A. or B. is the thief, naming all the persons you suspect. On naming the real thief, the sieve will suddenly turn round about.

To know whether a Woman shall have the Man she Wishes.—Get two lemon peels and wear them all day, one in each pocket, and at night rub the four posts of the bedstead with them ; if she is to succeed, the person will appear in her sleep, and present her with a couple of lemons ; if not, there is no hope.

To know what fortune your future Husband shall have.—Take a walnut, a hazel-nut, and a nutmeg, grate them together, and mix them with butter and sugar, and make them up into small pills, of which exactly nine must be taken on going to bed, and according to her dreams so will be the state of the person she will marry. If a gentleman, of riches ; if a clergyman, of white linen ; if a lawyer, of darkness ; if a trades-man, of odd noises and tumults ; if a soldier or sailor, of thunder and lightning ; if a servant, of rain.

To see a Future Husband.—On midsummer eve, just after sunset, three, five or seven young women are to go into a garden, in which there is no person, and each to gather a sprig of red sage, and then going into a room by themselves, set a stool in the middle of the room, and on it a clean basin full of rose-water, in which the sprigs of sage are to be put, and tying a line across the room, and on one side of the stool, each woman is to hang on it a clean shift turned the wrong side outward ; then all are to sit down in a row, on the opposite side of the stool, as far distant as the room will admit, not speaking a single word the whole time whatever they may see, and in a few minutes after twelve, each one's future husband will take her sprig out of the rose-water, and sprinkle her shift with it.

The Dumb Cake.—In order to make the dumb cake with perfection, it is necessary to strictly observe the following instructions : let any number of young women take a handful of wheaten flour, and from the moment the hand touches the flour, not a word is to be spoken by any of them during the rest of the process. Place it on a sheet of white paper ;

then sprinkle it over with as much salt as can be held between the finger and the thumb ; then one of the damsels must add as much water as will make it into dough ; which being done, each of the company must roll it up, and spread it out three times, and the last must then spread it thin and broad ; and each person must, at some distance from each other, make the first letters of her christian and surname with a large, new pin, toward the end of the cake (if more christian names than one, the first letter of each must be made) ; the cake must them be set before the fire, and each person must sit down in a chair, as far distant from the fire as the room will admit. not speaking a word all this while.   This must be done soon after eleven at night ; and between that and twelve, each person must turn the cake once, and in a few minutes after the clock strikes twelve, the husband of her who is to be first married, will appear to lay his hand on that part of the cake which is marked with her name.

SIGNS OF SPEEDY MARRIAGE, AND GOOD SUCCESS ATTENDING IT, BY SUNDRY SIGNS.

1. For a woman to have the first and last letters of her christian name the same as the man's surname, that makes love to her, denotes a great union and a generous love.

2. For a man to have the first and last letters of his christian name the same as the woman's surname, denotes the same.

3. To think on a party on a sudden awakening, without any meditation, on a Friday morning, that before had a place in the affection of man or woman, is a demonstration of love or extraordinary friendship.

4. If a ring falls accidentally off a man's finger, that is under no obligation of marriage, and runs directly to the feet of a maid or widow, it denotes that he is not only in love with the widow, but that a sudden marriage will ensue.

5. The singing of a robin-redbreast at your window, in the time of courtship, on a Wednesday, is a sign that you shall have the party desired.

6. If walking abroad with your sweetheart you perceive a pair of pigeons circle you round, it is a sign of marriage and happiness to ensue, with much content.

7. If a hare cross you on a Saturday morning, it promises happy days, riches, and pleasure.

SIGNS TO CHOOSE GOOD HUSBANDS AND WIVES.

1. If the party be of a ruddy complexion, high and full nosed, his eyebrows bending archwise, his eyes standing full

of a black and lively colour, it denotes him good-natured, ingenious, and born to good fortune, and the like in a woman, if born under the planet Jupiter.

2. If the party be phlegmatic, lean, and of a dusky complexion, given much to musing and melancholy, beware of such a one, of what sex soever.

3. An indifferent wide mouth, and full cheeks, smooth forehead, little ears, dark brown hair, and a chin proportionate to the face, is very promising.

4. An extraordinary long chin, with the under-lip larger than the upper, signifies a cross-grained person, fit for little business, yet given to folly.

5. A well-set broad chin in a man, his face being round, and not too great, and a dimple or dent in a woman's cheek or chin denotes they will come together and live happily.

SEVERAL QUERIES RESOLVED IN MATTERS OF LOVE AND BUSINESS, BY THROWING THE DIE, OR PRICKING AT A FIGURE, AFTER THE RULES OF THE FOLLOWING TABLE:

A	1	2	3	4	5	6
B	1	2	3	4	5	6
C	1	2	3	4	5	6
D	1	2	3	4	5	6
E	1	2	3	4	5	6

What number you throw, go to that, or else what number or letter you prick upon, they being covered with a piece of paper, through which you must prick.

AS TO WHAT KIND OF A HUSBAND A WIDOW OR MAID SHALL HAVE.

1. A handsome youth be sure you'll have,
   Brown hair'd, high nos'd ; he'll keep thee brave.
2. A man unto thy lot will fall,
   Straight, but neither short nor tall.
3. An honest tradesman is thy lot :
   When he proffers, slight him not.
4. Fair, ruddy, bushy-haired, is thy love,
   He'll keep thee well, and call thee still his dove.

5. A widower, though rich, thou'lt marry.
   You for a husband won't long tarry.
6. Proper and gay will be the man,
   That will thee wed, my pretty Nan.

WHETHER A MAID SHALL HAVE HIM SHE LOVES.

1. Be not too coy, he is your own,
   But through delay he may be gone.
2. He of your wishes does not know ;
   He'd soon comply if it were so.
3. Come, set thy heart at rest, I say,
   He will not plunder, and away.
4. Fear not, thy neighbour is the man,
   And he will have thee if he can.
5. Show him more kindness, he will speak—
   His heart with silence else will break.
6. Sigh thou no more ; he does relent,
   And his inconstancy repent.

HOW MANY HUSBANDS YOU MAY EXPECT, ETC.

1. Come in the town thou first shalt wed,
   A stranger next shall grace thy bed.
2. With one well lov'd, thy life shall be,
   And happy days, in marriage free.
3. The stars three husbands do presage,
   And thou shalt die in good old age.
4. Wed betimes, or else I fear,
   Thou wilt not much for wedlock care.
5. Too much pride will make thee tarry,
   Yet, after all that, thou shalt marry.
6. Accept the ring thy love doth give ;
   For long in wedlock he'll not live.

WHETHER IT IS BEST TO MARRY OR NOT.

1. Don't fear, thy husband will be kind,
   And it is one shall please thy mind.
2. If he be of complexion fair,
   For thee that man I do prepare.
3. Come, never fear, it will be well,
   Or say, I can no fortune tell.
4. Pray lose no time, for if you do,
   Age will come on, and you will rue.

5. If this match slips, you may long stay ;
   Then take kind Will without delay.
6. Cupid commands thee now to do 't.
   Then, prithee, make no more dispute.

QUERIES ABOUT FORTUNATE DAYS.

1. Each Monday in the year in different are,
   Yet the event thereof bids you beware.
2. On Tuesday cruel Mars doth reign ;
   Beware of strife, lest blows you gain.
3. On Wednesday witty projects make,
   For Mercury the rule does take.
4. Mild Jove rules Thursday, do not fear,
   'Tis prosperous throughout the year.
5. Fair Venus Friday does approve,
   And on that day does prosper love.
6. Saturn next does rule, beware,
   And take in hand no great affair.
   Lastly, Sol rules, whose golden aspect shows
   He all things mildly does to good dispose.

CHARMS, SPELLS, AND INCANTATIONS.

THE Three Keys.—Purchase three small keys, each at a different place, and going to bed, tie them together with your garter, and place them in your left-hand glove, along with a small flat dough cake, on which you have pricked the first letters of your sweetheart's name ; put them in your bosom when you retire to rest ; if you are to have that young man you will dream of him, but not else. This charm is the most effectual on the first or third of a new moon.

The Magic Ring.—Borrow a wedding-ring, concealing the purpose for which you borrow it ; but no widow's or pretended marriage ring will do, it spoils the charm ; wear it for three hours at least before you retire to rest, and then suspend it by a hair of your head over your pillow ; write within a circle resembling a ring, the sentence from the matrimonial service, beginning with, *with this ring I thee wed,* and round the circle write your own name at full length, and the figures that stand for your age, place it under your pillow, and your dream will fully explain whom you are to marry ; and what kind of a fate you will have with them. If your dream is too confused to remember it, or you do not dream at all, it is a certain sign you will never be married.

To know if a woman with Child will have a Girl or a Boy.—Write the proper names of the father and the mother, and the month she conceived with child ; count the letters in these words, and divide the amount by seven ; and then if the remainder be even, it will be a girl, if uneven, it will be a boy.

To know if a Child new-born shall live or not.—Write the proper names of the father and the mother, and of the day the child was born ; count the letters in these words, and to the amount add twenty-five, and then divide the whole by seven ; if the remainder be even, the child shall die, but if it be uneven, the child shall live.

To know how soon a Person will be married.—Get a green-pea pod, in which are exactly nine peas ; hang it over the door, and then take notice of the next person who comes in who is not of the family, nor of the same sex with yourself, and if it proves an unmarried individual, you will certainly be married within that year.

FORTUNE-TELLING GAMES WITH CARDS.

LOVERS' Hearts.—Four persons, but not more, may play at this game. Play this game exactly the same in every game, making the queen, who is to be called Venus, above the ace, the aces in this game only standing for one ; and hearts must be first led off by the person next the dealer. He or she who gets most tricks this way (each taking up their own, and no partnership) will have most lovers, and the king and queen of hearts in one hand shows matrimony at hand ; but woe to the unlucky one that gets no tricks at the deal, or does not hold a heart in their hand ; they will be unfortunate in love and long tarry before they marry.

Hymen's Lottery.—Let each one present deposit any sum agreed on, but of course some trifle ; put a complete pack of cards, well shuffled, in a bag or reticule. Let the party stand in a circle, and the bag being handed round, each draw three. Pairs of any kind are favourable omens of some good fortune about to occur to the party, and gets from the pool the sum back that each agreed to pay. The king of hearts is here made the god of love, and claims double, and gives a faithful swain to the fair one who has the good fortune to draw him ; if Venus, the queen of hearts, is with him, it is the conquering prize, and clears the pool ; fives and nines are reckoned crosses and misfortunes, and pay forfeit of the sum agreed on to the pool, besides the usual stipend at each new game ; three nines at one draw, shows the lady will be an old maid ; three fives, a bad husband.

Matrimony.—Let three, five or seven young women stand in a circle, and draw a card out of a bag ; she who gets the highest card, will be married the first of the company, whether she be at the present time maid, wife, or widow ; and she who has the lowest, has the longest time to stay ere the sun shines on her wedding-day ; she who draws the ace of spades will never bear the name of wife ; and she who has the nine of hearts in this trial, will have one lover too many to her sorrow

THE ORACULUM OR BOOK OF FATE.

Consulted by Napoleon Bonaparte.

How to work the Oraculum.

MAKE marks in four lines, one under another, in the following manner, making more or less in each line according to your fancy :

```
*  *  *  *  *  *  *  *  *
*  *  *  *  *  *  *  *  *  *
*  *  *  *  *  *  *  *  *  *  *
*  *  *  *  *  *  *  *  *  *  *  *  . . .
```

Then reckon the number of marks in each line, and if it be odd, mark down one dot ; if *even*, two dots.   If there be more than nine marks, reckon the surplus ones over that number only, viz :

The number of marks in the first line of the foregoing are *odd* ; therefore make one mark, thus .... *

In the second, *even*, so make two, thus................... **

In the third, *odd* again, make one mark only .... *

In the fourth, *even* again, two marks .... **

To Obtain the Answer.

You must refer to The Oraculum, at the top of which you will find a row of dots similar to those you have produced, and a column of figures corresponding with those prefixed to the questions : guide your eye down the column at the top of which you find the dots resembling your own, till you come to the letter on a line with the number of the question you are trying : then refer to the page having that letter at the top, and on a line with the dots which are similar to your own, you will find your *answer*.

The following are unlucky days, on which none of the questions should be worked, or any enterprise undertaken : January 1, 2, 4, 6, 10, 20, 22, ; February 6, 17, 28 ; March 24, 26 ; April 10, 27, 28 ; May 7, 8 ; June 27 ; July 17, 21 ; August 20, 22 ; September 5, 30 ; October 6 ; November 3, 29 ; December 6, 10, 15.

N.B.—It is not right to try a question twice in one day.

ORACULUM.

Numb.	Questions.	1	2	3	4	5	6	7	8	9	10	11	12	13	14	15	16
1	Shall I obtain my wish?	Q	A	B	C	D	E	F	G	H	I	K	L	M	N	O	P
2	Shall I have success in my undertakings?	P	Q	A	B	C	D	E	F	G	H	I	K	L	M	N	O
3	Shall I gain or lose in my cause?	O	P	Q	A	B	C	D	E	F	G	H	I	K	L	M	N
4	Shall I have to live in foreign parts?	N	O	P	Q	A	B	C	D	E	F	G	H	I	K	L	M
5	Will the stranger return from abroad?	M	N	O	P	Q	A	B	C	D	E	F	G	H	I	K	L
6	Shall I recover my property stolen?	L	M	N	O	P	Q	A	B	C	D	E	F	G	H	I	K
7	Will my friend be true in his dealings?	K	L	M	N	O	P	Q	A	B	C	D	E	F	G	H	I
8	Shall I have to travel?	I	K	L	M	N	O	P	Q	A	B	C	D	E	F	G	H
9	Does the person love and regard me?	H	I	K	L	M	N	O	P	Q	A	B	C	D	E	F	G
10	Will the marriage be prosperous?	G	H	I	K	L	M	N	O	P	Q	A	B	C	D	E	F
11	What sort of wife or husband shall I have?	F	G	H	I	K	L	M	N	O	P	Q	A	B	C	D	E
12	Will she have a son or a daughter?	E	F	G	H	I	K	L	M	N	O	P	Q	A	B	C	D
13	Will the patient recover from his illness?	D	E	F	G	H	I	K	L	M	N	O	P	Q	A	B	C
14	Will the prisoner be released?	C	D	E	F	G	H	I	K	L	M	N	O	P	Q	A	B
15	Shall I be lucky or unlucky this day?	B	C	D	E	F	G	H	I	K	L	M	N	O	P	Q	A
16	What does my dream signify?	A	B	C	D	E	F	G	H	I	K	L	M	N	O	P	Q
Numb.		1	2	3	4	5	6	7	8	9	10	11	12	13	14	15	16

A

* * * *	What you wish for you will shortly *obtain*.
* * * * *	Signifies trouble and sorrow.
* * * * *	Be very cautious what you do *this* day, lest trouble befall you.
* * * * *	The prisoner *dies*, and is regretted by his friends.
* * * * * * *	Life will be spared this time, to prepare for death.
* * * * * * *	A very handsome daughter.
* * * * *	You will have a virtuous woman or man for your wife or husband.
* * * * * * *	If you marry *this* person, you will have enemies where you little expect.
* * * * *	You had better decline *this* love, for it is neither constant nor true.

Decline your travels, for they will not be to your advantage.

There is a true and sincere friendship between you *both*.

You will not recover the stolen property.

The stranger *will*, with joy, soon return.

You will *not* remove from where you are at present.

The Lord *will* support you in a good cause.

You are *not* lucky—pray to God that He may help you.

■.

The luck that is ordained for you will be coveted by others.

Whatever your desires are, for the present decline them.

* * * * *	Signifies a favour or kindness from some person.
* * * * * *	There *are* enemies who would defraud and render you unhappy.
* * * * * * *	With great difficulty he will obtain pardon or release again.
* * * * * * *	The patient should be prepared to *leave* this world.
* * * * *	She will have a son, who will be learned and wise.
* * * * * *	A *rich* partner is ordained for you.
* * * * * *	By *this* marriage you will have great luck and prosperity.
* * * * *	*This* love comes from an upright and sincere heart.
* * * * * * *	God *will* surely travel with you, and bless you.

• • • • • • •	Beware of friends who are false and deceitful.
• ✴ • • • •	You *will* recover your property—unexpectedly.
• • • • •	Love prevents his return home at present.
• • • • • •	Your stay is *not* here : be therefore prepared for a change.
• • • • • • • •	You will have *no gain* ; therefore be wise and care-ful.

O.

• • • •	With the blessing of God, you *will* have great gain.
• • • • • •	Very unlucky indeed —pray to God for His assistance.
• • • • •	If your desires are *not* extravagant, they will be granted.
• • • • • •	Signifies peace and plenty between friends.

♦♦ ♦♦ ♦♦ ♦	Be well prepared *this* day, or you may meet with trouble.
♦♦ ♦♦ ♦ ♦♦	The prisoner *will* find it difficult to obtain his pardon or release.
♦♦ ♦ ♦ ♦	The patient *will yet* enjoy health and prosperity.
♦♦ ♦♦ ♦ ♦	She *will* have a daughter, and will require attention.
♦ ♦ ♦♦ ♦♦	The person has *not* a great fortune, but is in middling circumstances.
♦ ♦ ♦ ♦♦	Decline *this* marriage, or else you may be sorry.
♦♦ ♦ ♦♦ ♦♦	Decline a courtship which *may* be your destruction.
♦ ♦♦ ♦♦ ♦♦	Your travels are *in vain* ; you had better stay at home.
♦ ♦♦ ♦♦ ♦	You *may depend* on a true and sincere friendship.

✦ ✦ ✦✦ ✦	You must *not* expect to regain that which you have lost.
✦ ✦✦ ✦ ✦✦	*Sickness* prevents the traveller from seeing you.
✦✦ ✦✦ ✦✦ ✦✦	It *will* be your fate to stay where you now are.

D.

✦ ✦ ✦ ✦	You *will* obtain a great fortune in another country.
✦✦ ✦ ✦✦ ✦	By venturing freely, you *will* certainly gain doubly.
✦ ✦✦ ✦ ✦	God *will* change your misfortune into success and happiness
✦✦ ✦ ✦ ✦✦	Alter your intentions, or else you *may* meet poverty and distress.
✦✦ ✦✦ ✦✦ ✦	Signifies you have many impediments in accomplishing your pursuits
✦✦ ✦✦ ✦ ✦✦	Whatever may possess your inclinations this day, abandon them.

●● ● ● ●	The prisoner *will* get free again this time.
●● ●● ● ●	The patient's illness *will* be lingering and doubtful.
● ● ●● ●●	She will have a dutiful and handsome son.
● ● ● ●●	The person will be *low* in circumstances, but honest hearted.
●● ● ●● ●●	A marriage which *will add* to your welfare and prosperity.
● ●● ●● ●●	You love a person who does not speak well of you.
● ●● ●● ●	Your travels *will* be prosperous, if guided by prudence.
● ● ●● ●	He means *not* what he says, for his heart is false.
● ●● ● ●●	With some trouble and expense, you may regain your property.

You must *not* expect to see the stranger again.

E.

The stranger *will not* return so soon as you expect.

Remain among your friends, and you will do well.

You will hereafter *gain* what you seek.

You have *no luck*—pray to God, and strive honestly.

You will obtain your wishes by means of a friend.

Signifies you have enemies who will endeavour to ruin you.

Beware—an enemy is endeavouring to bring you to strife and misfortune.

The prisoner's sorrow and anxiety are great, and his release uncertain.

The patient *will* soon recover— there is no danger.

She will have a daughter, who will be honoured and respected.

Your partner *will* be fond of liquor, and will debase himself thereby.

This marriage will bring you to poverty, be therefore discreet

Their love is false to you, and true to others.

Decline your travels for the present, for they will be dangerous.

This person is serious and true, and deserves to be respected.

You will not recover the property you have lost.

F.

By persevering you *will* recover your property again.

** * ** *	It is out of the stranger's power to return.
* ** * *	You will *gain*, and be successful in foreign parts.
** * * **	A great fortune is ordained for you ; wait patiently.
** ** ** *	There is great hindrance to your success at present.
** ** * **	Your wishes are in *vain* at present.
** * * *	Signifies there is sorrow and danger before you.
** ** * *	*This* day is unlucky ; therefore, alter your intention.
* * ** **	The prisoner will be restored to liberty and freedom.
* * * **	The patient's recovery is doubtful.

✷✷ ✷ ✷✷ ✷✷	She will have a very fine *boy*.
✷ ✷✷ ✷✷ ✷✷	A worthy person, and a fine fortune.
✷ ✷✷ ✷✷ ✷	Your intentions would destroy your rest and peace
✷ ✷ ✷✷ ✷	*This* love is true and constant ; forsake it not.
✷ ✷✷ ✷ ✷✷	*Proceed* on your journey, and you will not have cause to repent it.
✷✷ ✷✷ ✷✷ ✷✷	If you trust *this* friend, you may have cause for sorrow.

Q.

✷ ✷ ✷ ✷	This friend exceeds all others in every respect.
✷✷ ✷ ✷✷ ✷	You must bear your loss with fortitude.
✷ ✷✷ ✷ ✷	The stranger will return unexpectedly.

✦✦ ✦ ✦ ✦✦	Remain at *home* with your friends, and you will escape misfortunes.
✦✦ ✦✦ ✦✦ ✦	You will meet no *gain* in your pursuits.
✦✦ ✦✦ ✦ ✦✦	Heaven will bestow its blessing on you.
✦✦ ✦ ✦ ✦	No.
✦✦ ✦✦ ✦ ✦	Signifies that you will shortly be out of the *power* of your enemies.
✦ ✦ ✦✦ ✦✦	*Ill-luck* awaits you—it will be difficult for you to escape it.
✦ ✦ ✦ ✦✦	The prisoner will be *released* by death only.
✦✦ ✦ ✦✦ ✦✦	By the blessing of God, the patient *will* recover.
✦ ✦✦ ✦✦ ✦✦	A daughter, but of a very sickly constitution.

* ** ** *	You will get an honest, young, and handsome partner.
* * ** *	Decline this marriage, else it may be to your sorrow.
* ** * **	Avoid this love.
** ** ** **	Prepare for a short journey, you will be recalled by unexpected events.

H.

* * * *	Commence your travels, and they will go on as you could wish.
** * ** *	Your pretended friend hates you secretly.
* ** * *	Your hopes to recover your property are vain.
** * * **	A certain affair prevents the stranger's return immediately.
** ** ** *	Your fortune you will find in abundance abroad.

⁂	Decline the pursuit, and you will do well.
⁂	Your expectations are vain—you will not succeed.
⁂	You will obtain what you wish for.
⁂	Signifies that on this day your fortunes will change for the better.
⁂	Cheer up your spirits, your luck is at hand.
⁂	After *long* imprisonment he will be released.
⁂	The patient will be relieved from sickness.
⁂	She will have a healthy *son.*
⁂	You will be married to your equal in a short time.

If you wish to be happy, do not marry this person.

This love is from the heart, and will continue until death.

I.

The love is great, but will cause great jealousy.

It will be in vain for you to travel.

Your friend will be as sincere as you could wish him to be.

You will recover the stolen property through a cunning person.

The traveller will soon return with joy.

You will not be prosperous or fortunate in foreign parts.

Place your trust in *God*, who is the disposer of happiness.

•• •• • •	Your fortune will shortly be changed into misfortune,
• • •• ••	You will succeed as you desire.
• • • ••	Signifies that the misfortune which threatens will be prevented.
•• • •• ••	Beware of your enemies, who seek to do you harm.
• •• •• ••	After a short time your anxiety for the prisoner will cease.
• •• •• •	God will give the patient health and strength again.
• • •• •	She will have a very fine daughter.
• •• • ••	You will marry a person with whom you will have little comfort.
•• •• •• ••	The marriage will not answer your expectations.

K.

● ● ● ●	After much misfortune you will be comfortable and happy.
●● ● ●● ●	A sincere love from an upright heart.
● ●● ● ●	You will be prosperous in your journey.
●● ● ● ●●	Do not *rely* on the friendship of this person.
●● ●● ●● ●	The property is lost for *ever* ; but the thief will be punished.
●● ●● ● ●●	The traveller will be absent some considerable time
●● ● ● ●	You will meet luck and happiness in a foreign country.
●● ●● ● ●	You will not have any success for the present.
● ● ●● ●●	You will succeed in your undertaking.

• • • ••	Change your intentions, and you will do well.
•• • •• ••	Signifies that there are rogues at hand.
• •• •• ••	Be reconciled, your circumstances will shortly mend.
•• • •• •	The prisoner will be released.
• • •• •	The patient will depart this life.
• •• • ••	She will have a son.
•• •• •• ••	It will be difficult for you to get a partner.

L.

• • • •	You will get a very handsome person for your partner.
•• • •• •	Various misfortunes will attend this marriage.

♦ ♦♦ ♦ ♦	This love is whimsical and changeable.
♦♦ ♦ ♦ ♦♦	You will be unlucky in your travels.
♦♦ ♦♦ ♦♦ ♦	This person's love is just and true. You may rely on it.
♦♦ ♦♦ ♦ ♦♦	You will lose, but the thief will suffer most.
♦♦ ♦ ♦ ♦	The stranger will soon return with plenty.
♦♦ ♦♦ ♦ ♦	If you remain at home, you will have success.
♦ ♦ ♦♦ ♦♦	Your gain will be trivial.
♦ ♦ ♦ ♦♦	You will meet sorrow and trouble.
♦♦ ♦ ♦♦ ♦♦	You will succeed according to your wishes.

● ●● ●● ●●	Signifies that you will get money.
● ●● ●● ●	In spite of enemies, you will do well.
● ● ●● ●	The prisoner will pass many days in confinement.
● ●● ● ●●	The patient will recover.
●● ●● ●● ●●	She will have a daughter.

M.

● ● ● ●	She will have a son, who will gain wealth and honour.
●● ● ●● ●	You will get a partner with great undertakings and much money.
● ●● ● ●	The marriage will be prosperous.
●● ● ● ●●	She, or He, wishes to be yours this moment.

●● ●● ●● ●	Your journey will prove to your advantage.
●● ●● ●● ●●	Place no great trust in that person.
●● ● ● ●	You will find your property at a certain time.
●● ●● ● ●	The traveller's return is rendered doubtful by his conduct.
● ● ●● ●●	You will succeed as you desire in foreign parts.
● ● ● ●●	Expect no gain ; it will be in vain.
●● ● ●● ●●	You will have more *luck* than you expect.
● ●● ●● ●●	Whatever your desires are, you will speedily obtain them.
● ●● ●● ●	Signifies you will be asked to a wedding.

● ● ●● ●	You will have no occasion to complain of ill-luck.
● ●● ● ●●	Some one will pity and release the prisoner.
●● ●● ●● ●●	The patient's recovery is unlikely.

N.

● ● ● ●	The patient will recover, but his days are short.
●● ● ●● ●	She will have a daughter.
● ●● ● ●	You will marry into a very respectable family.
●● ● ● ●●	By this marriage you will gain nothing.
●● ●● ●● ●	Await the time and you will find the love great.
●● ●● ● ●●	Venture not from home.

This person is a sincere friend.

You will never recover the theft.

The stranger will return, but not quickly.

When abroad, keep from evil women or they will do you harm.

You will soon gain what you little expect.

You will have great success.

Rejoice ever at that which is ordained for you.

Signifies that sorrow will depart, and joy will return.

Your luck is in blossom ; it will soon be at hand.

Death may end the imprisonment.

O.

The prisoner will be released with joy.

The patient's recovery is doubtful.

She will have a son who will live to a great age.

You will get a virtuous partner.

Delay not this marriage—you will meet much happiness.

None loves you better in this world.

You may proceed with confidence.

Not a friend, but a secret enemy.

* * ** **	You will soon recover what is stolen
* * * **	The stranger will not return again.
** * ** **	A foreign woman will greatly enhance your fortune.
* ** ** **	You will be cheated out of your gain
* ** ** *	Your misfortunes will vanish and you will be happy.
* * ** *	Your hope is in vain—fortune shuns you at present.
* ** * **	That you will soon hear agreeable news.
** ** ** **	There are misfortunes lurking about you.

P.

* * * *	This day brings you an increase of happiness.

●● ● ●● ●	The prisoner will quit the power of his enemies.
● ●● ● ●	The patient will recover and live long.
●● ● ● ●●	She will have two daughters.
●● ●● ●● ●	A rich young person will be your partner.
●● ●● ●● ●	Hasten your marriage—it will bring you much happiness.
●● ● ● ●	The person loves you sincerely.
●● ●● ● ●	You will not prosper from home.
● ● ●● ●●	This friend is more valuable than gold.
● ● ● ●●	You will *never* receive your goods.

✱✱ ✱ ✱✱ ✱✱	He is dangerously ill, and cannot yet return.
✱ ✱✱ ✱✱ ✱✱	Depend upon your own industry, and remain at home.
✱ ✱✱ ✱✱ ✱	Be joyful, for future prosperity is ordained for you.
✱ ✱ ✱✱ ✱	Depend not too much on your good luck.
✱ ✱✱ ✱ ✱✱	What you wish will be granted to you.
✱✱ ✱✱ ✱✱ ✱✱	That you should be very careful this day, lest any accident befall you.

Q.

✱ ✱ ✱ ✱	Signifies much joy and happiness between friends.
✱✱ ✱ ✱✱ ✱	This day is not very lucky, but rather the reverse.
✱ ✱ ✱✱ ✱	He will yet come to honor, although he now suffers.

** * ** **	Recovery is doubtful ; therefore, be prepared for the worst.
** ** ** *	She will have a son who will prove forward.
** * ** **	A rich partner, but a bad temper.
** * * *	By wedding this person you insure your happiness.
** ** * *	The person has great love for you, but wishes to conceal it.
* ** * **	You may proceed on your journey without fear.
* * * **	Trust him not ; he is inconstant and deceitful.
** * ** **	In a very singular manner you will recover your property.
* ** ** **	The stranger will return very soon.

● ●● ●● ●	You will dwell abroad in comfort and happiness.
● ●● ● ●	If you will deal fairly you will surely prosper.
● ● ●● ●●	You will live in splendour and plenty.
●● ●● ●● ●●	Make yourself contented with your present fortune

BOOKS OF INTEREST

BOOKS OF INTEREST

THE PSYCHOLOGY OF FATE
By Dr. UNITE CROSS

What has the future in store for you ? This guide to character and destiny in which the forgotten truths of ancient wisdom are applied to present-day need, will tell you how to control chance and attain success. To those who have failed in the past, this book will bring a message of hope, as it will convince them that life is always generous. Gain a knowledge of yourself, ascertain the right road, and success will follow as surely as the night the day. **2/6 net.**

NUMEROLOGY UP-TO-DATE
By KAREN ADAMS

A clear account of the science of numerology, which indicates by a system of numbers how the letters of your name and date of birth may determine the course of your life—past, present, and future. It helps you to analyse your own character and to solve the problems of your own life. **2/- net.**

THE GRAVEN PALM
By MRS. ROBINSON

A new and revised edition, with 251 illustrations, of this comprehensive work. It has been proved that the lines in the hand have a normal and natural position. The slightest deviation from the normal denotes unusual qualities or tendencies. With full knowledge proper precautions can be taken, which in themselves justify Cheiromancy. **10/6 net.**

WITCHCRAFT AND THE BLACK ART
By J. W. WICKWAR

The author has gathered into his pages a fund of fascinating material, covering the nature of the cult, black magic in earliest times, witchcraft in the Middle Ages, in Europe, England and America, the persecution of witches, which became so cruel a social and political factor in the history of the day. He cites many famous witch trials, and traces many of our popular superstitions and beliefs to the practices of witches in bygone days. **3/6 net.**

Will you let us send you, post free each month, " The Herbert Jenkins Wireless," that is, if you enjoy a laugh.

Printed in the United Kingdom
by Lightning Source UK Ltd.
107735UKS00001B/537